The Ocean of Grace

Tributes to Amma's All-Embracing Love

Volume 5

The Ocean of Grace

Tributes to Amma's All-Embracing Love

Volume 5

Edited by Rudran Degnan
Co-edited by Julius Heyne

Mata Amritanandamayi Center
San Ramon, California, USA

The Ocean of Grace – Volume 5
Tributes to Amma's All-Embracing Love

Edited by Rudran Degnan
Co-edited by Julius Heyne

Published by:
Mata Amritanandamayi Center
P.O. Box 613
San Ramon, CA 94583
United States

International:
www.amma.org

In India:
www.amritapuri.org
inform@amritapuri.org

Contents

"From a beggar, the guru lifts you to the status of the Emperor of the Universe.
From a mere receiver, he makes you a giver."

— *Amma*

Preface

astyuttarasyāṁ diśhi dēvatātmā
himālayō nāma nagādhirājaḥ
pūrvāparau tōyanidhī vagāhya
sthitaḥ pṛithivyā iva mānadaṇḍaḥ

In the northern quarter stands the Himalaya,
sovereign of mountains, a deity in essence.
Stretching into the eastern and western oceans,
he stands like the measuring rod of the earth.

This is the opening verse of *Kumārasambhavam* by the great classical poet Kālīdāsa. In it, he extols the Himalayas, which stand as tall as the sky and extend from the eastern ocean to the western ocean.

We have read and heard accounts of many who have travelled in the Himalayas, whose majestic grandeur is equal to that of the gods. Each traveller has unique experiences to share. What emerges is a tapestry of the paths they took, the sights they beheld, and the distinct impressions they carried away.

Those drawn to spirituality will speak of the sacred pilgrimage sites in the Himalayas and the mahātmās, the great souls who dwell there. A nature lover will wax eloquent on the region's breathtaking natural beauty. A tourist will describe its places of interest and sources of entertainment. A keen mountaineer, driven by adventure, will speak of the challenges and deep sense of fulfilment he receives from climbing the Himalayan peaks.

All these views and experiences of the Himalayas are valid. Together, they shape our picture of the mighty mountains. Yet even if we combine all these descriptions into a single painting in our mind, what emerges is only a faint outline, for the Himalayas are vast beyond measure. In the span of a single lifetime, no one can truly comprehend the Himalayas, whose soul is a deity.

When we think of Amma before such a background, what do we truly know of her? How can we ever comprehend Amma, who shines as both Creator and Creation, who is 'Pūrna-brahma-svarūpinī,' the complete embodiment of absolute truth?

We can only gaze upon the vast, resplendent, snow-clad peaks and say, "The Himalayas." In the same way, when we behold Amma in her simple white attire, all we can do is call out, "Amma..." To each, she bestows what they seek. This has been the experience of countless people who have come to her from every corner of the world, regardless of race, language, culture, or gender.

Bhagavān Śhrī Kṛiṣhṇa tells Arjuna of four kinds of devotees who turn to him: the distressed, those who seek wealth and pleasure, those who seek knowledge, and the ones who have realized God (*Bhagavad Gītā* 7.16). In these words, we can see the journey of every individual soul. Those who come for Amma's darśhan surely belong to one of these four categories. Reading their experiences during darśhan (Amma's divine embrace) brings us relief and reassurance. Moreover, it lessens the distance we feel between Amma and ourselves. When they share their experiences of Amma with us, they are, in fact, painting Amma's portrait before our very eyes. Yet, if we were to call the totality of all these experiences Amma, it would still be only an incomplete and fragmented glimpse of the whole.

When a small child standing at the seashore points at the water and says, "Look, the ocean," what he says is true — he does see the ocean before his eyes. Yet can the ocean be limited to what he sees? Who can truly plumb its unfathomable depths, its limitless breadth, and its immeasurable vastness?

We can never fully know Amma, but even so, when we learn about her children's experiences, they add beauty to and deepen our own experiences and understanding. Through their descriptions, we behold numerous bhāvas, or moods, of Amma that we ourselves may never have experienced. Their experiences will guide us, helping us to anticipate and avoid many obstacles on our path to her.

Through the accounts of others, we will be able to mature, to understand, and to hold Amma within us, however slightly. We will come to realize and experience that Amma truly is 'Hṛidayēśhvarī,' the Goddess who dwells in our hearts. This realization will give us the strength to overcome the challenges and tests of life. *The Ocean of Grace,* a compilation of the experiences of Amma's children, is a book that will guide us in this endeavor.

Swami Jnanamritananda Puri

Concentration

A Message from Amma

Many people complain that they are not able to concentrate while meditating or praying. True, it's not easy to concentrate. To make the mind one-pointed, we need to practice constantly. That said, not being able to concentrate should not stop us from meditating and praying. Unwavering enthusiasm and a focus on the goal can definitely help us gain concentration.

Amma remembers a story: There was a lad who did not possess any skill. His father earned his living by climbing coconut trees and plucking coconuts. When he died, people started calling the son to do his father's job. But what could he do? He needed to learn how to climb a tree first. Not seeing any other way of making a living, he decided to learn how to climb coconut trees.

He knew that he had to be very careful. If he fell down, he would break his arms and legs, and then, earning a livelihood by climbing coconut trees would be out of the question. So, he started practicing with great care. He hugged the tree tightly and started climbing slowly, placing each foot carefully on the trunk. After climbing a short distance, he would come down. After many days of concerted effort, he mastered the art of climbing coconut trees. Through practice, he was able to climb up and down quickly.

A spiritual seeker ought to think like this: "God alone is true. The goal of life is to attain God-realization; that is the only road to eternity. But there are impediments on the way. If I'm not careful, I'll slip and fall. Then, I'll lose my life." We need to have this attitude in order to gain concentration.

In truth, the mind is already pure and focused. But until yesterday, it has been home to innumerable worldly emotions. Hence, we are not able to concentrate when we sit down to meditate. These emotions are like tenants. We gave them the space to build a house on our land, which until then had been a vast and open tract. When told to leave, the tenants not only refuse but also fight with us. We must struggle hard to evict them by filing a case in court. Similarly, to evict the tenants occupying our mind, we must take the case to God's court. It will prove to be a constant battle, and we must fight until we gain victory. Our inability to concentrate is of our own making. But through unceasing effort, we can regain concentration.

Thinking about our parents, relatives, friends, or tasty food is not at all difficult. If asked to think about them, they will at once appear clearly before our mind's eye. We are able to spend as much time as we like with them because we have forged a strong bond with them through long association. Hence, we don't need to teach or train the mind to think about them. The mind is already familiar with them.

We can create such a strong bond with God also. This is why we must do japa (repeated chanting of the mantra), meditate, and listen to satsangs. We must practice remembering God constantly. Then, the form of God and the mantra associated with Him will arise in the mind as spontaneously as thoughts of worldly objects. Everything we see and think will be filtered through the perception of the divine. There will be no world for us other than that of God. This is true concentration. Through alertness and unremitting effort, we can gain such concentration of the mind. Children, may you all be able to do so.

1

Three Fingers Pointing Back

Shalini Nair - USA

In the autumn of 2021, Amma was sitting on the steps of the Kālī Temple, laughing and smiling with her children as they joked, told stories, and sang — and then it happened. Amma began serving her children chocolate cake and coffee. I was glued to the screen, watching online, but when I saw the cake and coffee, I thought, "Now I have to go to Amritapuri."

Recently, Amma sang the bhajan, *Manasigē Kachchikoḷuva Āse*. Part of the lyrics say, "The mind is tempted to taste anything it sees, and to hold onto everything it likes." In the same way, Amma took my animal mind, my longing for coffee and cake, and used it to lure me towards her, like a master fisherman catching an unwitting fish with tasty bait. Thank you Amma for bringing this fish back to these sacred waters after fourteen and a half years away!

Like many, I had grown accustomed to the clock-like regularity with which Amma visited us on her world tours. In December 2019, after the Michigan program, I had no idea it would be years before I could see Amma again. That time away created a precious opportunity to deepen my relationship with my inner Amma.

I was born in Kochi, and when I was four years old, my family moved to Dallas, Texas. We faced struggles early on, yet time and again, we felt God watching over us, carrying us through. As Amma says, challenges drive us to God more than favorable situations, and so it was with us.

This reminds me of a story of Lord Kṛiṣhṇa and one of his childhood friends. Once when his friend was slapped hard across the face, Kṛiṣhṇa stepped forward. There were no marks on the boy's face; the marks appeared on Lord Kṛiṣhṇa's face. God compassionately accepts the blows meant for us.

In 1990 my aunt took our family to the Dallas program to meet Amma. I was quite young and had never been to an event like that. I didn't yet understand who Amma was or the significance of that first meeting. We continued to occasionally see Amma in Dallas, but back then we couldn't perceive the changes Amma was bringing about in our lives.

It was around this time that my aunt gave me a book called *A Book of Daily Thoughts and Prayers* by Swami Paramananda, who lived in the early 1900s. The book contained translated verses from the *Bhagavad Gītā* mingled with verses of the Swami's own poetry. The poems were filled with a deep longing for God. "What is this longing?" I thought. My child's mind could not grasp having longing for God and God alone. Little did I know that Amma would eventually be answering these unspoken thoughts.

Reflecting back on that decade, I can clearly see that Amma planted seeds in me, and some were beginning to sprout. I started doing community-focused volunteer work in junior high and high school. I became sensitive to the needs in our community and began to see the plight of the homeless and disabled for the first time, as if with new eyes. In high school, I took an opportunity to work with disabled students and began to understand the challenges their parents were facing. I felt extra compassion for these students and did my best to make sure they had fun, felt included, and knew they were loved. I truly believe the seeds of compassion, the ability to recognize others' struggles, and the enthusiasm to serve, were planted by

Amma. Even so, Amma had not yet lifted the veil to show me who she truly is.

***

It was not until 2003, after I started fervently praying to Amma to resolve a difficult situation that I was dealing with at the time, that a lightbulb went off. Amma happened to be in Dallas for her annual visit at the time when the veil was lifted just a little, and over the course of two months, Amma answered my prayer. The complicated issue completely fell away, and all was well again. My faith in an unnamed and formless God began to strengthen as it solidified around Amma. Around that time, I also discovered the Dallas satsang community and began to regularly attend their programs. My quest for understanding more about who Amma is was starting to gain steam.

I have always felt God speak to me through books. So it was only appropriate that two spiritual classics soon came my way: *Autobiography of a Yogi* and *Amma's Biography.* Both were incredibly eye-opening. Amma was starting to lift the veil even further. By reading Paramahansa Yogananda's and Amma's life stories, I started to understand more about longing for God. Through these books, I learned about self-realization and what the ultimate goal of human life is.

There is one line in *Autobiography of a Yogi* that still stands out in my memory. It is when Yoganandaji cries out in agony about the death of his biological mother. Suddenly, the Divine Mother appears before him and says, "It is I who have watched over thee, life after life, in the tenderness of many mothers!" This is the same assurance that Amma gives us: she is the one watching over us, life after life.

Over the next few years, I started to relate to life and the world differently. I no longer fit in with my co-workers. They were focused on promotions, gaining status, buying new homes and cars, and enjoying life. "But what about the needy?" I kept thinking. What happens to them if people only focus on gaining things for themselves? I didn't belong in this type of environment anymore and yearned to find my true path and purpose in life.

When Amma saw my plight in November 2007 as I asked her if I could spend a year at her Amritapuri āśhram to figure things out, she suggested I come on the 2008 North India Tour instead. I was surprised, since at the time I didn't understand how that would solve my dilemma. Miraculously, my job granted me a leave of absence with a verbal assurance that I would get my job back when I returned.

So I set off for India and joined the tour, hoping I would be able to stay on in India once it was over. In New Delhi, Amma looked at me quite fiercely and asked if I had left my job! This was my first experience of Amma's Kālī Bhāva (fierce form). Amma also expressed concern about how my family would cope during my absence. I stammered, saying, "No Amma, I can go back to the same job." She told me to go back as early as I could. I was shocked and confused. I wondered if I should leave the tour immediately or wait until it finished. Since there was a long road trip to Kolkata coming up, and I didn't want to try to catch a flight in the middle of nowhere, I decided to wait until the tour ended. Amma's grace helped me get through the tour without much trouble, but I still felt disillusioned about the world and did not look forward to going back to the same life so quickly, but the bigger lesson was yet to come.

When I boarded the bus for the long trek back from Kolkata to Amritapuri, I was early to get a seat and noticed a *Matruvani* magazine in one of the back seats I had selected. When I opened it at random, I was stunned. There, right on the page in front of me, was a list of Amma's advice on how to treat work in the world as karma-yōga — how we should turn our work into an offering to the divine! Through eyes blurred by tears, I read the following lines:

> *However high your position in life may be, always have the attitude that you are just a servant of your fellow beings. Think that God has placed you in a fortunate position as an opportunity for you to help those in need. When you work with the attitude that you are serving God, then your work becomes spiritual practice.*
>
> *Never think you are just working for your boss or for a company. Do your duty with the attitude that you are serving God. Then you will be sincere and attentive in your work. We should always be willing to do more work than is required by the rules. Only such additional work, done without any desire for praise or reward, qualifies as selfless service.*
>
> *If you place a picture of your beloved deity, or spiritual master, in a clearly visible position in your workplace, this will help you keep your focus on God. There is no need to be ashamed of this. Your good example will serve as a model for others.*
>
> *With constant effort, we should be able to mentally repeat our mantra while doing any type of work. Only the actions that are done while remembering God, or the actions that are offered to God, can be considered real karma yoga. The work we do with the attitude that it is God's work won't cause any bondage. No matter where we are, let us always repeat the divine name and pay homage to God and to the spiritual master.*
>
> (Excerpt from *Immortal Light*, reprinted in *Matruvani*, December 2007)

In true Amma fashion, Amma had created the perfect circumstances on the tour for me to witness firsthand the suffering that people all across India were enduring. It was like a microcosm of the larger world, as these circumstances are mirrored in many places around the globe. Then, came the lesson in written form.

Amma showed me I didn't need to change my physical circumstances in order to help others — I could help right where I was! I had been trying to fit in, but I realized I didn't need to fit anyone's expectations. I didn't need to change or defend who I was inside, but I had to change my attitude. I could be in the world and stay true to my values. Amma had given me full license to be who I was and to stand up for what I believed in. It only took me a trip around the world to see that.

***

During the last fourteen-and-a-half years since that incredible lesson, I have done what I can to serve in my workplace. While I still struggle to follow Amma's guidance, my small steps in that direction have definitely brought grace. While coordinating Mother's Kitchen[1], doing āśhram sēvā (selfless service), and coordinating food service for the Dallas program, the attitude that I am an instrument in Amma's hands helps to deflate any ego and allows grace to flow.

It is not always so easy to have that attitude. We easily get attached to our sēvā, and if things do not go according to our plans, we can quickly become frustrated. A sense of frustration is a clear sign that an unannounced Amma pop quiz is taking place. I tend to fail most of these pop quizzes, but occasionally I

---

[1] Mother's Kitchen groups in North America prepare, cook, and serve 150,000 meals for the homeless and hungry each year. Some groups also collect and distribute clothing, household items, or food staples for communities in need.

spot one while it's happening and respond appropriately to the situation. Are we watchful enough to avoid getting trapped into a sense of doer-ship when it comes to our sēvās?

In 2004, I was asked to help coordinate the food areas for the Dallas program. I had no idea what I was signing up for and innocently agreed. I threw myself into this sēvā with enthusiasm, but I was a complete case study on how not to get attached to the work! Just like with all aspects of the tour, there were so many things to coordinate and so many people to work with, and I started getting caught up in the drama. And on top of it all, I felt sad to be away from Amma for so much of the program. At the time, I did not fully understand that sēvā brings us closer to Amma. I cried a bucket of tears. By the end of that Dallas program, I felt like a failure who had missed the chance to be with Amma. Over the years though, I have found that I am better able to let things go and be a bit more detached.

As we grow in our lessons, Amma throws more challenging situations at us. She knows we can handle them, even if we ourselves do not believe so. During the last summer program in Dallas, the food-area-team was told that we could not use the areas between the kitchen and the delivery dock for veggie chopping. The new executive chef was used to following extremely strict guidelines. In his opinion, chopping veggies in an open area was not up to code! Thankfully, someone thought about contacting the city health department and having an inspector come out. This way, we could explain all the safety measures we were taking. The executive chef agreed that the guidance from the city inspector would be the final verdict.

In the meantime, we looked for alternative ways to do veggie chopping, which is so essential to provide fresh, tasty, healthful meals to Amma's guests. We explored chopping at nearby facilities like the local Indian temple. This was problematic though, as we would need to transport both food ingredients and sevites to and from the main program venue to the veggie chopping venue.

With all of our effort came grace. After exploring every possible option and praying fervently to Amma, the health inspector agreed to let us do our veggie chopping where we had originally planned! This was a real test to see if we could stay calm and find a good solution under pressure. With grace, the program was a success.

***

This year, Mother's Kitchen has been able to deliver wholesome meals to a shelter in downtown Dallas every month. Instead of cooking at the shelter, as we did before the pandemic, we cook ahead of time and then deliver the food. Doing this was directly inspired by Amma's door-to-door food delivery program, which is on-going to this day, as are Mother's Kitchens all around the U.S. During the pandemic, Mother's Kitchens continued to operate in creative ways to keep serving the needy.

As for my work in the world, I now understand that the different circumstances I encounter are only for my own spiritual growth and that my attitude towards each one makes all the difference. Let me tell one last story to illustrate the importance of maintaining a good attitude.

Some time back, I had a co-worker who was older and had a great deal of work experience but was new to our team. I was his peer, but always felt he was competing with me. I did my best to soften this by being helpful and supportive, but often felt myself slipping into silent criticism of him. Amma always tells us that when we point our finger at someone, three fingers are pointing back at us. Thanks to this teaching, I was able to cultivate more patience with this colleague.

After three years of working together, I became his boss. The competitive energy went away, but I was concerned about how this would affect our working relationship. I was sure he would use this as a reason to retire or leave the company. I decided that I would continue to be as supportive and helpful as possible. To my surprise, he reciprocated with a supportive and helpful attitude. I truly believe that it was Amma's three-fingers teaching that helped transform this relationship.

I still struggle with letting things go at work and with knowing when to speak up and when to stay quiet. In this struggle, it is very easy for criticism to creep in. At its heart, criticism has a sense of superiority behind it, a feeling that 'I know better.' It can be compounded when others join in and we all commiserate together. Then the criticism becomes a community activity and an even more ingrained habit. The best way to get out of this downward spiral of the ego is to bring back the attitude that I am just a servant of my fellow beings. This ideal is tough to maintain, especially in a critical work environment. But with effort, we can make progress and become receptive to grace. I pray that the work of all of Amma's children becomes karma-yōga for the world.

Recently, I noticed a devotee in Amritapuri, who looks exactly like the co-worker I was just mentioning. They could be twins! I was so shocked the first time I saw him that I stopped to take a hard look to make sure my co-worker hadn't somehow followed me here. Is this a coincidence? Are there coincidences around Amma? I personally do not think so.

Every time I see this devotee, I imagine it is my co-worker doing sēvā, and meditating, and singing bhajans for Amma, and I send that energy back to my co-worker in our workplace in the U.S. Like this, I hope and pray that I continue to imbibe Amma's teachings and put them into practice in my own life.

Amme, please open my heart more so that I may more deeply integrate your lessons and teachings. Please give me the strength to handle any circumstance that you send in my direction. Please help me to light the inner candle and step forward in the world to share its small glow. And please continue to lead me on the path to you as the final destination.

2

Home at Last

Divyananda Puente – Spain

It is my good fortune to have been born into a pious and wise family. My parents and my grandparents have been powerful examples of sacrifice and kindness towards all their children and towards society. They inspired me to lead a spiritual life based on simplicity, renunciation, and surrender to the guru. My most sincere thanks to them.

Amma once said, "The teachings of Sanātana Dharma are imperishable jewels that selfless ṛiṣhis (seers) have given to the world, out of their compassion. No one seeking peace can avoid the principles of Sanātana Dharma. Sanātana Dharma does not ask us to believe in a God who lives up in the sky. What it says is, 'have faith in yourself; everything is within you.'"

Sanātana Dharma is the light of the world. If the human race really wants to save our beautiful and divine planet, we need to put the teachings of Sanātana Dharma into practice. Everything is included in it.

I remember the moment I arrived in India for the first time in 2001. As I was walking through the Delhi airport, I felt such a sense of homecoming — that I was returning to my real home. Twenty years later, I understand that it was the beginning of my journey from untruth to truth, from ignorance to knowledge of the self. When I met Amma in 2006, I knew almost nothing about the self, our true nature.

After many experiences with different spiritual teachers from the East and West, I can say that traveling on the path of spiritual life without a guru is like driving an old car through the high mountains of the Himalayas during a heavy monsoon. Our journey may be impeded for a long time due to landslides, bad road conditions, and poor visibility — and this is in the best of cases. However, if we travel the path accompanied by a spiritual master who knows the way, it is like traveling in an airplane. The journey becomes faster and easier. Amma is piloting us in her divine vehicle at the fastest speed towards permanent peace and liberation from suffering. She is guiding us to knowledge of the ātman, our true self.

Of course, there will be many difficulties. But if we surrender sincerely, hold tightly to her holy feet and try to be an instrument of her will, the highest goal of life can be fulfilled. Amma once said that a true satguru is able to give mōkṣha (liberation) to thousands of people. She is like a huge ship that can carry thousands across the ocean of saṁsāra (the cycle of birth and death).

I got my first darśhan (hug) in Barcelona in 2006. I had heard about Amma from a devotee I met in Anantapur, Andhra Pradesh when I was volunteering in 2002. He told me that he had just come from Kerala where he had been with a holy woman who gave hugs. My first thought was that "it is not right in India for a woman to hug everyone, especially men." I didn't ask any questions and forgot about Amma until I received her darśhan in Barcelona four years later.

I remember so clearly that upon entering the pavilion where Amma was giving darśhan, I felt an electric power run through me, and all my hairs stood on end. This happened before I had even set eyes on Amma. The friend with whom I had come told me that he could see the aura, or subtle body, around people. He told me that he had never seen a being surrounded by as much light as Amma.

After receiving darśhan, I clearly understood the next step I had to take during that time of confusion in my life. I made the decision to return to India to continue my study and practice of the science of yoga and to continue my practice of Buddhist meditation.

When I arrived in Amritapuri for the very first time, I almost instantly wanted to return to Rishikesh to continue my yoga training. This was due to my attachment to holy sites in the Himalayas, but instead I decided to join Amma's South India Tour. After that pilgrimage, I knew that Amma was my guru.

Nowadays I clearly understand what Amma means when she says that there is no need to go to the Himalayas to do tapas (austerities). Once we have found a perfect teacher, a satguru, we do not need to go anywhere else. He or she will guide us to the final goal of liberation from suffering. The key is to surrender to her lotus feet, where the supreme truth abides and to recognize that we really do not know anything, even if it seems to us that we know a lot.

As many of you know, it can be very difficult to surrender and obey the guru completely. Living in Amritapuri long term is a very tough life. We get up at 4:30 a.m., take a shower, put on clean clothes and go to archana to chant Sanskrit mantras. I heard that Amma once asked, "Why aren't people chanting archana (the divine names) loudly?" She added, "Why aren't they clapping their hands during *Mahiṣhāsura-mardini Stōtram* (the concluding song)?" Since then, I try my best to chant more loudly than before.

I found out that it has been scientifically proven that chanting Sanskrit out loud is very beneficial for the brain cells. Those who chant regularly become more intelligent. I really need that myself. I sometimes feel that my brain is getting dried up. I do not know if it is something to worry about or if it is part of the purification process. I hope that Amma is doing a deep cleaning of my mind, especially removing my ego, selfishness, arrogance, and anger.

***

I was born and educated in a modern society that exalts the ego and rejects the traditional knowledge of our ancestors. It chooses to blindly follow American fashions and business practices obsessed with materialism and consumerism, without taking into account the spiritual life or practices that help us to know who we really are and what our true nature is.

In my case, my spiritual journey began with Buddhism, followed by yoga and Sanātana Dharma. This is where I found the answers to questions like, "What is the goal of life?... How can I achieve that goal?... Who am I?"

Let me share an experience I had during that first Indian tour with Amma. I was preparing the fruit Amma gives to some devotees during darśhan. As I was working, another person doing the same sēvā (selfless service) told me not to allow anyone to sit in our work area. I was on the stage right behind Amma. All of a sudden, many brahmachāriṇīs (celibate female disciples) came up on the stage, and one of them sat next to me. My legs and feet were touching her; there was no space at all. I thought, "This is too much! I cannot do my sēvā like this." I was sitting on a chair, and she was sitting on the floor. I told her that she couldn't sit there and insisted that she go away. She ignored me and didn't move even a centimeter, so I thought I would try and push her away with my foot.

At that very moment, I looked towards Amma and clearly saw the face of the goddess Kālī in her most ferocious aspect looking at me. Her eyes were full of anger and her tongue was hanging out of her mouth. I was having the darśhan of Amma in her fiercest form. When Amma or Kālī continued to give darśhan to the devotees, I looked around and realized that no one else was experiencing this. I was the only one seeing Kālī; everyone else was seeing Amma giving darśhan as usual. Amma appeared to me in the frightening form of Bhadra Kālī to destroy my ego. My face changed completely, I was in shock. I did not tell anyone at that moment; I was just slowly digesting this terrifying experience.

Nothing like this had ever happened to me before or since. Amma is the Mother of the Universe, fiercely protecting all her sincere devotees from the selfish and evil actions of others. My impulse to move the brahmachāriṇī with my foot was terrible. In the Indian tradition, if our foot touches another person, we touch that person with our hand and bow to them with respect to apologize. I honestly apologize to that brahmachāriṇī. Please, I ask all of you to forgive me. It will not happen again.

I had the great fortune to experience the culture and traditions of India for several years in the Himalayas both before and after meeting Amma. I have traveled with authentic yōgīs and visited some of the most sacred pilgrimage places in India, like Badrinath and Gangotri. So, I now understand the customs and rituals of India a little bit better than before. The scientific Indian tradition is still alive and vibrant, especially in its sacred places and villages. The basic essence of the Indian tradition is to maintain peace and harmony all over the planet.

Up until 2015 I continually asked Amma if I could marry a traditional Indian woman and live in my own yoga center in the Himalayas. There my beautiful wife and I could give yoga classes to Westerners or Indians and put the practical aspects of Amma's teachings into practice. When I first asked Amma she said, "Think about it, and then make the decision." For me, that was a clear, "Yes!" For the next three years my only goal was to make money for that purpose. I worked as a yoga instructor near my home in Spain, and by Amma's grace got 108 students every month. I used to give one free yoga class every week and got very good feedback from my students. However, I learned that the vast majority of them just want physical exercises and nothing else. This is like going to a rich man's house and asking for just ten rupees!

Whenever I made enough money, I returned to India hoping to marry and build my yoga study center. However, after spending months traveling by train from the Himalayas to Amritapuri, back and forth, I got exhausted. Every trip, I would take pictures of my potential future Indian wife to show to Amma, and each time Amma would say, "Fine, ok, if you like." But no matter what I did, I could not get a bride. Amma had other plans for me.

So, I decided to become a renunciate. During my renunciate trial period, the āśhram asked me to go to the AIMS hospital for a blood test. There, they found out that I had Hepatitis C, which I had forgotten since I was first diagnosed with it when I was twenty-five years old. When I found out about this, I became very sad and nervous, thinking that I would not be accepted by the āśhram. At AIMS they told me that they would need to do a more accurate test. From that moment onward, I stopped eating eggs and focused on sēvā, sādhanā (spiritual practice), morning archana, bhajans (spiritual songs), and meditation. When I received the test results a few months later, the doctor told me that there was no trace of the virus. He said, "It's a miracle from Amma."

***

My biological mother had several falls over the past few years. Recently she told me that in the very moment of falling, Amma came to her mind and miraculously nothing bad happened to her. During a time when my biological mother was living in fear due to the bad actions of my brother-in-law, three women dressed in white clothes came to visit her. She thinks they were Indians because of their dark skin. I told her that it was Amma accompanied by her lady saints. They had come to bless her and protect her. My mother answered that I could be right. My mother is a humble, courageous, and righteous woman. From these experiences, we can affirm that our beloved Amma is always protecting our parents from all kinds of danger.

Amma accepted me as a renunciate in June 2016, after I had passed my six-month trial. During those months I understood for the first time in my life that āśhram living and spiritual practices are the ideal way to know our mind and how it works. I have become much more aware of my negative thoughts during my time here.

In the beginning of my āśhram life, my ego told me, "You have been teaching yoga successfully. You have also been one of the best trainers in Spain. In two schools you were selected to lead the classes. The āśhram will have to assign you a sēvā suited to your high level. Actually, you should be teaching yoga at Amrita University." So I decided to ask Amma about my sēvā assignment during one of my early room darśhans. The swāmī who translated Amma's words said, "The āśhram will let you know when to teach yoga." Thanks to Amma, I no longer have that desire to teach, which clearly came from my ego.

Here in the āśhram we are much more aware of what we do, say, and think than in the outside world. This gives us a precious opportunity to correct our mistakes, while surrounded by many wonderful brothers and sisters. The āśhram gives us so many opportunities to put spiritual teachings like compassion, love, and acceptance into practice.

Due to the good qualities Amma is developing in us, the āśhram has become a paradise on Earth. Thank you Amma for letting us be a part of this divine and joyful community of God. Even if we are in other places working, taking care of our parents, or doing sēvā for the āśhram, we can feel that you are with us, guiding and protecting us all the time. I have no doubt about it.

***

I would like to conclude by talking about my favorite scripture, a great epic — the *Mahābhārata*. Amma has said that all situations that humans pass through in life are described in this scripture.

In the *Mahābhārata* a great war looms between opposing sides of the same family, the Pāṇḍavas and Kauravas. The Kauravas had taken the kingdom by force, by cheating the Pāṇḍavas at a game of dice. By the conditions of the game, the Pāṇḍavas were exiled to the forest for twelve years, followed by another year in hiding. But even by the end of the thirteenth year, having met all the conditions of exile, the Kauravas still refused to return the kingdom to the Pāṇḍavas.

Śhrī Kṛiṣhṇa, who was the cousin of both the Pāṇḍavas and Kauravas, visits the Kauravas' palace hoping to negotiate peace without success. He subsequently chose not to fight in the war, but became Arjuna's charioteer and guided Arjuna safely through the war.

The *Mahābhārata* represents the war within the human mind, which has both good and bad qualities. The five Pāṇḍava brothers represent the few good qualities in man. The hundred Kaurava brothers represent the much larger number of negative forces in life. But God, here in the form of Śhrī Kṛiṣhṇa, always supports dharma or righteousness.

Just as the war is about to start, Arjuna, overcome by the sight of his own family standing before him as enemies on the battlefield of Kurukṣhētra, lays down his weapons and refuses to fight. He hesitates to wage a war with his close relatives, his teachers, grandfather, uncles, and cousins. Arjuna's mind came up with intelligent and convincing excuses not to follow God's command and fight for dharma (righteousness).

It's at this point that Lord Kṛiṣhṇa shares the profound advice now known as the *Bhagavad Gītā*. The Lord advises Arjuna to perform his duty and fight without any attachment to the outcome, to make the work an offering to God, leaving the results to the Lord.

The Lord teaches Arjuna to face the war and to not run away from it. Kṛiṣhṇa explains that one can run from the battlefield, but one can never run from the self. Similarly, it is possible to ignore your conscience for some time — but you can never escape it. Therefore, we have to fight our negative inner qualities using the Lord or the divine as our guide and charioteer until we reach self-realization.

In order to bless Arjuna with total knowledge and convince him beyond any doubt, Kṛiṣhṇa reveals his universal form to him saying: "Whenever there is a decline in righteousness and a rise in false religious values, O son of Bharata, I will incarnate Myself." (B.G. 4.7)

I believe that Amma is Śhrī Kṛiṣhṇa reincarnated 5,000 years later in a beautiful female body, here in front of us right now. She has come once again to restore dharma to the face of the Earth. Please Amma, may we all be instruments to serve you in this mission.

3

She Who Melts the Moon and Drinks Its Light

Vaishnavi – Switzerland

In 1991 in a small room in Switzerland, it was not so much Amma herself, but the music that enveloped me like a hug. I don't remember Amma very well, but everything around her was so pleasant. It was a magical world.

"What do you want to be when you grow up," my relatives continually asked me as a child. I replied, "I want to retire young and have somebody teach me the secrets of the world." Of course, they laughed. My grandma, who was very sweet, always said she was retired, so to me that looked like the path to happiness. The desire to learn the secret teachings of the universe was just an idea in my head, or so I thought.

I grew up with a secret script in my mind. It was a kind of hieroglyphics that represented everything I thought. Every Monday afternoon I shared the stories behind these magic symbols with our housekeeper, in her room full of laundry and the smell of starch. I felt most at home in that small room, even though we had a big, beautiful apartment filled with stylish furniture.

Not many had the right to enter my secret world. A few outside words, however, penetrated the closed doors of my fantasy world. One was yoga. I loved this word: I love all words that have a 'y' in them. 'Yoga,' 'yogurt,' and 'New York' were my favorite words.

My first yoga class was in New York. My second one was in Zurich with Aviva. Her studio had a blackboard with writing on it. "That looks like my secret writing," I thought.

"What kind of script is that?" I asked her.

"It's Sanskrit," she replied. "We have a Sanskrit study group. Why don't you join us?"

> 'That which is beyond caste and creed, family and lineage; devoid of name and form, merit and demerit; transcending space, time and sense-object — that brahman art thou; meditate on this in the mind.'
>
> *Vivēkachūḍāmaṇi 254*

This was the first verse I ever heard in Sanskrit. Those first verses I studied, verses 254 through 265 of *Vivēkachūḍāmaṇi*, are still my very dearest treasure. Aviva had studied with Swami Chinmayananda. I came to know him through her, and it was also through Aviva that I came to know about Amma.

"How can it be that Amma dislikes no one?" I asked myself when I saw Amma in Zurich the following year. She touched every person so intimately, some of whom obviously had not bathed in a long time. She showed no disgust. Another verse from *Vivēkachūḍāmaṇi* kept echoing in my mind:

> 'That which is free from duality; which is infinite and indestructible, distinct from the universe and māyā, supreme, eternal; which is undying bliss; taintless — that brahman art thou; meditate on this in thy mind.'
>
> *Vivēkachūḍāmaṇi 261*

'Free from duality' — these words were too much for me. Not only was I incapable of accepting people as they are, free from fear and aversion, but I also experienced many contradicting feelings within myself. As fate would have it, I experienced violence both as a child and as a young woman. Women who have experienced what I did are often called 'survivors.' Whenever I closed my eyes, I was haunted by unpleasant images where my perspective varied: sometimes seeing from within my body, and at other times witnessing from outside. Unlike me, Amma was always aware of her true nature, even when the world was crashing in on her from left and right, in front and behind.

> 'But one who controls the mind, keeps their senses restrained, and is free from both attraction and repulsion, even while using objects of the senses, attains peace.'
>
> *Bhagavad Gītā, 2.64*

Despite my inner turmoil, I felt the peace that Amma radiated. The world around Amma in the early 90's was quite peaceful. You could sit on the floor for hours and watch Amma closeup. No one shooed you away. Getting a token to be hugged by Amma? That was unimaginable. Whenever you felt like it, you could just sit in the darśhan queue and slide forward cross-legged towards Amma. At the programs, I simply observed and enjoyed.

In 1998, at Amma's London program, I realized my peaceful Amma life was over. I went from being a spectator to an actor and made a hundred million mistakes in the process. One of the Swiss organizers asked me if I wanted to help with media work. They decided to approach me because they knew I worked in a publishing house. "Sure," I said. Then someone else asked me to go through a curtained door into a room. I immediately felt at home, as if I was back in the little room with the squeaky ironing board, where I told our cleaning lady my secrets. The room had the exact same smell of freshly ironed laundry and although the room was cluttered and full of things, I had the same relaxing feeling in my body. I felt like a child completely at home.

An American from Amma's public relations team, who was working for Walt Disney in Paris at the time, approached me and said, "Amma is coming to Switzerland soon. Can you try to invite the media to Amma's program? It would be nice if more people in Switzerland knew about her before she arrives."

"Sure," I replied.

Back in Switzerland, I got in touch with some of my contacts, among them was a PR agency I had worked for. Swiss television had filmed a piece about my boss there a few years back. I called the TV journalist who had done the story to see if he was interested. No sooner had I said Amma's name than he interrupted me. "Amma? I know her. I was in India for a long time. Ah, she's coming to Switzerland... Unfortunately I can't come." At that moment, another journalist walked by his office. He asked her if she could cover Amma's visit and without hesitation, she replied "Yes, we're coming." It was the main news program.

A few days later, a cameraman, a sound expert and the journalist were standing in front of the hall where Amma's program would soon begin. I had, as they say in German, "Keine Ahnung von Tuten und Blasen," (Absolutely no clue about what I was doing). Camera crews always make a big impression at Amma's programs. It was so new for most of us back then. They filmed Amma as she gave an interview and recorded clips with some of the visitors.

The program was broadcast in the evening. Because the piece about Amma was on the main news program, she became the story of the day. It was a very beautiful program. The next day, one after another, newspapers and television channels started coming. I still had no clue what I was doing, but suddenly, I was Amma's PR woman.

I was no longer sitting on the shore of Amma's world, I was fighting in the middle of the sea, surrounded by huge waves.

How many mistakes can you make when you're showing a camera crew around? Millions! How many people can you drive crazy with this sēvā? Everyone, including your closest friends. How many journalists can you irritate when you try to take care of them around Amma? Almost all of them!

And Swamiji, who translated the interviews with Amma, had to endure it all. "Vaishnavi, why do all the journalists have to come at the same time?" "Vaishnavi, please tell them to ask fewer questions" On one particular occasion, he simply said, "Vaishnavi, that was very, very bad!" That was when I allowed a photographer in Barcelona to stand on Amma's pīṭham (meditation seat), just before the start of the special Dēvī Bhāva program to photograph the packed hall. My sincere apologies to all. I must say that I did not know how sacred Amma's pīṭham was — but of course, I should have known!

When talking with the media, I avoided the word 'saint' as much as possible. In Christianity, the main religion in Europe, there are no living saints. There are also no living incarnations and no living prophets. They may exist, but they are not recognized by society. And, unfortunately, gurus do not have the best reputation in Europe. So, how could I help people understand Amma? How could I explain that Amma is more than the "Indian woman who embraces everyone"?

Sometimes we referred to the *Bhagavad Gītā* because it so clearly defines what a great soul is. At other times, we referred to India and its ancient spiritual tradition. In many cases, this helped us work around the possible misconception that Amma is a self-proclaimed spiritual master with a big ego. We also tried to explain that Amma was born in a rather poor community and that from a young age she just naturally wanted to help the people in her village. Over time, more and more people began to feel that this girl, who only had four years of schooling, was very special. They felt peace, love, and closeness to God in her presence. They felt Amma could guide them on their spiritual path. Organically, over time, masses of people began coming to Amma.

In India, there have always been enlightened beings who were recognized and called mahātmās. Most journalists accepted that. What was harder for them to grasp, however, was why Amma was being worshiped. I tried to explain that the prayers were not being addressed to Amma as a personality, but to the ideal she embodies: the higher consciousness, without which no experience in life is possible; that which is the essence of all beings, which has neither a beginning nor an end; that which is the same in Amma and every person she embraces. Amma please forgive my ignorance in attempting to express your greatness. Only you know your own glory.

In the *Bhagavad Gītā* Arjuna asks Lord Kṛiṣhṇa how we can recognize a mahātmā:

> "What, O Kēśhava, is the description of one who has steady wisdom and who is absorbed in the self? How does an enlightened person talk? How do they sit? How do they walk?" (2.54)

Lord Kṛiṣhṇa replies,

> "One who remains unattached in all situations, and who neither rejoices on encountering the pleasant nor despises the unpleasant — such a person's wisdom is firmly established." (2.57)

Sometimes there were beautiful articles and TV reports about Amma, but some were shallow. I was always afraid that there would be an unfavorable article. Once Amma asked me why my face looked so worried. I replied that I was afraid the journalist's report would not be good. She simply said, "Don't worry. Today's newspaper is tomorrow's waste paper."

Despite Amma's compassionate reassurance, I was constantly stressed out. First and foremost, I worried about whether the wording of the press release would inspire journalists to cover Amma's program. I was as afraid of the question, "No cameras today Vaishnavi?" as I was of the question, "Why so many reporters today?" I also worried about whether the media people would come on time, and about how the interviews with Amma would be coordinated. I found myself in a lot of trouble again and again. I kept losing my bag, my pens, and my papers with the interview questions I was supposed to give to Swamiji. "Where is my phone?" "Where did I keep my shoes, again?" "Again, why is the internet not working?"

Eventually, Irmgard from Germany joined to support me in this sēvā. That was a great help, as she was excellent at speaking with critical German journalists. The team continued to grow, which made things run much more smoothly.

Amma gave me the most beautiful sēvā: to talk about her. But by doing so, she also catapulted me into the greatest conflicts of my inner being: "What should I accept in a situation and what should I try to change about it? Where is surrender needed and where initiative? Why do I always turn into the bad guy? Why can't I be a good girl? Why does it seem like I do everything wrong? Why am I not the kind of person whom the people around Amma love?"

Being loved is a big topic in the West. Unconditional motherly love is something some of us don't know. Not that our mothers were extra evil, but they themselves were abused by their mothers and fathers, and they passed it on. When did this vicious cycle begin? No one knows. The only thing that is certain is that when you are in that cycle, you must heal so that you can become capable of love.

Amma says,

> "There is pure love in everyone. All of us have the capacity to love others without expectations. As love is our very nature, we can never lose it. A diamond left lying inside a bottle of oil may seem lusterless. But if we wipe away the thick coating of oil, we can restore brilliance to the diamond. Similarly, if we eliminate the impurities of the mind, we can regain the most pristine form of love."

The way to Amma is through the heart, and when our hearts are closed due to past experiences, Amma heals them incredibly tenderly, darśhan by darśhan; even if we do not always feel it immediately. Amma's beauty is her magic remedy for me; I just find her beautiful, beautiful beyond comprehension. Amma is radiant. Her radiant presence heals and transforms.

> 'She who knows all, understands all, and to whom belongs all the glory in the world — She, the ātman, is placed in the space within the effulgent abode of brahman. She assumes the forms of the mind and leads the body and the senses. She dwells in the body, inside the heart. By the knowledge of *that* which shines as the blissful and immortal ātman, the wise behold Her fully in all beings.'
>
> *Muṇḍaka Upaniṣhad 2.2.7*

No matter how good or bad sēvā goes, sitting in front of radiant Amma is the greatest happiness.

> 'The sun does not shine there, nor the moon and the stars; not even lightning flashes there, let alone this

> earthly fire. When She shines, everything shines after Her; by Her light all is illumined.'
>
> *Muṇḍaka Upaniṣhad 2.2.10*

The more you drink of this beauty, the more yearning you get. It is a paradox. Although your thirst is quenched, you get even more thirsty. Amma does not speak my language, but she speaks to everything in me.

I have been blessed to do many Europe and U.S. tours with Amma. Even though some days I could only spend a few minutes near Amma, every time I sat close to her, I felt this beautiful inner light. As I sat there, I tried as much as I could to focus on this light and not on the suffering. Amma shares her light without any if's or but's. Amma does not see us as separate from her. There is no small 'I' putting up any barriers. This light, this love flows to us spontaneously. During Amma's darśhan, it's as if our petty little stream of thoughts gets flooded away by Amma's river of love.

Despite all my difficulties and insecurities, I have always been inspired by Amma's beautiful presence — in each and every moment Amma simply radiates such peace, effortlessness, and beauty. I have also been profoundly touched by Amma's concern for the poor. Amma understands the needs of society like no one else, for she has directly listened to the concerns of millions of people. She knows exactly what is lacking. She simultaneously runs the best private university in India and two massive state-of-the-art hospitals. She runs these institutions, along with countless others, while receiving people for darśhan in a hall jam packed with mountains of clothes and food for the poor. During the Corona period, while Amma was conducting the evening bhajans, chili peppers, wheat, rice, and other essential items were being packed in the back of the hall for families who had fallen on tough times.

In a recent speech in New York, Ramu Damodaran, Chair of the United Nations Academic Impact Committee, highlighted the profound contributions Amma's university has made to the United Nations Development Program in the areas of poverty, discrimination against women, sanitation, wastewater management, water resources, infectious diseases, biodiversity, and social cohesion.

On the subject of higher education, Amma says, "Nowadays, universities and their researchers are judged mainly by the amount of funding they receive and the number of publications produced. But one should also consider whether or how research benefits people at the bottom of society. The development of the world is only sustainable if the people at the base of the pyramid are empowered. Only then will society be healthy."

Amma is so much more than the "Hugging Saint" that is depicted in the tabloid press. She is a visionary leader, whose world view fits beautifully with Europe's vision of human competences promoting democratic culture as outlined by the framework developed by the Council of Europe.[2] Amma's teachings directly address competences such as "Tolerance of Ambiguity," "Valuing Human Dignity and Human Rights," "Empathy," "Conflict Resolution Skills," and "Knowledge and Critical Understanding of the World" — all of which are needed for the thriving of a healthy democracy.

Another characteristic of a country's democratic strength is the relationship between the various social classes and the ability to shift from one to another. According to the OECD (Organization for Economic Co-operation and Development), this so-called "social mobility" is declining worldwide. This means if you are poor, you are more likely to stay poor. Not with Amma.

---

[2] The Council of Europe Reference Framework of Competences for Democratic Culture (RFCDC).

Amma brings together people from every possible social class and culture. The diversity reflected around Amma is something that almost every single journalist notices when they come to Amma's programs. In Amritapuri the same diversity thrives. Academicians and laborers, rather conservative people and quite free-spirited people, people from rich and also poor families, all live and work together in a spirit of unity and love.

When Amma addressed the United Nations Alliance of Civilizations in Shanghai in 2015, she said, "We have to acknowledge the fact that even though we are one in essence, externally, we are different [...] An awareness of the need for coexistence amidst diversity is the only way to alleviate the suffering of others."

Even renowned thinkers, like the French sociologist Bruno Latour, are coming around to the fact that humans do not have the world, especially nature, under control. Rather it is nature that determines the course of humanity. For centuries, the conviction prevailed in Europe that man is the supreme being and can and must control everything. Now we must rethink this with spiritual wisdom as our guiding star.

Amma has always emphasized the intimate relationship between people and nature. On her sixty-sixth birthday she said,

> "It is nature that nurtures and raises not only humans but all beings in creation. If we really think about it, we will see that our existence is always dependent on nature — even before our life was conceptualized as a thought in the minds of our parents, even when we were born as an embryo within our mother's womb, and even after the death of our body. Hence, nature is mother and father to us; nature is everything. We are the children of that revered Mother Nature. She only

> ever has love and compassion for us. We, on the other hand, have just stomped all over her and kicked her in the chest. Now that loving mother has fallen ill and is exhausted."

***

Amma, we need you so much. It is 2022 and there is war in Europe, which no one ever thought would happen again. There are so many people on the run. In Africa, and so many other places, more and more people are falling into poverty. The whole world is in deep trouble. We need Amma's peace. We need Amma's wisdom. We need Amma's love.

Amma, please help us to realize that love is our true nature. Please Amma protect us and shower your white flower petals of peace on all of us. I pray that Amma helps us to develop a burning desire for mōkṣha — the liberation from our ego. Because only when we have fully realized that we are one, can we truly serve.

Let me close with Amma's words,

> "A drop of water cannot become a river on its own. A river is born from countless drops flowing together. The true current of life is unity, the oneness that springs from love."

4

The Greatness of Satsang

Devidas – USA

> *ōm sachchidānada mūrtayē namaḥ*
>
> "Salutations to Amma who is existence, knowledge, and bliss."

This is the second mantra in *The 108 Names of Amma*. 'Sat' means existence. It is truth itself and is eternal in nature. Being in Amma's presence is the greatest form of satsang (spiritual company) that we can have, as she is always radiating pure sat-chit-ānanda. Amma's satsang and darśhan have changed my life. Before I met Amma, I was an ordinary person who only wanted wealth and worldly pleasure, but Amma's grace has lifted me up to a higher path focused on dharma (doing what is correct) and liberation.

There is a beautiful story that illustrates the profound greatness of satsang and darśhan with a satguru, a true master like Amma, which I would like to share.

One day long ago, while sage Nārada was visiting Lord Viṣhṇu in his abode, Vaikuṇṭha, he asked the Lord, "What is the greatness of satsang?"

Lord Viṣhṇu replied, "See that baby worm over there down on Earth? Go ask that worm your question."

So Sage Nārada went down to Earth with his yogic powers, approached the worm and asked, "Hello little worm, can you please tell me the greatness of satsang?"

Great celestial sages like Nārada can speak with any being, so it wasn't a problem for him to speak to the worm. The little worm looked up at Nārada and dropped dead! Nārada was shocked! He went back to Lord Viṣhṇu and reported what had happened.

The Lord said, "No problem, go back down. A baby parrot was just born in that house over there; he will give you the answer to your question."

So Nārada once again flew back down to Earth and approached the baby parrot. "Hello little parrot," he said, "Can you explain the greatness of satsang to me?"

The baby parrot looked over at Nārada, and just like the worm, he too fell over dead!

Nārada rushed back to Lord Viṣhṇu very distraught and told the Lord what had happened. And once again the Lord said, "Ok, no problem! There is a baby calf being born down in that cowshed there. You go ask him."

Trembling with fear, afraid of what would happen to the baby calf, he went down to the cowshed and approached. Nārada spoke somewhat timidly, "Hi little calf, can you tell me the greatness of satsang?"

You can probably guess what happened next. The baby calf took one look at Sage Nārada and died instantly! Nārada was shaking with grief, for killing a sacred cow is a terrible sin.

Feeling quite miserable he went back to Lord Viṣhṇu, and the Lord asked, "What's the matter?"

Nārada replied, "You know, I don't think I actually want to know the answer to this question anymore," but the Lord was not about to let him off the hook so easily.

The Lord pointed and said, "This time go to that palace. There is a prince being born, and he will definitely tell you the answer to your question this time. I promise."

So, Nārada went to the palace, paid his respects to the king and queen, and only then approached the baby prince. He then leaned over into the cradle and said, "Hello little prince! Can you tell me the greatness of satsang?"

The little prince smiled up at Nārada and said, "Don't you recognize me, Nārada? I was a baby worm when I first had your darśhan, and then because of that I was born as a parrot, where again I had the good fortune to have your darśhan. Then I took the body of a sacred cow. After receiving your darśhan as a sacred cow, I reached the highest birth as a human being with spiritual tendencies! And now because I'm getting your darśhan again as a human, I'm sure that I will obtain liberation in this birth itself!"

That is the transformative power of true satsang and darśhan with an incarnation such as Amma! Although we don't have the same powerful presence as Amma, we certainly have the ability to share a tiny bit of her light with a friendly smile, or a kind word or deed.

***

At the age of twenty-two, a friend introduced me to yoga asanas and, along with a daily practice at a local yoga shala, I soon found myself sitting for half-an-hour after class enjoying the inner bliss of meditation. My life began changing quickly, and I started reading spiritual books. When my friends asked me to go out at night, I would usually say no. I preferred to stay home and read spiritual books or meditate. I started to think about moving to the Hawaiian island of Kauai, where I could live off of wild fruits and vegetables in the forest like a yōgī (spiritual adept). It was quite an innocent plan.

I found out there was a beautiful, undeveloped coastal paradise on the island. An eleven mile hike would take you to this special valley. That was it! I booked my ticket, gave away what little I had, and went with a backpack to Kauai! When I made it to the valley, reality struck me. I didn't really know much about living out in nature and foraging for food. Unlike our Amma, who befriends all animals, I was worried that an animal was going to have me for its dinner. In fact it's Amma's grace that I was trying this experiment in Hawaii, where there are no dangerous predators or snakes.

It didn't take too long for me to realize that I was not ready for this. After a few weeks, I headed back to Reno with my head hung low, having failed in my life as a 'forest yōgī' and got my old job back at Whole Foods. I was sad, but at least I still had my yoga practice. My new plan was to find a meditation teacher and an āśhram or spiritual center to live in.

Amma heard my call and sent one of her darling children to come and get me. As I was filling the grocery shelves one day, a lady asked me a question about one of the items.

As I was talking with her, I noticed that the name on her work badge was, "Ananda."

"Oh that's a great name!" I said. I recognized it from one of the spiritual books I was reading.

Ananda replied, "My guru, Ammachi, gave it to me." She then told me about Amma and said, "You know Amma will be coming to the Bay Area in a few months. Why don't you come and meet her and receive a hug?"

I said I would try, but did not really think much of it at the time.

Several months went by, and my longing to live in a spiritual community was becoming intense, so I started making plans to quit my job. Just then, guess who came back into the store? Yes, by Amma's grace, Ananda came back and said, "Amma is coming in a few weeks, do you still want to come?" I couldn't believe it! This was perfect timing! I said yes, and within a few weeks I had quit my job and traveled with Ananda and another devotee, Neelima, to the San Ramon program.

They were so gracious. Not only did they drive me four hours to the program, but they also let me stay in their car, as I had very little money and could not afford accommodation. My heartfelt gratitude goes out to the both of them for their kindness in bringing me to Amma.

Getting to know Amma was a slow process for me. It seemed that Amma would reveal a little more about her true nature each day during darśhan, which I experienced as a deep presence. It was a presence that had always been there right behind my thoughts, feelings, and emotions. I began to feel a big sense of relief and security knowing that Amma was always with me through the good times, and the challenging ones too. I started to do some sēvā (selfless service), which became a good way for me to pass time during Amma's long programs.

The bliss of working alongside devotees who had spent a lot of time traveling with Amma and living in India was uplifting and inspiring. I decided to travel to the next city. By Amma's grace, a devotee I was doing pot washing sēvā with found me a ride and accommodation for Amma's next stop. Actually, this devotee found me rides and accommodation for all of the cities and stops on that U.S. tour! Again, my heartfelt gratitude to this brother, another of Amma's many embracing arms. Of course, he was the dishwashing supervisor that year, and I finished a lot of his shifts for him, so there might have been a little self-interest in keeping me around.

After that tour, I was invited by a devotee to come back to Amma's San Ramon āśhram for the Karma Yoga program. The Karma Yoga program was supposed to last a few weeks to a month, but again by Amma's grace, I was allowed to stay on until the November tour! Living in Amma's San Ramon āśhram was bliss for me, as there were bhajans (spiritual songs) every night. On the weekends there was a large satsang with hundreds of devotees, which saturated the whole property with Amma's divine presence!

When the next year rolled around, I was most fortunate to move to Ron-ji's house, where Amma stayed when she came. This marked a big shift in my life, as Swami Dayamritananda was living in that house as well. Observing how Swamiji spent his time, always chanting, and never engaging in unnecessary conversation, set an example for me. He always flipped off the lights when not needed, saved water whenever possible, and did not waste a single thing. Just being in his presence helped guide me in the right direction.

To be honest, I was making plans to move to India and become a renunciate, but it seems Amma had another plan for me. Soon, I would be taking care of Ron-ji, which would last for the next seventeen-and-a-half years!

***

Please allow me to briefly share about Ron Gottsegen or Ron-ji, as most of us affectionately call him. Ron-ji was a very successful businessman before meeting Amma. He invented a security system that is being used today all around the globe. His company grew rapidly in the late '80s and was publicly traded on the stock exchange. It was on its way to going international, but lucky for him, he had a far better opportunity ahead. He came to Amma, who offers the only real security in life, self-realization — the direct experience of the eternal self as one's own true nature. The *Bhagavad Gītā* describes this self (the ātman) in the following way: "The self is uncleavable, cannot be burned, cannot be moistened, nor dried. It is eternal, all-pervading, stable, immovable, everlasting." (2.24)

Many years ago Ron-ji received an unpublished manuscript, *On The Road To Freedom*, from his cousin, Swami Paramatmanada Puri, who had been living with Amma in India for several years. Ron-ji cried as he read the book. He knew he had to meet Amma and did so during Amma's first World Tour in 1987. Ron-ji fell in love with Amma at first sight. Soon after, he sold his company to tour with Amma full-time.

After a trip to India, Ron-ji, along with some of the other early devotees, decided to build an āśhram in the U.S., where Amma could hold her programs. They wanted to bring a bit of Amritapuri to America by holding daily satsangs, bhajans, meditation, and chanting. Over the years, Amma has spent more time in the San Ramon āśhram than anywhere else in the world, other than Amritapuri.

In 1995 Amma asked Ron-ji and Dr. Prem Nair to build AIMS hospital in Kochi[3]. Ron-ji stayed there serving as the administrative director until 2005, when he was diagnosed with a serious and rare illness called Primary Amyloidosis. He returned to the U.S. for treatment. At that time, it was thought he had six months to live at the most. What follows next is purely Amma's miracle and grace: Ron-ji's life was extended for another seventeen-and-a-half years!

During those years, Ron-ji continued to serve Amma as President of MA Center USA. He was instrumental in establishing many other new centers as well. All the while, Amma kept Ron-ji as the administrative director of AIMS. Although he was not in the best of health, Ron-ji served from the U.S. as much as possible and even made a trip to India in 2008. During the last

---

[3] Amrita Hospital, formerly known as the Amrita Institute of Medical Sciences (AIMS), is a mutlispeciality hospital with an over 1,300 bed capacity and an attached medical college that is a part of Amrita University.

seven years of his life, Ron-ji was instrumental in purchasing a lot of the equipment for Amma's new hospital in Faridabad.

When Ron-ji arrived at San Ramon in 2005, Swami Dayamritananda asked me to start looking after his needs. A few months later, Swamiji told me that I would have to stay back from the U.S. tour to take care of Ron-ji. Little did I know the grace that was in store for me! I was able to be in Ron-ji's house during the U.S. tour for fifteen years, which meant that twenty days a year I lived in the same house with Amma and her swāmīs! I have so many blissful memories and cherished moments from this time.

In 2010 Swami Dayamritananda held programs on all of the islands of Hawaii and invited Ron-ji to join him. We both accompanied Swamiji for this amazing tour! Hawaii is beautiful, with flowering trees and shrubs everywhere you look. It was the most beautiful place I have ever been. Actually, it's a lot like Kerala. Many of the plants and trees are the same. The island of Maui is especially quiet and peaceful. It has a healing atmosphere, and Ron-ji really felt quite good there. After having suffered the effects of chemotherapy treatments and severe neuropathy for five years, he was now in need of comfort and healing.

Ron-ji suggested that we should get a house there and spend some time. To be honest, I didn't really like this idea. I was very attached to being at the āśhram with Swamiji, but the island seemed to be really good for Ron-ji's health. A few months later, we returned to Maui to look for a home and found a place that was perfect. It was large enough to host Swamiji's annual program of sixty to seventy people as well as the local satsang group. That was Ron-ji's condition for the purchase: the house should be used for Amma, not just for his comfort.

We purchased the house during Amma's summer tour that year. After the tour was over, we went to Hawaii to spend some time in the new house. I would have preferred to be in San

Ramon, but didn't get any sympathy, as most people would jump at the chance to live in Hawaii!

***

In 2011, the local Amma group in Chicago found a property that they were very interested in. Amma asked Ron-ji to take a look at it. We flew to Chicago and met the group at the property, which was an old Christian boarding school. It was in the rural suburbs on the far edge of town in farmland surrounded by corn and soybeans. This school had been built in the 1950s, so most of the buildings were in poor condition. Some needed to be knocked down altogether! There were twenty homes on the property, but they were also all in bad shape. It was not looking good. To repair and maintain a 144-acre property with multiple buildings, houses, roads, and a water tower seemed impossible.

Ron-ji reported back to Amma and recommended that she not buy it, but Amma could see beyond the apparent flaws and shortcomings. She had a vision for her children. As Amma often says, "The sculptor alone can see the beautiful statue hidden in the rough stone." Amma instructed us to go ahead and purchase the property. Without hesitation, Ron-ji and the local group moved forward with the purchase.

Despite all the difficulties that come with an older property, Amma's grace was flowing and removed obstacle after obstacle. The property was purchased in time for Amma to hold her 2012 Chicago program there. The Governor of Illinois came to meet with Amma and addressed the audience. Here are some excerpts from his speech:

"It is so important that our state of Illinois is the home of an MA Center! Amma is one of the world's great humanitarian leaders! All of us have learned a life of service from the example and life of Amma! MA Center follows the principle that service to others is the rent we pay for our place on God's Earth... We are honored by the presence of Amma in our state... She knows how to reach out and hug and love everyday people... [We are honored to host] such a wonderful person who is serving all the people of our Earth!"

Not long after that, Amma asked Ron-ji to spend time at the Chicago MA Center to supervise housing, construction, and the renovation of one of the dormitories. After the work began, we split our time between Chicago and Hawaii.

There was an amazing amount of work to do. It seemed like an impossible task, as none of us were trained in these areas, except for Ron-ji. Usually, on a campus like this, you would have a huge staff, along with a few maintenance people, groundskeepers, and engineers, but we, like the Pāṇḍavas[4], had only Amma and her grace!

Things were happening, but at a slower rate than we anticipated. There were many challenges. One of our neighbors even filed a lawsuit to try to stop our construction projects. This reminded me of the opposition that our Amma faced from the locals long ago when the Amritapuri āśhram was starting to form. Recalling Amma's early struggles gave us strength to face the challenges without fear. The Divine Mother was with us!

By this point, we were spending so much time in Chicago and so little time in Maui that Ron-ji asked Amma if we should sell the house in Hawaii. Amma replied that we should keep the house and rent it to a devotee. Her advice did not make sense to us at the time. Who would want to stay at the house, then move out when we wanted to come back? Maybe Amma hadn't understood our question. Yes, that thought was there for

---

[4] The five heroic brothers of the *Mahābhārata* epic who, bereft of their kingdom and wealth, always depended on Lord Kṛiṣhṇa as their ultimate support to overcome any obstacle they faced.

a second, but our all-knowing Amma knew exactly what was needed! The Maui satsang coordinator needed a place to stay at the time. It was a perfect fit. She took good care of the house and held the satsangs there while we were away.

After Amma's 2019 Tour, we went back to Maui with plans to return to Chicago in March 2020. But seeing the direction things were going with Covid, we decided to ask Amma's advice. Amma told us to stay in Hawaii, as it would be safe there for Ron-ji. Now I understood why Amma hadn't wanted Ron-ji to sell the house. She wanted to ensure he had a safe place to stay during the whole pandemic!

At last, Amma called Ron-ji home to Amritapuri for his final days before merging in her lotus feet on October 7th, 2022.

There's a famous saying in Kansas, the farming state I was born in, "Make hay while the sun shines." It means to cut the alfalfa hay, dry it, roll it into balls, and store it for the cows to eat during the winter when no rain is expected. This way the alfalfa can dry properly. Seizing the opportunity, the farmers work intensely and "make hay while the sun shines."

We must do the same. We must seize this opportune moment. We have the great fortune of a human birth, with spiritual qualities, which is highly praised in the scriptures. This is hard to obtain and most precious! Most importantly, and even harder to obtain, we have a realized master in our lives. We are blessed beyond measure to have an incomparable divine incarnation such as Amma here to guide us to the final goal of self-realization. Thus, may each one of us, "Make hay while the sun shines."

Our most beloved Amma creates so many opportunities to be in her presence with daily meditation, satsangs, bhajans, hours and hours of darśhan, and plenty of sēvā opportunities for us to develop purity of mind. There has never been such an incarnation, who spends so much time with so many people, personally guiding each one of them. Amma is always there for each one of us.

5

From Death to Immortality

Rasika Debronsky – USA

I often wonder how it is that I found myself here. How is it possible that a being like Amma is here on this Earth at the very same time we are? How truly fortunate it is that this simple girl from East Los Angeles gets to experience being in her presence. It's pretty awesome that out of the billions of people who will never meet Amma, we find ourselves here. I know that I have found the jackpot of all jackpots.

Years ago I suddenly had a strange thought — I want a guru. I have no idea why I thought this. I began to wonder where I could find one. I imagined my guru would be an old man with a long white beard. But then I started to wonder if there were any women gurus.

Maybe she would be somebody who helps the poor. I had no idea how I even conjured up the idea of wanting a guru to begin with, as I had no real concept of spirituality. But, as soon these thoughts began, I met Amma. What a blessing!

I met Amma for the first time in 2007, in my hometown. I had no knowledge of spirituality — none whatsoever. Zero. Nada.

But, for some reason, just a few months later, I found myself in Amritapuri.

I remember placing my bag on the temple steps and thinking, "What am I doing? I don't even know this lady. I met her once in L.A., and now I'm traveling thousands of miles away from home just to see her!"

The next evening, a woman holding a pitcher stopped me and asked, "Would you like some pāda pūjā water?"

I replied, "Some what? Pada what?"

She stared at me and said, "Put your right hand out."

I did, and she filled my hand with a spoonful of a strange liquid. I stared at her blankly, unsure what to do.

After a pause, she said, "You drink it."

So, I did.

Still confused, I asked, "I'm sorry, but what exactly am I drinking here? I mean, it's tasty and all, but...what is it?"

She said, "It's pāda pūjā water." She further explained, "It's consecrated water consisting of the offerings used in the worship of the guru's feet."

Then the lady hurried away. Little did I know that shortly after this, I would fall so helplessly in love with Amma that I'd find myself running through the crowds and pushing everyone out of my way, like my life depended on it, to get some of that liquid gold. If you are one of the people I have pushed in the past, I just want to say sorry, but I can't promise it won't happen again.

Then I went on my first India tour. I was about twenty-eight at the time. Let's just say I was suddenly faced with my own mortality. Of course, sickness and death are a part of life. Without any prior signs, they can happen to anyone at any time, in any place. We often forget this fact.

During that stay in India, I became friends with a woman, and we made plans to spend some more time together. But when I last saw her, she wasn't feeling so well. I didn't make much of it — it didn't seem serious. After not seeing her for a couple of days, I found out that she had passed away. I was totally shocked and became confused. How could this have happened so quickly?

I began to think of something I had never given much thought to, something that always seemed to happen to other people, in the far distance. I thought, "Well, if she can suddenly just die, I can suddenly die, too. Oh my God!"

From that moment on, it seemed that I was being reminded of my mortality at almost every corner. It also seemed as if others were reminding me, constantly. Someone would bring up a story of a family member dying, or a fatal car accident. This went on and on.

My own mortality was something I had never given much thought to. Suddenly, fear struck me at the core. I, this, me could not only actually die at any moment, it is bound to happen at some point. This thought ran through my mind over and over. I started to have anxiety attacks and so much fear. I was waking up with heart palpitations.

After my trip ended and I returned home, I thought, "How can I ease this new fear I've acquired? What can I do? What can I learn? Where can I go? I mean, this is important; it's the one thing that will happen to every single one of us for sure." Then, a thought came to my mind — hospice!

Hospice is specialized medical care for terminal patients that helps them with pain management and end-of-life care. It also provides support to the family members of the patient.

I thought maybe doing some hospice work would help me overcome my fear. What better way to learn about dying than to jump right into situations where it is constantly happening. I thought maybe through that, I could ease my fear a little and bring some of Amma's light to these patients.

So I became a hospice volunteer, then a nurse, and eventually a hospice nurse, which I've been doing now for many years. If it wasn't for Amma and that first tour, I wouldn't be doing what I am doing now. The fear of death was actually a gift that would change my life. Has my fear completely vanished? I would say, no. But I have learned a lot and am slowly becoming a tiny bit more comfortable with the idea. Obviously, I would prefer that this event happens much, much, much, much later for me!

***

When I was a new hospice nurse, I remember meeting with my supervisor outside the home of a patient who had just passed away. It was the first time I would see a patient who had just died. Her body was still warm, and we would have to clean and prepare the body for transport. Before we entered, I told my supervisor that I was scared, and that I had no idea what I was doing. Now looking back, I have no clue how I even got hired! I had no prior hospice experience as an actual nurse, and they knew it. Yet somehow they agreed to hire me and didn't mind teaching me. My supervisor said something to me that night, right before we went in, that has always stayed with me. She said,

> "Don't worry. I will show you what to do. Just observe and follow my lead. But you must always be courageous and willing to face any situation, especially in this line of work. You must always act confident, even if you are not feeling that way on the inside. And you must never let the patients or family members know that you are afraid or uncertain. Because they are looking up to you for answers and guidance."

Her words reminded me of how Amma always says that we must be courageous and confident like lion cubs when facing life's challenges. It was as if Amma was speaking through her.

Years of hospice work was also preparing me for the first time in my life when a loved one would die — my grandmother. Because of Amma's grace, it was not sad for me. When I cried, I was crying not because I was sad, as I had the feeling she'd be taken care of. I was crying out of love, devotion, and gratitude for her. It was actually quite a magical experience. While intense, there was so much love and so much presence. I felt gratitude for the gift she had been in my life, and realized how very lucky I was that I got to take care of her during her transition. Even during her dying process, she left me with a gift. My grandmother showed me I had more to learn about hospice care. The experience showed me that I should care for each and every patient I come across with the same presence, love, and intensity as I did for her.

Over the years, I have become interested in people who had near-death experiences. I even joined online communities where people share their experiences and ask each other questions. The one common thing I see is that they all say they are no longer afraid of dying. While each of their experiences is unique, one thing most of them seem to have in common is that they see death as a beautiful experience, not to be feared. They now know that our lives don't end at death. They all seem to have the notion and understanding that the process happens naturally, in its own divine timing and on its own terms, and they are no longer afraid.

Amma also says that death is a blissful experience, like jumping into a pool of water. Just because a light bulb breaks doesn't mean the electricity gets destroyed. Pure consciousness is eternal and never changes. The forms come and go, but the consciousness remains.

Another thing they seem to come back with is the realization that loving and serving others is the most important thing — that it is one love that pervades the entire world.

As a hospice nurse, I'd like to think that I bring some of Amma's light to my patients. I love when they ask me why I travel so much. They haven't even finished the question when

I'm already holding a picture of Amma up on my phone. I tell them I'm going to see Amma, this super cute Indian saint. They stare at Amma's picture, curiously.

***

Before becoming a hospice nurse, I was a pediatric home health nurse. Many of my patients were on ventilators. They depend on these ventilators to breathe and could not live more than a few seconds without them. I would often say a prayer before my shifts. I would pray for Amma's guidance and the grace that everything runs smoothly during my shift. I also prayed that if anything went wrong, Amma would be there to help me.

I once had a patient whom I accompanied to school. I would ride the school bus with her and stay by her side throughout the day. The ventilator would beep if something was wrong – perhaps there was not enough air running through it, or perhaps it had become disconnected somewhere. My patient once told me that she had an emergency signal: if I ever saw her smacking her lips together, it meant I needed to act quickly.

One day we were on the school bus with lots of loud children. The ride was bumpy, and the bus would beep every time the ramp lowered to load children. Every few seconds, I turned around to check on my patient, who was seated behind me. That day I got distracted – and would soon learn a big lesson.

Suddenly a child on the bus loudly shouted, "Excuse me miss, but someone is trying to get your attention! Hello!"

I immediately turned around and saw my patient smacking her lips and frantically wiggling her head in great distress!

In a panic, I rushed over, trying to figure out what was wrong. The tubing had somehow disconnected. I quickly reattached it – but honestly, I nearly lost it. Had just a few more seconds gone by, she could have died, and I would have probably ended up in a dark, damp jail cell. Amma's grace truly saved both of us that day!

Thank you, Amma.

***

Amma never fails to show us she is beyond her body and knows us even better than we know ourselves. She knows our thoughts and our hearts.

Once when Amma was giving darśhan in the temple, I looked around and thought, "Should I go today?" I wasn't sure.

As soon as I looked back at Amma, she moved her head to the side, raised her eyebrows, smiled and nodded, "Yes," as if saying, "Come come." I thought, "Wait, what? Did Amma just answer me? No!"

I looked all around to see if maybe the look was meant for someone else. When I looked back up at Amma, she did it again. Again I thought, "Nooooo, it can't be for me." Suddenly the woman sitting next to me smacked my arm and said, "What are you doing? Don't just sit there, Amma is calling you. Go!"

With that confirmation, I rushed to the darśhan line. The woman managing the line stopped me, saying darśhan was finished and that I should come tomorrow.

Stuttering in panic I said, "No, but...but, I...I...I have to go today!"

She replied flatly, "No, tomorrow."

Frantic, I blurted out, "But Amma called me!"

She took one step back, looking at me suspiciously, and asked, "When? When did Amma call you?"

How could I explain all that had happened in a few seconds? "Amma waved at me!" I said. (Yes, that was an exaggeration, but I was desperate.)

Her gaze softened; she believed me! "Okay," she said, "Go!"

Amma was taking me one step closer to becoming one of her confident and courageous lion cubs.

***

Once, I invited a friend to come meet Amma in New York City. I hadn't seen her in years. While waiting for her to arrive, I kept thinking about how I wanted to sit near Amma. But every time I tried, I kept getting blocked, either by people or by the lack of empty chairs. I was getting frustrated. Eventually, I tried to sit near Amma's chair, but the stage monitor stopped me and told me there was no room.

That was it. I'd had enough no's.

Upset and defeated, I ran to the bathroom, locked myself in a stall, and cried and cried like a child. My heart hurt. I kept asking, "Why, why, Amma? I just want to be close to you... just a little bit."

Then I remembered that my friend would be coming soon and I had to stop crying. I did not want her to see me in that state. She came towards the end of the program and went for darŝhan. Right after her hug, I motioned for her to sit next to me because I knew that Amma would be passing that way to go back to her room. In those days, Amma would give darŝhan at ground level, just in front of the stage.

As we were standing, waiting for her to pass, Amma got up from her chair and walked straight over to me. She motioned with her beautiful glowing face and hands as if saying, "What's wrong?" She looked at me with such beautiful, compassionate eyes that I lost myself in them. She then looked at my friend and took us both into her arms at the same time. My friend was shocked. She said it was amazing but was puzzled as to how Amma knew that we were friends. Whenever the subject of Amma comes up, my friend just loves telling this story.

***

Amma also never fails to let us know when we are getting too attached to the concept of 'mine.' Several times on the Western tours, during the special Dēvī Bhāva programs, I have been blessed to give some light snacks to Amma. Once on the Europe Tour, I invited a friend to join me. At one stop, I decided to make french fries. By the time we got to the stage, the fries were soggy and cold. Amma ate some nonetheless, and said "You need to go to the University of French-Fry-Making."

At the next stop, I decided that I would find the perfect french fry recipe. I spoke to a Belgian woman who said she had the perfect recipe to make them crispy. When I told my friend that I wanted to make french fries again, she disagreed. She wanted to make zucchini fries. I didn't say anything to her, but I was very annoyed.

I thought, "How absurd! Who likes zucchini fries better than french fries anyway? Certainly not Amma! And who is this friend of mine to change my plan?" I insisted that I wanted to make french fries. She came up with a solution: I would make french fries, and she would make the zucchini fries. We could both take them up together. I agreed. I was certain Amma would not like the zucchini fries.

When we got to the stage, Amma didn't even look at my now perfect, warm, crispy, right-out-of-the-frying-pan fries. She picked up the zucchini fries instead and said, "Amma *really* likes these!" She definitely emphasized the *really*, or at least that's how I heard it. Not only did Amma *really* like the zucchini fries, she wanted the leftovers wrapped up to take with her on her way to the next stop. I realized my mistake. I had become too attached to the concept of *mine*. In the end, I laughed at my own foolishness. When I saw what joy Amma's response brought to my friend, I was able to forget my attachment and enjoy the moment right along with her.

***

Over the years, I've seen many people pass away and have often wondered why some seem to have a harder time than others. Some people have a lot of anxiety and die in distress, while others go with such peace and ease. I once read that you die how you lived.

But Amma always says that what matters more than how we die is how we live.

May we all live our most magnificent life full of love, gratitude, and service to our beautiful Amma and to our brothers and sisters around the world.

May Amma bless us with more patience and śhraddhā (alert attention), so that we may treat each other with more love and less judgment.

6

Growing Past Spiritual Misconceptions

Raghunath - France

I often thought that if I wrote a satsang, it would be about my various misunderstandings about spiritual life. Unfortunately, I have plenty of material on this topic. But perhaps our greatness is not measured by our successes alone, but also by our failures. If we are willing to introspect and learn from our mistakes, we can grow spiritually.

My first misconception became clear while trying to write this satsang. Because I am fairly disciplined with my spiritual practices and listen to satsangs every day, I thought that writing a satsang would be relatively easy. I was wrong. As I wrote, I found it very difficult to put the connection between my life and Amma's teachings onto the written page. I had to cut back all of my daily activities to the bare minimum, so I could focus on writing and finish before the deadline. I felt deeply discouraged more than once. Writing a satsang is definitely an art, one that takes a lot of practice. I wish to thank all my brothers and sisters who have helped me in one way or another to focus on this difficult task. It is in no small part due to their help that I have the immense privilege of having completed the endeavor and am able to offer it to Amma.

I was born in France and grew up as an only child without my father, but with all the love and care that a mother could possibly give. Since I was young I have been preoccupied with what I would become when I grew up. At first, my life-plan was to become an ice cream seller, but even at that young age, I felt this might not be enough to make me truly happy. So, I asked my mother if it would be possible for me to work several jobs. As her answer was positive, I added "become a car-mechanic" to my list. The list kept growing until I met Amma in 2013. It's not really that my list of life-plans stopped there, but that my life-direction was no longer the same. My goal to "be happy in the world" had changed. I now longed to "be happy in Amritapuri."

The common goal of all beings is to be happy; it is completely natural. However, most people tend to believe that if something is pleasant, it is good for us, and if it is unpleasant, it is bad for us. But happiness in the āśhram doesn't follow this logic. To be happy here, we must be happy with ourselves, and the path to that doesn't always coincide with what we like.

When I became a resident in Amritapuri in 2016, I didn't know what I needed to progress spiritually. The few spiritual books I had read recommended being alone and quiet; whereas, we are mostly surrounded by crowds and noise at the āśhram. I had grown up alone with my mother and was always the center of attention. I now found myself in a spiritual family with thousands of "toddlers" shouting, singing, and sometimes even dancing! At times, this aspect of the āśhram disturbed me, and I often thought of running away to a hermitage at the top of a mountain! But Amma had other plans.

When I went to Sri Lanka with my āśhram brother Vishakh to apply for a new Indian visa, Amma taught me a valuable lesson. While there, we stayed in a Buddhist monastery for two weeks. This place was ideal for silence and solitude. In the afternoon, we taught French to a sixty-five-year-old European monk, but we noticed that he was thirsty for conversation. He jumped on any visitor who came within fifty meters of him. Eventually, our French classes became nothing more than a way for him to talk for whole afternoons. One day he decided to share about his pre-monastic romantic exploits. He even brought a small stack of photos of his ex-girlfriends to show us.

I'm not saying this to criticize him; we all have weaknesses. I felt Amma was showing me the important lesson that real silence and solitude have to be found within. Like Amma says, we should have equanimity even in the middle of the marketplace. That is the real yardstick for spiritual growth.

***

Like many Amritapuri residents, Tuesday was my day of 'silence and solitude.' When Amma was on tour, I would take a vow of silence, meditate, and fast until 6:00 p.m. To be honest, I dreaded this day all week! When Tuesday finally came around, and I started my tapas (austerities), my main focus for the day was on what I would buy at the Indian canteen at 6:00 p.m. If there was nothing I liked at the canteen that night, I would feel miserable.

I am not saying that meditation and the practice of silence are not needed — they are very important. At the same time, for most of us, meditation alone is not sufficient to get rid of our deep-rooted vāsanās (mental tendencies). That's why we need Amma to put us in her "rock-tumbler". It may not always feel like the most pleasant of experiences, but it is what we need to lose our rough edges, so we can become pure.

Believe it or not, I was obese as a kid. By the time I was thirteen, I weighed 112 kg (247 pounds), and I was bullied at school. It was at fourteen that I decided to lose weight. What caused this change in me? I desperately wanted to be loved by others, but on an even deeper level, I wanted to love myself. Since coming to the āśhram, Amma has put me in many situations to help me overcome what I perceived as my own limitations, and through that I have gained self-confidence. For example, when I came to the āśhram, my English was a disaster. Simply ordering food at the Western Café was quite an adventure, and I couldn't understand the translations of Amma's satsangs.

When I learned that classes on the *Bhagavad Gītā* were being given by Br. Atmaprakash Chaitanya, I knew I could not miss them. One of my French brothers and I made a deal. As long as I was present at the 9:15 p.m. class, he would share his French notes with me. I did not miss a single class. After three months, I realized that I no longer needed his notes to follow the class. I consider it Amma's miracle to have learned English this way.

Before Covid, whenever Amma would go away on tour, she used to meet with the residents in the Kālī Temple to give instructions. The topics ranged from not putting large flower pots on the rooftops because they damaged them, to increasing the time we dedicated to spiritual practices. One time before she left, she asked everyone to learn Sanskrit. Going back to my room, I felt totally discouraged. I thought, "I don't even speak English well. How can I possibly learn Sanskrit?" But because Amma's saṅkalpa (divine resolve) was there, and I put in my best effort, within one month, I had learned the Devanagari script and was able to read slowly. Within one year, I seamlessly joined the āśhram Sanskrit class, which had started four years earlier. I feel Amma guided me through such experiences to help me build self-confidence and to be more accepting of myself.

***

In the āśhram, sēvā is the best place to become aware of our vāsanās (negative tendencies) and put an end to them. Amma's method is to make them more and more apparent until they become unbearable to us. This gives us the motivation to defeat them.

The sēvā that highlighted my vāsanās best for me was cashiering at the Western Café. My role was simply to collect the money when devotees paid for their food. Most interactions were limited to a "Namaḥ Śhivāya,"[5] a smile with eye contact, and a "thank you." But each person's character is unique, and often my interactions would go beyond the meal being paid for. Some customers would add a few nice words in French, others would try to offer me a piece of cake or a cookie, others would have specific requests and get angry when I didn't satisfy them. Others would completely ignore me. After several months at this sēvā, I realized how vulnerable I was.

Amma always says that our lives depend on the words of others. I realized how true this is! Each person coming to get their meal or to buy a cake had the power to make me happy, if they complimented me; to make me impatient, if they were angry; or to demoralize me, if they ignored me. Even though I waited impatiently for each shift to end so I could return to an activity more comfortable for me, I never gave up. By observing my own shortcomings, and through continuous practice, I gained some detachment, and now my opinion of myself is less dependent on what others think.

Amma often tells the story of the beggar who goes around to receive alms from different homes. Someone may give him five rupees, the next may give ten rupees, and the third may spit in the beggar's hand, but he says thank you to everyone. This is the attitude we should aspire to attain.

There was a visitor to the āśhram who always seemed to avoid social interactions. One day our eyes met when I gave her back her change. As I said, "Namaḥ Śhivāya" to her, I managed to push past my inhibition and give her a wide and sincere smile.

---

[5] 'Salutations to Śhiva, the auspicious one, the inner self,' a famous mantra and the common greeting used in Amma's āśhrams.

She smiled in return. I remember the little light of joy in her eyes at that moment. At the end of the day, we all are the same; we all want to be treated with love. Even if we can't always give what others expect from us, we can at least understand them and have compassion, maybe add in a nice little word in French, and give a sincere smile.

***

As mentioned before, I was unpopular and isolated as a child. But 'the fat boy' grew up and became popular and hip. By the time I started working, I was the youngest stock manager for a famous American clothing brand with more than 270 stores across twenty countries. But, was I happy with this life? You all know the answer; I was not at all content.

By that time, my mother had been going to see Amma at the French program for several years. Every year, she invited me to join her, and every year I refused. One year, though, I found myself facing the fact that my life had no meaning; I felt I was wasting my life. Looking for meaning, I became interested in the problems of modern society and in the solutions offered by different spiritual traditions. However, meeting an authentic satguru seemed beyond my reach. Since Amma did not sit in a cave in the Himalayas, I did not consider her a real spiritual master. It was only in 2013, when I found myself completely bogged down by depression, that I accepted my mother's advice and went to India to meet this 'Amma' lady.

***

In 2015, I did my first India tour with Amma. After two-and-a-half months of touring, while at the Kochi program, I suddenly realized that Amma is the pure love I had been searching for in the world. I had finally found a person who sincerely wanted to reach out to all, a person who endlessly caressed, consoled, and wiped away the tears of each and every individual who came to her. I realized that her promise to do so for as long as she has enough strength in her arms, until the end of her mortal frame, was a scientific certainty. As Amma arrived on stage to start the Kochi program, I burst into tears. I had found meaning in my life.

I was drawn to the monastic lifestyle of the āśhram, and after spending three years in Amritapuri, I asked Amma if I could be a renunciate. Amma grimaced and asked me to think about it again and again and again and again. She added that, "People take renunciation but keep their desires for the world." Still, I was sure that was what I wanted, so I was disappointed. My interpretations of her words ranged from, "She is testing me," to, "I'm not good enough to be a renunciate."

But Amma knew me better than I did, and she knew what I needed to grow spiritually. She knew that a part of my motivation was based on resentment for "what the world did to me." My desire for renunciation wasn't the deep kind of vairāgya (dispassion) that is needed to live a monastic life. Amma knew my weaknesses and the difficulties I would encounter in facing the many obstacles on the monastic path.

Again I had misunderstood, thinking that only the life of 'a perfect renunciate' reflected the greatness of God and could make Amma happy with me. This was yet another big misunderstanding I had about spirituality!

Swamini Sanatanamrita Prana once told me, "Being a renunciate is not what matters. What's important is the place we give Amma in our hearts." Swamini's words became a rich source of contemplation for me. They prompted me to ask, "What really matters?"

In Chapter 9 of the *Bhagavad Gītā*, Śhrī Kṛiṣhṇa says that when someone devoutly offers him a leaf, flower, fruit, or water, he receives this offering, imbued with the devotion of this pure-spirited person. He continues by saying that whatever we do, whatever we eat, whatever we sacrifice or practice, whatever we give, whatever austerity that we follow; we do it as an offering. In this manner, we will be liberated, and we will come to him.

To explain these verses, our Swami Paramatmananda Puri tells a story. Three boys lived in Italy in the 1600s. Their names were Salvador, Julio, and Antonio. Salvador was a very good singer, and Julio accompanied him very well on the violin when they performed around town. Antonio also loved music, but his voice squeaked like a creaky door hinge, and all the children laughed at him. But Antonio also had a talent; he could carve very pretty little things using his grandfather's pocket knife. One day, when Antonio was sitting with a heavy heart because he was unable to sing, an old man placed a gold coin in his hand. Later, his brothers told him that this old man was Amati, probably the best violin maker in all of Italy. Antonio became determined to find Amati and brought with him some of the beautiful figurines he was carving. When he found the old man's house, Antonio showed Amati his handiwork, asking him to teach him to make violins. Amati admired his little figurines for a long time and asked him, "Why do you want to make violins?"

Antonio replied, "Because I love music, but my voice squeaks like a creaky door hinge. You heard the other day how well my brothers sing... I want to bring music to life too!"

Amati looked Antonio straight in the eyes and said, "The most important thing is the music in your heart. There are many ways to make music — some play the violin, others sing, and others paint beautiful pictures. Each helps to add beauty to this world. You are a carver of wood, but your music will be as noble as the others."

For the rest of his life, Antonio Stradivari made violins, trying to make each even better than the last. Today, whoever owns a Stradivarius violin has a treasure worth millions of dollars.

Paramatmananda Swami concludes that perhaps we are not all great seekers or perfect renunciates, but we can all offer God what we have, and he will always be satisfied. Amma knows each one of us, along with our weaknesses and imperfections, and compassionately accepts any efforts we make on the path, each at our own level.

***

In October 2021, after I had been living in Amritapuri for six years, the Indian government reauthorized international flights. My situation at the āśhram did not allow me to stay. My wife, Padma, and I went to France, hoping to turn this unfavorable situation into a favorable one. We decided to use the time working to earn money for our life at the āśhram. Without this push, neither of us could have imagined leaving Amritapuri. Using our sēvā at the Western Café as a reference, Amma's grace quickly got us a job in a restaurant, and we worked there for a year.

It can be disconcerting to find yourself in the world after six years in Amritapuri, but it was impossible to complain because we had received so much. Would we be able to share some of what Amma had given us?

We haven't had the opportunity to explain to our bosses and co-workers why, "He who knows the absolute becomes the absolute" ('*brahmavid brahmaiva bhavati*' – the famous declaration from the Upaniṣhads that Amma asked us to comment on during the Covid period). It was complicated enough explaining to them why we were called "Raghunath and Padma" as we enjoyed our green salads, and they savored their beef steaks.

It seemed to us that the best thing to do was not to talk about Vēdānta (the supreme truth) or give moral lessons. The best thing we could do was to try to put Amma's teachings into practice.

I was still trapped a few times by my tendency to suppress my emotions in the face of the chef's anger. But later, after tempering my negative emotions — keeping a gap between my thoughts and my actions — I would return to him and ask him to talk to me, so that we could try to understand each other. Between the loud techno music and the workplace gossip, the conditions there were far from ideal. However, by doing regular sādhanā, watching the daily livestreams of Amma's evening program, and speaking with our āśhram family through WhatsApp, I never felt disconnected from Amma, her teachings, or Amritapuri. By her grace, I have always found a way to stay in her presence.

***

We are returning to France in a few days to work for another year-and-a-half. Last month, we were able to ask Amma for her blessing to go back to earn the money needed. Our goal is to settle in the āśhram for good and dedicate our lives in service to Amma. Amma replied with an eager, "Yes!" The image of her shining eyes and enchanting smile in that moment will give us the enthusiasm and strength we need for the year ahead.

I don't have the great qualifications given by the scriptures, such as vivēka (discernment) or vairāgya (detachment), but Amma has remained in my heart and in my thoughts. It is through love for Amma that I was able to work in a challenging situation in France without being pulled down by it. At the end of each seasonal contract, with tears in my eyes, I raise my arms and shout, "Amma, we did it!"

As you can see, I have held many misunderstandings about the spiritual path. I'm deeply grateful to Amma for illuminating so many of them — and I pray for her grace to continue guiding me through those yet to be revealed. May Amma bless all of us with untainted vision so that we may ever abide in eternal peace and her immutable love.

7

L.O.V.E. — The Path of Bhakti

Seema – USA

This wonderful series of satsangs all started after Amma asked the āśhram kids to explain the twenty-four gurus that the great sage Dattātrēya encountered during his wanderings as an ascetic. Well, I've found the twenty-fifth guru. When this twenty-fifth guru came to me, it meant that I had to work on my satsang throughout the night in my friend's room. A few days later while procrastinating in my room, I received another visit from the twenty-fifth guru. As I was writing, a furry flash ran past me and disappeared under the door! It was Lord Gaṇēśha's vehicle, a rat; he was my twenty-fifth guru. I suppose the late night snacking may have invited this divine encounter. More importantly, I had an epiphany — if only I could be as aware of Amma's underlying love in all areas of my life, including my work, as I was of the rat scurrying around my room, my life would be full of love.

Love is the essence of life. Love inspires popular novels, movies, great historical epics, art, and music. Love is the fundamental power of creation governing each being. We can see love at work every day between family members, friends, and even pets and their owners. This type of love is familiar, but there is another type of love — the pure, eternal love of Amma.

Amma's love has touched all our hearts in one way or another: Amma's love is the cord that tethers us to her. Whatever our path may be, whatever our life goals are, our center point, our home is Amma's love.

The master of pure love knows exactly how to reawaken this pure love in us. It all starts with a spark. For me, it was that first darśhan.

We all come to Amma in different ways. Some of us were drawn through bhajans, *Matruvani* (Amma's monthly magazine), Amma's books, or her photos. For my parents and me, it was a family member, a documentary, and a flier. Let me explain.

My parents had been yearning to meet a satguru (true master) for over a decade, but they believed that such a mahātmā would never come to the West. Little did they know our Amma travels around the world just to meet her children, to alleviate their sufferings, to hear their woes, and to spread love. We came under Amma's wing in Toronto, Canada when I was twelve years old.

That first hug woke up an almost obsessive love. I became what many of Amma's children would term "Amma crazy," or "Amma vaṭṭē," as it is called in Malayalam. Like many of my friends, I obsessed over Amma's photos, bhajans, videos, books, sēvā, saris Amma has worn for Dēvī Bhāva, old Amma stories, Amma's walk, Amma's eyes, Amma's hands, Amma's smile, Amma's laughter — everything about her.

Every year at the retreat, I wanted to buy the entire set of newly released bhajan albums, but my dad would step in and say that I didn't need so many albums. So naturally, I devised a plan.

Step 1: Politely ask my dad to buy the two CDs in our native languages, Hindi and Telugu.

Step 2: Give a compliment to my mom, saying, "Wow mom, did you do something with your hair? It's so nice," then ask for two more CDs, omitting the fact that my dad had just bought two.

Step 3: Complain of hunger. Ask for money for food. Buy the remaining set.

I think my plan was quite savvy because I usually ended up with the whole set of albums. Those tracks were my playlist for the rest of the year. I listened in the car, on the bus, while walking.

I know there are many who wait for Amma's darśhan once a year, and I know that there are many 'off-the-grid' Amma crazies like me out there who didn't get a chance to grow up around Amma but longed to. The battle between keeping a grateful mind for having Amma in my life and the longing and sorrow that came from being physically distant from her is a real pain that many of us face. Even though it hurt so much, and I don't ever want to be apart from Amma like that again, it was a necessary first step in opening my heart to Amma. Her love inspired me to live my life on the path of bhakti (devotion).

The learned often say that bhakti is the sweetest path. Even though I don't yet fully comprehend this, Amma has made it so easy for me to follow this path.

Amma says,

> "Bhakti is love — loving God, loving your own self, and loving all beings. The small heart should become bigger and bigger and, eventually, totally expansive. A spark can become a forest fire. So to have only a spark is enough, for the spark is also fire. Keep blowing on it, fanning it. Sooner or later it will burn like a forest fire, sending out long tongues of flame."

Lord Kṛiṣhṇa teaches Arjuna about the path of bhakti in the *Bhagavad Gītā.*

> *ananyāśh-chintayantō māṁ yē janāḥ paryupāsatē*
> *tēṣhām nityābhiyuktānāṁ yōga-kṣhēmaṁ vahāmyaham*

> For those who always think of me, worship me, and are ever absorbed in me, I provide whatever they lack and preserve what they already possess. (9.22)

When we open our hearts to Amma, we become completely open and drop any sense of shame or fear. Love becomes our greatest strength because it opens up the space in our heart for Amma to shine through. With faith, surrender, and acceptance, we know Amma will take care of us. We know that she is with us despite everything, and that we can tell Amma anything. We establish our relationship with Amma as our guru, our mother, our friend. We make Amma ours. And perhaps that's the key in bhakti. It is to live normally, do everything that you have to do, and add God into every moment of it. The feeling should be intimate; we should think of God as "mine." Slowly God will start to spill over into all aspects of our life. God in turn, takes us as her own and protects us, guides us, and gives us whatever we need most. Amma has shown this in not just my case, but in every single heart she has touched.

I think there is a lot more Amma is teaching us here. I have come to understand that bhakti means L.O.V.E.

L - Live, O - Open-Heartedly, V - Vigorously, E - Entirely

Those of us on the bhakti path are called to live with an open heart, vigorously, and entirely for the Lord. Let me break it down a little further. We will start with O, V, E and end with L.

'O' represents Opening our hearts to Amma

On January 6, 1984 during evening bhajans in Amritapuri, Amma asked one of her daughters to sing, but, out of her shyness, she did not. After bhajans, Amma lovingly approached her daughter during supper and told her that shyness should be the first thing a spiritual aspirant gives up. When one comes to spiritual life, assertiveness should be developed. (from *Awaken Children* 2)

Even though Amma spoke to her daughter in 1984, her words were really for all of her children from around the world, through all time.

I know that Amma was speaking directly to me as I read about becoming assertive. In many ways I am still shy, but Amma is slowly cracking my heart to not be shy around her. It's a work in progress.

It was during my first U.S. tour that I got to see how much my shyness was affecting my relationship with Amma. Watching other devotees' open relationship with Amma made me examine my own relationship with her. I realized that my shyness around Amma came from the feeling I should conduct myself in a proper way with her because she is my guru. She is Dēvī, the Goddess. A friend on tour told me that I shouldn't think like that and should just open my heart up to Amma. "Forget everything else," she said. "All Amma wants is your heart." It wasn't until my second world tour that I realized what these words meant.

My first trip to India marked my first time traveling without friends or family members. The South India Tour made me talk to Amma more in my mind than I ever had before. I argued with her, I complained to her, I cried to her. But every time I was ready to quit, Amma found a way to fill my heart with love. She looked after me that entire trip. Anytime I felt lonely, she found a way to give me sēvā close to her. The dust and smog, which should have triggered my sinus issues, was no problem at all.

Because of my shyness, not knowing Malayalam, the fast pace of darśhan, and my lack of assertiveness, I never talked to the outer Amma. On the other hand, I have always talked to Amma in my head, and this trip was proof that she was listening. I felt Amma with me at all times. It was during this South Indian Tour that Amma became *mine*.

Love is a funny thing. The ego, which takes lifetimes of effort to overcome, simply drops away in love.

'V' represents loving Vigorously

With a sincere heart full of love and conviction, we act dynamically for love, in love, and through love.

In the *Gītā* verse mentioned above, Lord Kṛishṇa mentions two key words, yōga (union) and kṣhema (protection), which represent two ways of living. Yōga is the energy we spend trying to unite with an object of desire. Kṣhema is the energy we spend in trying to protect that which we have already acquired. When we turn to the Lord through devotion, God will look after both yōga and kṣhema for us. When we surrender our worries, we gain mental clarity. It frees up our energy to live in the moment, to focus our undivided attention on our duties, and to live wholeheartedly.

Almost every Amma devotee has had two lives: B.A. and A.A., i.e., before meeting Amma and after meeting Amma. Most positive transformations we make happen A.A.

In my B.A. life, academics were the most horrible nightmare. I really struggled with learning and with school. Every year, I failed the standardized exam and would have to take a remedial class to make up for the poor marks. Although I had a lot of help from my parents, teachers, and even tutors, the struggle still persisted. However, the academic year after meeting Amma, something happened. I started picking things up more easily and for the first time in my life, I made straight A's. It was as if some sort of block lifted, and I was able to grasp things.

The next school year, I was selected to tutor remedial kids. With Amma's grace, I graduated in the top 3% of my school, went on to finish my undergraduate degree in engineering, and received a competitive job. I am not saying all of this to brag. Far from it, I know in my heart that it was Amma who studied for me, who completed the degree, who hired me, and who earned enough money so I could go on tour and travel with her. I am not an engineer; I don't even consider myself as one. Amma is the engineer in my life, in all aspects.

The *Awaken Children* series was Amma's way of silently teaching and guiding me. It was my *Bhagavad Gītā*, my scripture. When I was a kid, my mom enrolled me and my brother in cultural and spiritual classes at the Chinmaya Mission, and I would use Amma examples from *Awaken Children* during my exams. My teachers were quite impressed with the stories.

In my B.A. life, I could never understand concepts in Sanātana Dharma like bhakti, brahman (the absolute), or the satguru. But after meeting Amma, I started to understand them by relating everything back to Amma. It was like every aspect of Sanātana Dharma was describing Amma; whatever I learned was embodied by Amma's actions. Amma was right there with me, and the flame of Amma's love rekindled in my heart.

When the Orlando satsang community started and our AYUDH (Amma's youth-wing) chapter began, there were just a handful of us who had this desire in our hearts to serve Amma, but we didn't know what to do. Within a year, not only had we managed to plan a sēvā activity every month, we also started the first Southeast Regional Camp together with AYUDH Atlanta!

Growing up, I always felt that Amma was with me, but it was my secret. Wherever I went, whatever I did, I had this subconscious awareness of Amma. Talking to Amma in my head or relating something in my life to the Amma-world grounded me. If anything good happened, I wanted to tell the world that it was Amma, the Amma within my heart, who did it.

Our vision is to live fully, to face life and its challenges, to be dynamic and fearless, to plan with clarity and to work selflessly. With no other thoughts, without doubts, demands, or desires — not even the desire for liberation — we love God. God takes the throne in the lotus of our heart and our being becomes an offering to God.

'E' represents Entirely

There is only one ultimate dharma or duty in life and that is: to know God. When God is the goal, then the love we have for God will trump any desire. As human beings, we all strive to find meaning. Once we discover what that is for us, we redirect our energy to achieve the goal. The path of bhakti guides us to channel this energy so that our mind becomes completely absorbed in God. When we do this, all our secondary goals in life get displaced. This does not mean that we give up our duties, rather we understand the nature of worldly goals and stop wasting energy worrying about something that God will take care of. With a mind that is fully absorbed in God, our entire being becomes a wellspring of love for God, and it is that love that merges us with God.

Sādhanā, or spiritual practice, is a tool which reminds us to remember the Lord. But as love builds within our heart, sādhanā becomes more than that. It becomes an outlet to express the longing in our heart. Amma gave me a glimpse of this during Covid. For many of Amma's children around the world, the notice that Amritapuri was closed until further notice because of the pandemic was heartbreaking. Uncertainty about the future added fuel to the fire, but a blessing came from it. We all got a chance to find Amma within. We had to, it was our only way to be with Amma. There were no tours, no Amma family, no sēvā. Nothing.

The intense longing made me fully open my heart to Amma. I don't know if this was the best thing for Amma because there was a lot of heartbreak, sobbing, and accusations. I heard that when you do archana[6] with full sincerity, Amma sees your face. If this is true, Amma was seeing my face very often. Archana became my bond with Amma; it allowed me to pour out my longing into chanting her names. It was as though I was giving Amma a call and so I began to immerse myself more and more in spiritual practices. In addition to archana, I took up fasting and meditation, and soon I got more and more online sēvā. From the moment I opened my eyes to the moment I closed them, my thoughts were filled with Amma. I stopped watching TV and reading books because it took me away from her. In many ways, I experienced the intensity of vairāgya (dispassion) and love. Sēvā became my way of channeling the burning love and gratitude in my heart towards her.

Amrit Ganga, Amma's Hindi television series, has reached tens of thousands of people in India and around the world. During Covid, I began writing scripts for special episodes. While writing promos and scripts, I had to put myself in the shoes of those who don't know anything about Amma and figure out how to present Amma to them. For example, how would you respond to prompts like: 'What is Amma's love?' or 'Describe Amma's darśhan.'

Actually, writing is not my forte — I have the grades to prove it. But focusing on Amma's love in my heart helped me to write creatively. For the first time in my life, I was able to write, and by Amma's grace it wasn't bad! The more sēvā I did, the more I felt Amma's presence in my heart, however exhausted I felt. I didn't care if something was feasible or out of my scope. I simply tried my best with Amma in mind. I did it for her. Amma gave me the confidence that if I do something with utmost sincerity, and I do it with love, Amma's grace will flow.

---

[6] Chanting of the names of a particular deity, especially the *Śhrī Lalitā Sahasranāma*, the thousand names of the Divine Mother.

Even though I was suffering the sweet misery of yearning for Amma, I felt alive. Amma's love lifted me. I found her in everything that I did, and I found Amma within. She gave me a strength that I don't think I would have found otherwise.

'L' means to Live our Life with God in every breath

Every thought, every word, every action should be coated with the fragrance of the Lord. Only when we live a life of love can we be happy.

To really live, the heart must be filled with pure love, and the soul with compassion. Pure love allows us to see past our own needs and into the needs of others. Amma says, "Compassion can shoulder the suffering of the entire world without feeling the slightest pain." When we see Amma in those that we are serving, the love in our hearts will grow until we surrender to the flow of love. That is when we are truly living, when we become connected to the source of love.

So, what is bhakti? Bhakti is living a normal life with pure love for Amma. However, pure love doesn't come all on its own; it takes effort. It takes an open heart, a vigorous spirit, and a mind absorbed entirely in Amma. I am still learning on my journey, so I realize that this definition will grow and develop over time. One thing that remains unchanging though, is Amma's love.

Falling in love with Amma is falling in love with existence, with everyone and everything around us. When we do everything out of that place of love, our actions become an offering to the world. This love is all I have to offer, however limited.

I love this very moment in your physical presence, Amma, even though it will last only a moment. In a couple of days, I will go back to the U.S. — just as all of Kṛiṣhṇa's gōpīs also had their lives to return to. But maybe the key is to find this profundity in every moment of our lives: to offer our every thought, word, and action in service of Amma, to that brilliant love that she is.

On the path of love, or bhakti, we give up the right to be unhappy. In the awareness that God is taking care of all of our problems, we realize that there is nothing to be sad about, and *that* is all Amma wants. She wants to see us love and live happily. That is her purpose.

I will conclude with Amma's words:

> "Children, you are Amma's treasure. When Amma renounced everything, there was only one thing that could not be renounced — that was you, my children. It is only when Amma sees you becoming the light of the world that Amma truly feels happy. Amma does not require your praise or service. Amma only wants to see you acquire the strength to bear the burdens and sufferings of the world."

Amma, please slam open the doors of our hearts. Pour in waves and waves of your love until there is only your love. Steal our hearts. Make our lives yours and fill them with opportunities to serve you. Merge us in the flame of your love, Amma.

8

Returning to Our Sacred Roots

Mangalan – Germany

I was blessed to have met Amma in my early youth in 1994 at the age of eighteen.

Having been born in Germany to parents who were devoted to Paramahansa Yogananda, I grew up with the presence of a guru in my life. Even though my parents didn't practice meditation, they talked about and embodied spiritual principles.

Despite having had a very blessed childhood, from an early age I always felt that something essential was missing, not only in my personal life, but in Western society as a whole. I remember that the only reason I agreed to be confirmed in the Protestant Church was to receive the gifts and the money that would be presented to me on that day. I have always had a deep reverence for, and close relationship with Jesus Christ, but I did not experience his essence as being alive in the Church in any way. No matter how hard I tried, the Church remained empty for me. In fact, I felt the same emptiness about the education system and basically all other aspects of life, as well.

In my youth, the only places left for me to find meaning were the laser-lighted discotheques of the freshly blossoming Techno (electronic music) scene. What started out as joyful experiences of love, family, and friendship (in what was *not* a substance-free environment) soon transformed into a disastrous one-way street of self-destruction. Even so, I was still consciously searching for the truth. I read spiritual books and often visited a Buddhist lama. I could feel the truth in those teachings but was never inspired enough to follow those paths.

I still have a vivid memory of sitting outside a discotheque with a good friend of mine in the early hours of the morning uttering, "I need to know if God exists." I knew that if my search did not take a serious positive turn soon, I would not be around much longer.

Shortly after this, my brother came back from a journey to India and I could see that he had completely changed. He told me of how he met Amma and his experiences in Amritapuri. A few months later, we hit the road together to meet Amma in Germany for one of her early Europe tours.

> After my first darśhan, that was it!!!
> The unique experience of her divine embrace
> Made me forget the outer world.
> I merged in Her.
> Into my own Self.
> Oneness.
> Unity.
> Peace.

Coming back out of this timeless moment, I knew that this was what I had been searching for. I had found my origin, my goal. It was simple yet profound. During the following week on tour, I received my mantra and asked Mother if she was my guru. She confirmed with a clear, "Yes!" and a sweet smile.

Some months later I found myself in India, staying in Amritapuri for six months.

The Divine Mother herself had come to pull me out of a dark ditch and had brought me home to her own abode of eternal bliss. The time that followed was the best time of my life. My soul was drinking in the bliss of Amma's divine presence like a little baby sucking milk from its mother's breast.

Ah yes, God does exist! And that, too, in a beautiful form far beyond anything I could have ever dreamed. I was home, forever at home in the love of Amma's feet. I was blessed with bhakti (devotional love) that must have been equal to what the gōpīs, Lord Kṛiṣhṇa's milkmaid devotees, experienced long ago in Vṛindāvan. Whenever the bell rang to let us know Amma was coming out to spend time with us, I would sprint to make it to the front row and find a place right next to Mother's seat.

During bhajans in the Kālī Temple I would always sit in front, literally one or two meters away from Amma, drowning in the sea of bliss and her divine beauty. The two weekly Dēvī Bhāva programs were the heartbeat of Amritapuri; they were the divine rhythm that aligned our hearts with Mother.

***

By Mother's grace, I went back for a seventeen month stay soon after. I was actually allowed to do my German Civil Service in Amritapuri, in place of compulsory military service. My journey of bliss continued.

Thanks to my brother, who had lived as a brahmachāri (celibate student) for a long time, I found myself spending more time with the Indian monastics than with the few Westerners staying in the āśhram. During the North India tours, I would travel in the brahmachāri bus and help with the sound system. In those days, there were sometimes two programs in completely different locations on the same day in big cities like Mumbai or Delhi. We would take down the sound system and bookstall after the morning program and set it up in the next location for evening darśhan.

On many occasions, I was lucky enough to squeeze into one of the few vehicles that were following Amma's car for house calls. She made these after finishing her public programs in the early hours of the morning. Actually, it was more like a divine car race, with Amma's white car shooting along the deserted streets, escorted by the police, as we struggled to keep up. The renegade cars were always filled with devotees giggling with divine madness. I was so lucky to see Amma bless many devotees' pūjā rooms where she would perform a small pūjā (worship ritual) and sing a bhajan or two. She would then head for the kitchen to boil milk and distribute it as prasād (blessed food) to those present.

Many times on these tours we would stop for a chai break, or even go swimming in a nearby river. On one such occasion, Amma blessed me with a glimpse of her divinity. At that time I was still wondering who Amma really was. Inwardly I had been asking her to show me her divinity. We had just stopped by a beautiful river. It was the girls' time to bathe with Mother, and so we boys stayed away on the far side.

I remember casually thinking, just as Amma and the ladies were coming back to shore, "Oh no, I have no soap. So I guess I will just have to wash myself without any today." Out of nowhere Amma came directly towards me. As she walked by me she softly asked, "No soap?" My mind was puzzled. She has continually shown me her all-knowing, omnipresent nature over the years. Slowly I was beginning to grasp a bit more of the nature of her being.

All of these are unforgettable memories. I am so thankful for this moment, to be able to breathe life back into these stories by sharing them with you.

Back in the āśhram, when Amma was away on tour, I would sometimes wake up at two or three o'clock in the morning and lock myself in the old Kaḷari Temple. Then I would dance, as Amma had advised us to do. Well, to use the Kaḷari for that purpose was my own idea, but it was the perfect place to merge into that joyful practice. So many times during bhajans, tears of bliss and sweet longing for God flowed and flowed.

Back in those days, there weren't many buildings. There was no darśhan hall, no Amrita Darśhan building. Only the Kālī Temple had already been constructed. The site of the Big Hall was all islands of sand and palm trees surrounded by backwaters that we would fill up bit by bit on the occasions of the famous sand sēvā.

Many times I would sense, or wish, that Mother might come out at night, and I would sit near her room and wait. And sometimes, if the few of us waiting there were lucky, she would come, walk down the stairs and go to the ocean. Sometimes we were allowed to follow. Those are the most precious moments of eternity, as we sat at the seashore meditating with her. There were never more than ten to fifteen people. And often Amma would start to sing epic bhajans like *Kōṭānu Kōṭi*, *Sṛiṣhtiyum Nīyē*, or even *Hē Giridhara Gōpālā*, and we would sing along. Then the silence would drop again, and we would hear the ocean sing its sacred song of praise. Like that, the days passed. For some months, some of us were even blessed to stay in a room directly under Amma's room. But my tears of joy were mixed with sorrow, too.

***

Even though no other life made any sense to me at all, and there was no other place to go, I could not reach a clear decision to become a renunciate. Even though I cried my eyes out, it just would not happen. Until one day, with the help of a good friend who was offering amazing healing sessions, a decision was reached.

Together we discovered that my path in life was that of a healer. Upon realizing this, my soul knew that this was the right way forward for me. I was not destined to be a sannyāsin (monk) in this lifetime. I had always prayed to become an instrument in Amma's hands, and in these troubled times, I knew that this was how I could best serve the world.

After that, I stayed in Amritapuri for some more months and then made my way back to Europe, where I began my studies to become a naturopath. For many years I studied different techniques like acupuncture, a gentle form of chiropractics, the use of plant remedies, homeopathy, and many other things.

My relationship with Mother changed profoundly over the years. It became much more inward, focused on a connection to her all-pervasive being, that inner presence. She later confirmed this path by answering my earnest question with the soothing words, "I will guide you from within."

I started a naturopathy practice in Stuttgart, Germany, and when it was just about to really blossom, I realized that life was calling me to something else. Everything was going well. With Mother's grace, people who would come to me with intense pain would, after one hour of hard work, leave pain free. But somehow this didn't satisfy me. The clients were not changing on a deeper level. They would just continue to tread through life as they had done before. My work was not helping to create the change that the world really needs to happen.

People are stuck in a rut. They keep on consuming and hurting the Earth, and basically nothing has shifted. As Paracelsus stated in medieval times, "All times have got their own diseases and their own remedies." I felt that the horrific state of the world needed a different medicine than what I was offering at the time. And so, the calling of a long-trodden path became louder and louder in my soul.

The Medicine Path, the cultures of the Old Ones, was calling me once again. I asked for Amma's blessing to walk the Medicine

Path with shamans and medicine men and women from ancient tribal cultures. A mystical weaving of events brought me to the Cusco region in the high Andes mountains of Peru.

It was actually one of Amma's children who opened the doors for me to enter into the remote world of the Andean shamans, the Qéros, the last descendants of the Incas. They had been hiding up in the mountains for the last 500 years and had only recently opened up again to share their knowledge with the world. They realized this was the only way; otherwise, humanity probably wouldn't survive. Like many other tribes around the world, their hearts are strong enough to continue giving, in spite of all the horrors of their history.

Their culture holds amazing healing techniques centered on restoring balance on both the personal and physical levels, and their knowledge of medicinal plants is a living tradition rooted in guarding and nourishing Mother Earth. The main medicine that we work with are the mighty Apus, the mountain spirits, who are winged, angel-like, pure beings. They are spirits of the Earth that are willing to work with us.

The rituals we perform are very similar to the traditional vedic hōmas (fire ceremonies) of ancient India, which are practiced even to this day all over India and in Amritapuri.

It seems to me it is no coincidence that the Sanskrit word 'śhama' means, 'complete control of the mind.' I always used to say that Amma is the *Mahā Śhāman*, the mother of all shamans — and she truly is. When Amma used to inaugurate her Brahmasthānam temples, at the very moment the doors were shut with her inside, eagles would appear out of the clear sky. They would fly their rounds of praṇāms (salutations) directly above, only to vanish again as mystically as they had appeared. When the doors opened again, we would see that the huge granite mūrti (stone idol) that had been carried in by several strong swāmīs had been installed in place by Amma's hands — by her magnificent power alone.

One day after the sea had been very agitated for several days, Amma said, "I need to go and talk to the ocean." Her words had an immediate effect. The ocean completely changed its mood and became perfectly peaceful and tranquil. This reminds me of the story where, at her request, the ocean itself splashed right up to Amma's hands to receive a garland that she had made for it.

All of her loving interactions with each and every animal she meets are an expression of that mystical oneness with nature, a state we can only understand with our hearts.

***

I have been graced to meet amazing elders and wisdom-keepers during the last six years of traveling around the world. As I've studied and learned from these different cultures, I've found the underlying principles of dharma, oneness, and respect for all life to be the same everywhere. The ways they are expressed may seem to differ, but essentially they are the same. The principles of life, the imprinted natural laws, are made by God, not man — a concept the modern Western world seems to have completely forgotten. In Germany, our old roots have been almost completely extinguished. In order to reestablish this tradition, which was very strong in ancient days, I am eager to learn as much as I can from genuine elders from all the four directions of this beautiful Earth.

Amma says she is "requesting everyone to do their part in restoring harmony in nature." Her message is crystal clear, but to emphasize it even more, she recently said, "You only truly love me, when you can see and serve me in all living beings and all of life." These words help to remind us that she is Mother Earth and all of nature.

At this point, I would like to recall the last sentence of Swami Purnamritananda's satsang, given at Amma's recent birthday celebration: "May Amma bless us all to be able to see her form in all different aspects of nature." Is not the 955th name of Devi that we chant everyday, "*ōm dharāyai namaḥ*" — Salutations to she who is Mother Earth?

Walking down from Snow Mountain, Apu Ausangate, where we had spent the night for my second Karpay Initiation, my dear teacher Don Vincente Quispe told me in a gentle voice, "*Somos guardianes de la tierra*" — We are the guardians of the Earth.

And that, in short, is what all the ancient cultures are based on. They are doing their part to guard our Mother, the Earth. Isn't that what each and every single one of us in modern culture should be doing too?

There is so much to be learned from the ancient ones. Our human life here is hanging from not much more than a hair. As Amma herself has said on various occasions, we have essentially already crossed the point of no return. Just look at the Amazon! Can you believe that friends of mine are organizing projects to provide clean and healthy drinking water to the communities there — in the Amazon, Earth's treasure trove of water and oxygen?

In America, an underground lake of unimaginable dimensions, which took some billion years to form, has been pumped completely dry within sixty short years. Amma has been warning us from the beginning to use water with utmost care. When will we, myself included, finally listen and really start to practice her teachings?

As one of my amazing teachers, Elder Mamo Senchina, from the ancient tribes of the Sierra Nevada de Santa Marta in Northern Columbia put it, "See, we are all drinking water, but no one sings to the water anymore. Everything in life has its own song. The lakes have their song. The rivers have their song. Rice, potatoes, and corn have their songs. But everybody only takes, takes, takes without making offerings to them, or singing their sacred songs."

Everywhere I traveled, the elders were saying the same thing: "The youngsters don't listen anymore. They don't want to learn the ancient ways, the good ways." Most of the youth, even from the tribes, want to live a Western lifestyle in the city. So tempting is the deadly glitter of false gold!

Amma says the same thing: "We need to realize where the junction is, where we took a wrong turn. It was clearly when we decided to chase after unnecessary luxuries."

Let us lead a simple and happy life. When we look at how Amma is living, we see that it is most simple. She is living in a single room — simple as that — and she shares even that small space with others.

This world can be a heaven; we can have heaven here on Earth. There is enough for everyone. Look at nature — such abundance! Have you ever seen a mango tree in fruit season? So many fruits come from only one tree. Giving is Mother Nature's very nature. There is enough for each and every one of us!

The elders say that in 2020 a new Earth was born; the Australian aboriginal elders call it 'Christal Earth.' I pray that we may all walk ourselves home — home into a new story, home into a state of harmony and oneness with Mother Nature, a paradise here on Earth.

As I sit here today, a representative and a child of the white race, I pray for forgiveness for all the horrible mistakes and adharmic (unrighteous) deeds that have ever been done by my ancestors. I am so sorry for all that has happened! I pray that the

'White Light' may be fully reintegrated into the Tribal Rainbow once again, and that this may happen fast.

I bow to Amma's lotus feet and pray from the depths of my heart that all the gold (and thus the power), all tribal land and sacred sites be returned; may all the stolen artifacts and bones of the ancestors be returned to their original people. Finally, I pray that we all may start to listen again to the wisdom and the knowledge of the elders and learn once again our songs and dances. May we return to communicating with nature and dance our blissful dance in harmony with all of creation.

9

The Transformative Power of Sēvā

Padma – USA

In the summer of 2013, a friend invited me to a popular amusement park north of Chicago. He added that he would be seeing his spiritual teacher Amma afterward, and that I was welcome to come along to meet her. I had seen photos of Amma all around his house but had never thought more about her then. I was eighteen and waiting to start a new job... I agreed to come.

Later, he called to tell me that the trip to the amusement park was canceled, but I could still come along to meet Amma if I was interested. To both of our surprise, I spontaneously replied, "Yes, I would like to meet Amma."

Three months before the Chicago program, and one month before this phone call, I had a dream in which I encountered a black jaguar. He gazed at me with deep knowledge and love, and I was profoundly moved. Each night after that, I remembered him in my dreams, calling out with a deep longing to meet him again and learn the secret knowledge of identity that he possessed.

One morning as I rose from my bed, I felt that the world we live in is another dream. I became confident that I could find my guide here, if I longed for him as much as I had longed to meet the panther in my dreams again. For the next three months, my heart continued to reach out to him, willing him to take form in my life and to guide me.

I had no background knowledge in any religion beyond the strict Christian denomination I was raised in. The concept of a spirit animal, guru, or even a living saint was completely foreign to my upbringing. By longing for this guide I was in uncharted territory, and I was a little concerned that I was developing some sort of psychosis.

At the same time, I continued my life as normal — working in a bakery at a farmer's market and living with my sister and her husband. I had small comforts that made me happy: a bright yellow bike to commute to and from work with, a safe place to stay, and as many movies, TV shows, and video games as I had time for. I didn't put much attention into self-care, let alone caring for others. I basically did whatever I wanted, whenever I wanted. My only discipline was my job in the bakery.

As my pining for my spiritual guide continued to grow, the pleasures I found in my daily routine gradually lost their shine, much like the faint glow of a candle fades in the light of the rising sun. I grew bored of cigarettes, which I had tried to start smoking. The TV shows and video games I had once enjoyed were now replaced with long walks and bike rides in nature where I began mentally speaking with my guide, who always felt close. I felt confident that he would manifest in my life to guide and care for me in some tangible way. It was during this time that I agreed to meet Amma, though I had no idea who I was agreeing to meet.

I arrived at the Chicago āśhram in a van full of Colorado satsang members. As we arrived, the resident swāmī playfully called out to us from the entrance of the hall saying, "Are you here to help, or to just hang around?" We enthusiastically jumped into sēvā with the other devotees, who were setting up small outdoor structures for the program near the main hall.

The whole āśhram was abuzz with activity. The joy and love of the devotees was infectious. I felt as happy as a child with a new toy as I did heavy manual labor in the noonday summer sun! Later, one of the food supervisors found me and invited me to work with her in the kitchen. Even today, I continue to serve in the kitchen of the Western Café in Amritapuri. Throughout the Chicago program, other devotees encouraged me to go for darśhan and to sit near Amma. They patiently answered the many questions I had about *what* was going on.

I had met my guru before seeing her in person, but I didn't recognize her at first. By the end of that program, however, I knew Amma was my jaguar. As I was standing with everyone at the end of the Dēvī Bhāva program, Amma casually glanced at me. Her eyes reflected the knowledge I had seen in my dreams. I gazed back at her like a toddler trying to mimic her mother, like a musician trying to tune to the note she hears. Like this, at different times in the middle of busy programs, Amma's gaze would find mine, and I would strive to merge into that knowledge.

I approached Amma to receive a mantra near the end of the Dēvī Bhāva in Chicago. I was so late that the supervisor panicked and immediately took me to Amma's side. In the rush and excitement, I couldn't clearly hear Amma chant the mantra in my ear, but I received a small paper with my mantra afterwards, and a brahmachārī taught me how to pronounce it properly, syllable by syllable.

Once while sitting in the hall listening to Amma give a satsang, I wondered about my past births with her. A thought immediately came to me, like a reply, "Why be concerned about your past lives when your current life is all around you?" Looking around, I was struck by the awareness of 'being' everyone (and everything). This experience was a big support for me in years to come.

Chicago turned out to be the first of many stops, and I followed Amma to every program I could for the rest of the U.S. tour. I immediately felt part of the family. I had many sisters and mothers looking out for me, reminding me to eat, drink, and sleep. They taught me how to do sēvā, helped me find rides and accommodation, and invited me to come along to the next stop, and the next one, and the next, and then on to India.

By Amma's grace, I was sponsored to come to India that same year, for Amma's sixtieth birthday celebration in September, 2013. Because of my persistence and the welcoming support of Amma and her children, I was able to stay in Amritapuri long term. The 'Karma Yoga' program helped me to remain in Amritapuri for several years until the end of the Covid lockdown in October 2021.

***

It is said that the āśhram is verily the body of the guru. I love tuning into Amma's divine presence by imagining her as the very world around me: the ocean sands of the beach, the trees and plants growing throughout the āśhram, even the Café building. This mood energized my sēvā, and I felt I could work endlessly. Of course, I couldn't, as my older sisters here continually pointed out with loving scoldings. More often than not in those first years, I was floating in the clouds, unaware of my surroundings. Sometimes I did not drink water for days at a time, and I would only eat meals when someone sent me away to do so. Sometimes laundry would not get done until it was too late to salvage the clothes from the stinky bucket. I was a mess. My respect and gratitude to all the Western Café supervisors for their patience and hard love with me. It can only be with the inspiration of Amma's love and patience that Amma's children at the Café have been so accepting and patient with me over the years.

My supervisor often said I was "a very good sevite when I managed to show up!" This is because if someone asked me for help, I would immediately run to help them, leaving my station at the Café unattended. This often left my supervisor running around everywhere looking for me! At one point, my supervisor even put up a 'sign in' sheet to help me become more aware of what I was doing and to make me think twice before just running away!

Another sister kindly pointed out several sēvā details I needed to pay more attention to in the Café. She taught me to wipe the *entire* counter instead of just randomly moving the rag around, to actually look at the dish I was washing to see if there was any food left on it, to tie my hair back properly to keep strands from falling in the food, to *not* wipe my face or nose on the aprons...the list goes on and on! One day, she practically dragged me by the ear to Amma, telling her that, "this daughter is doing fifteen hours of sēvā a day!" To my delight, Amma pinched that sister's nose and laughed happily, giving me a big, loving smile and darśhan.

At the time, I thought Amma's gesture meant that this was between Amma and me, and my brahmachāriṇī sister should keep *her* nose out of *our* business. However, I later realized that Amma probably meant that she shouldn't worry, that Amma was taking care of me, and that I would learn moderation over time. My elders in the Café had kept warning me that I would crash, but by Amma's grace, nothing terrible happened to me. Very soon after this darśhan, I joined the Karma Yoga program and cut down on my sēvā hours. Eventually, I became more moderate and began to take up the other practices Amma encourages us to perform like morning archana, scriptural classes, haṭha yōga, and Sanskrit studies.

I not only learned the proper way to do things, but also the proper way to approach work as sēvā. In the last few years, I have been doing more sēvā in the bakery, where I had previously not been allowed to serve due to the high level of awareness required there.

One Sunday morning during the archana, I arrived at the bakery with bleary eyes to roll out the dough for the cinnamon rolls with some of the other bakers. I was feeling unenthusiastic that day about making rolls. To make cinnamon rolls, a large lump of dough is flattened with a pin across the entire surface of the metal table. This is done so that the butter, cinnamon, sugar, and plumped raisins can be spread across the dough before rolling it up and slicing out the individual portions.

On this Sunday, the dough had mistakenly been left in the fridge overnight, so it was very cold, hard, and difficult to roll. I thought we should just make something else for breakfast, but the supervisor began to place three equal portions of the dough on the three tables, one for each of us. Seeing the large, hard lump of dough resting like a mountain on the table before me, I rebelled.

"We can't do this!" I said, my eyes filling with tears.

But the supervisor's enthusiasm was infectious. To cheer me up, Apoorva dramatically performed each roll of the pin across the dough, as she loudly chanted along with the archana coming from the speakers: "*ōm parāśhaktyai namaḥ* (I prostrate before the supreme power!)... *ōm parāśhaktyai namaḥ... ōm parāśhaktyai namaḥ...*"

Watching her made me laugh through my tears and I began to roll out the dough along with her. We completed the work in the usual amount of time, despite my original misgivings. When our mind is connected to God, it remains enthusiastic, open, and sees the best way to overcome seemingly difficult situations. This supervisor showed me it was not only possible to work with this 'unmanageable,' hardened dough, but also with my own hardened mind.

When I was in France this last year, working with my husband, Raghunath, I was hired by a small restaurant as a dishwasher. The chef and owners were so pleased with the quality of my work that I was quickly promoted to the position of sous-chef. Little could they know of the quality training we received in the Western Café, where Amma turns rusty iron into gold!

***

Amma often says that we should think of the inner Amma as our own, but the outer Amma as shared with the world. It was during darśhan in Amma's room that I had the precious opportunity to see the inner Amma outside. In my first 'room darśhan,' I entered as soon as the door opened, smiling widely at Amma. Amma took one look at me and burst out laughing, "Ātmā-viśhvāsam, ātmā-viśhvāsam!" My thought was something like, "Yes, ātmā-viśhvāsam! You are the ātmā (the self) that I have viśhvāsam (faith) in!" As I cried, Amma fed me roasted chana dhal (split chickpeas) from her hand.

It was through my love for Amma, that I was coming out of depression during that time. When Amma praised my 'ātmā-viśhvāsam,' which is the Malayalam word for 'self-confidence,' I felt she was acknowledging my confidence in her and also encouraging me to have confidence in myself.

These room darśhan experiences with Amma have deepened my conviction that she knows me intimately and is supporting me. This has made me more open to listening to her teachings and trying to implement them in my life.

At times, my relationship with the outer Amma has been a little challenging for me due to my relationship with my birth mother. My mom had ten children, four of whom were teenage sisters who had been rescued from an abusive household. My father brought her fresh flowers every few days to replace the wilted ones, which she would keep in a vase on the dining table. She prepared home-cooked meals for the entire family every night, homeschooled all the younger children, myself included, and managed the daily affairs on the four-acre family farm while my father was away at work. In most of my memories of her, she has a smile on her face. In my eyes, she was a distant Wonder Woman.

Due to complications during pregnancy and birth, I came home from the hospital weeks after she did and was cared for mostly by my elder sisters and grandmother, who lived with us. My mother and I never managed to bond well. My few memories of her and me are, unfortunately, memories of rejection. I remember her locking me outside when I was just a toddler while she used a public restroom, telling me to turn away when I embraced her because my breath smelled bad, and hitting me for spilling something when I tried to help her.

I have many sweet memories of her, but not of her and me. She passed away when I was eight years old while giving birth to her sixth child. While my family mourned, I didn't cry; I hadn't known myself as hers. I carried this pain of rejection with me as I grew older, unconsciously keeping myself at a distance from mother-figures, though I was desperate for motherly love and affection. With so many loving mothers and elder sisters in Amritapuri, this resistance has been worn down to a great extent. However, this baggage has often closed me to Amma's direct affection, especially in public.

During the Covid lockdown, when nobody was entering the āśhram, Amma gave us darśhan on the stage in the big hall. As we moved up the queue, I watched Amma speak with little Lalita. I noticed the intimacy they shared and felt jealous. I started to scold Amma within, "See how beautiful? Why can't we have that? Why do you ignore me? I want your affection too!"

As I approached Amma, the inner scolding became quiet. Amma took me and held me purposefully at arm's distance. Her full attention was on me, and she was smiling widely. But, my eyes and heart were squinted shut, like when the sun is too bright to look at. If she hadn't been holding my arms so tight, I would have raised them to block the glare. Though she was trying to offer me something, I couldn't take it. After a hug, she let me go, satisfied that I had understood. I playfully pouted as I walked away, admitting responsibility for the situation. It isn't that Amma is not offering her love fully — it is that I am not prepared to accept it.

This feeling of neglect and rejection is something I still struggle with. Preparing this satsang at Amma's request has made me sift through precious memories and experiences that had started to rust over in my mind. I hope to shine them regularly from now on, remembering the value they have in my life on the path.

***

In closing, I have one recent experience to share. Near the end of the Covid lockdown period in October 2021, my husband Raghunath and I took the opportunity to earn money in France to support our āśhram life in Amritapuri. For most of our time there, I felt focused and did my daily spiritual practices with gratitude and my work with an attitude of sēvā. I attended Amma's online program almost every day. However, in the heat of the busy summer season, I became lax. Once my schedule cleared up, my spiritual practices did not return. Instead, I spent time reading books, watching YouTube videos, researching topics that interested me, and shopping online. I was 'pretending to sleep' (i.e., choosing to ignore the call of waking up to a higher purpose), and I knew it.

It was only when I returned to Amritapuri, and started up my practices again in Amma's presence, that my mind cleared. For eight years, developing devotion to Amma had been my identity. Now, I had to accept that I had set Amma aside, if only for a little while. This has been a hard pill to swallow, and I have been facing a lot of fear about returning to France to work for one more year. Guilt, fear, and lack of confidence have been gnawing at my mind. However, I must remember that Amma and her teachings are wonderful and unchanging. Amma guides us to discover acceptance and joy in life.

Even though I didn't use my last month in France wisely and failed to actively contemplate the scriptural teachings, the flowers of acceptance, forgiveness, patience, and love that Amma has planted are already blooming inside me. Their fragrance is sweetening over time.

When Raghunath and I shared our plans to return to work for one more year in France, Amma enthusiastically said, "Yes!" This inspires me to approach our time there with courage and discrimination rather than fear and doubt. For a solid decade, Amma has made it clear that she wants me to have self-confidence as I move ahead in life. Her faith in me reminds me to develop faith in myself.

Although I came to Amma as a young adult, my faculty of discrimination was as immature as that of a young child. Both directly and through her children in the āśhram, Amma has raised and supported me for almost a decade now, giving me both theoretical and practical lessons to help me grow up. I take this chance to thank her for her impact in my life, and pray to be near her always, both externally and internally.

I pray that we may all know where our feet are, and take steps forward on the path; that we may know where our hands are, and take support and guidance from Mother, as she takes us towards the goal.

10

Surrendering as Best as We Can

Adarsh (Søren Andersen) – Denmark

In my childhood and youth, spirituality did not mean much to me. But still, there was something in me that I couldn't define, something higher that couldn't be immediately understood — the divine. But back then, I spent neither time nor energy pursuing it.

Instead, I threw myself into trade union work, believing it was important for everyone to have good working conditions. I set my sights on ensuring a good working environment for my colleagues. I was also politically active and focused on providing good living conditions for the poor and vulnerable in society.

Meeting Amma

I met my wife Varada in 1979, and through her passion for spirituality, I came to know a little bit about the path. But spirituality didn't really wake up in me until I met Amma in Amritapuri during Christmas 2005. I was attracted by Amma's pure love and her great charitable work. It fell nicely in line with issues I had previously been passionate about. In a way, Amma's humanitarian work became a bridge between me and spirituality.

My wife is the daughter of a Christian priest, but she had been searching for a spiritual tradition that felt authentic to her for years. When Varada attended a workshop in her hometown in 1999, she happened to see a photo of Amma on the wall. Varada did not know who Amma was but felt an unusual attraction to the lady in the photo. During her lunch break, she asked for permission to take the photo out of the frame, so she could get a copy made at the nearest copy center. This was a very wise move on my wife's path. In fact, Amma says that seeing a photo of a true master, a satguru — even once — influences that individual's entire life path for the better.

Varada met Amma in person in 2001 in Munich. She felt that she had come home, that her spiritual search had come to an end. During her first meeting with Amma, Varada felt that she recognized the energy of love that she had encountered in Assisi, where Saint Francis lived. My wife and I both appreciate Saint Francis, and we are touched that Amma has referred to him several times as "the real thing," and to Assisi as a kind of spiritual "perfume factory" where the spiritual fragrance lingers on after one has visited.

From the time she was a young girl, Varada has had the feeling that she would go to India one day. In 2004, Varada made her childhood dream a reality and traveled to Amritapuri for the first time, but I wasn't ready. I didn't think India was for me and stubbornly said, "I will never go to India. There are too many people and too much poverty." In 2005 an inner shift happened, and I decided that I wanted to accompany Varada to India. My wife had one condition: I had to promise to stay in Amritapuri for at least two weeks without grumbling. I promised! You'll be happy to know that now I have a big love for both Amma and Mother India.

My very first meeting with Amma was when she was handing out cake on Christmas Eve. It was an overwhelming experience for me with so many people huddled so close around Amma. I became very worried about Amma's safety. It was hard for me to understand how it was going so well. At that time, I didn't have the experience I have today. Obviously, all situations around Amma function well in accordance with her will.

The next day I got my first darśhan in the Kālī Temple. What a wonderful and powerful experience! I had never been in direct contact with so much love and power before. Later I realized that Amma had given me an incredible gift; she had woken up my slumbering spirituality. After darśhan, I staggered up to our flat and lay down on my mattress. I was unable to do anything for the next three days, until Varada finally helped me down the stairs for another darśhan. In the meantime, I had a dream in which my head was chopped off by a guillotine. For me it was a clear message that my ego was to change somehow, one of its many heads had been cut off. Something new was opening up inside me.

When I returned home to work, my friends and work colleagues told me that I had changed, that my behavior was more pleasant after my "holy-days" in India.

The following year we came back to Amritapuri after traveling around India. For both of us, it felt like coming home. We could finally relax in Amma's peaceful oasis in the midst of busy, chaotic India. My expectations were high when I went for my first darśhan. I expected Amma to give me a unique darśhan because I had decided to come back to her. I looked forward to coming home in my mother's lap. Amma toppled my expectations and gave me a short darśhan. At first I (my ego) was very disappointed. Later I realized that Amma was showing me not to have big expectations and to calm down. I felt like one more head of my ego was being cut off. My ego still enjoys raising its hood, but sometimes, when I'm lucky, I remember what Amma says: "To become a zero is to become a hero." I hope to remember and practice this in my day-to-day life.

Getting a Spiritual Name from Amma

I soon realized that some devotees received not only a mantra from our beloved Amma, but also a spiritual name. I didn't understand the concept. To me it looked like children playing in a kindergarten, using names they had learned from a fairy tale. Soon, though, spiritual naming came closer to me. My wife had been asking Amma for a name once a year for three years. That year she succeeded. Varada received her name from Amma and was deeply happy. I told Varada that it was fine with me, but not to expect me to ask for a spiritual name.

Despite myself, a few days later a deep longing arose within me to get a name from Amma. I couldn't resist the tug. When I asked, Amma's response was, "Later," but I couldn't wait until later. After seven days had passed, I thought, "Well, Amma said later, and it has been a full week. I will go and ask Amma for a name again." This time the answer was, "Okay." I joined the name-line right after darśhan and received the name 'Adarsh' from Amma. What had happened to me during this process? How could my feelings have changed so quickly from having no desire for a name to having an intense longing for one? How had my stubborn ego changed so rapidly? Did my deep longing for a name come from Amma? Was it actually Amma who created that longing? To this day, I still don't know what happened, but I am sure it was a gift.

Having a satguru like Amma, you never know what is going to happen next in your life, and that it is both challenging and wonderful.

Glory Be to the Memory of Vimukta

Vimukta was a Danish renunciate here in Amritapuri for about thirteen years, until she left her body. Vimukta was passionate about spreading awareness of Amma in Denmark and had the steel-firm goal that Amma should visit Denmark. In 2005, Vimukta strongly encouraged Varada to start an Amma satsang group in our home city, Aarhus.

In April, Swami Shubamritananda Puri visited us for the first time. By Amma's grace 115 people came for the program held in a small theater — a fantastic start. From that time, we held weekly satsang meetings in our home, following Amma's guidelines. We learned from experience how important it is to participate in a satsang group when you are physically away from Amma most of the year. It helped us to keep the connection with Amma alive. We were still new to Amma, but Vimukta kept pushing us. She made us join the board of the Amma-Denmark Association. Our first task was to help create the formal framework for the association, which was later to be the platform for us to invite Amma to visit Denmark. A short time later, after having only known Amma for a year, I became chairman of Amma-Denmark. When I look back, I am still amazed how it all fell in place.

Over the next twelve years, Amma-Denmark invited Amma to come to Denmark again and again. In 2017, we yet again invited Amma to come to Denmark. This time we could tell Amma that we had found a hall, collected the necessary funds, and had begun planning for the food we would serve. We brought a large basket of vegetables from devotees' gardens and a glass jar of honey to seal the deal. As Amma took a big bite of a leek, a strange look washed over her face. She dipped a finger into the jar to rinse her mouth with honey. After all this Amma said, "Amma will come. Swami Ramakrishna will arrange."

Amma visited Denmark in 2018 and again in 2019. We are so grateful to Amma for fulfilling the dreams of so many Danes, to Vimukta for her persistent pushes, and to Swami Shubamritananda Puri for supporting us throughout the process. Finally the right timing, effort, and grace came together to make the program a huge success.

Awareness of Vāsanās

In my life, many things have come to me without me having to make much effort. Ironically, this blessing has fed into one of my many weaknesses. I am often too loose with handling things and don't always follow up on time. Maybe this is because so many of the challenges and problems I face solve themselves. But that is not always true, and my behavior sometimes brings me big troubles.

I know Amma has been focusing on correcting this tendency in me. She made this clear during a darśhan on the South India Tour in 2019, just after it was confirmed that she would be visiting Denmark later that year. I was one of the main organizers and looked forward to getting her blessing before leaving the tour to go back and help organize her visit. When I came to Amma, she suddenly grabbed my ears, turned my head from side to side, and then burst out laughing — and soon, I was laughing too.

Amma, of course, was doing this in an affectionate manner. Nonetheless, her playful gesture was done with so much physical power that it surprised me. Four years later, I think my ears are still glowing a little. I clearly felt Amma was treating me like one of her small children and telling me 'to be alert, aware, and awake with my sēvā and responsibilities.' It was wonderful, clear, and powerful guidance.

Amma: The Giving Principle

When I talk about Amma to people who don't know much about her, I often quote Dr. A. P. J. Abdul Kalam, former president of India. During the *Amrita Setu* Inauguration, the official ceremony opening the bridge between Amritpuri and the mainland, President Abdul Kalam spoke. He shared what he had learned from Amma — the critical importance of giving, both for our own spiritual evolution and for the good of society as a whole.

When I close my eyes, I can still hear Abdul Kalam's voice saying, "Amma's message is to give and give, and then to go on giving."

It was such a wonderful encapsulation of Amma's whole life, of her holy example of giving love to the world and all its creatures. His words celebrated Amma as both a spiritual master and as an incomparable humanitarian leader. The talk deeply touched my heart and reminded me to make full use of the privilege we have to serve others. I believe that the principle of selfless giving that Amma embodies is the best way to build a bridge between Amma and those who don't know her yet. And for those who think they have nothing to give, Amma provides the perfect solution: "If nothing else, we can always give a warm smile, a compassionate glance to our fellow human beings."

King Shivaji's Example

Over the years, we have learned to do our daily tasks at home in Denmark as sēvā for Amma. This is an effective way to counter the ego, which again and again tries to claim that it is the doer. Years ago, we heard Amma tell the story of King Shivaji from ancient times to illustrate the ideal attitude of sēvā. The short story goes like this:

Once long ago, King Shivaji gave his whole kingdom to his guru because he had grown weary of war and responsibility. The guru said, "Now the kingdom belongs to me." Shivaji felt a big relief, feeling that the weight of the world had been lifted from his shoulders. Later the guru said to Shivaji, "I want you to take care of the kingdom, to rule this kingdom as my representative." Thus Shivaji remained as the ruler of the kingdom, but his attitude was completely different.

He told himself, "This is not my kingdom anymore. I am just a caretaker who is serving his guru." In this way all his tension was removed, and there was much more love and attention in his actions.

As Swami Ramakrishnananda Puri says in his book, *The Blessed Life*, "If we can think Amma has given us our work and do it as a service to her, we will be able to discharge our responsibilities with love and sincerity."

While doing sēvā at the Recycling Center in Amritapuri, we learned the following helpful prayer given by Amma:

> *Om Amriteshwaryai Namah*
> *I am going to do this work.*
>
> *Please give me enough mental, physical, and emotional strength to do this as a worship of you.*
>
> *Help me to do this work with the right attitude, knowing this is yours, not mine.*
>
> *I am doing it with your power, not mine.*
>
> *Help me to work sincerely, with concentration and as best as I can, without thinking of its result.*
>
> *Help me to derive happiness from the spirit in which I am working.*
>
> *Thank you for your blessing and guidance.*
> *I surrender both the actions and fruit at your feet.*

We say this prayer every day before we start our sēvā at Blushojgaard.

Longing for My Master

Since the pandemic started, our life with Amma has been more intense than ever. We have faced many challenges and haven't had an opportunity to communicate with Amma directly. This has strongly encouraged us to seek Amma's guidance in our hearts. We have been steadily learning, as Amma often says, that we should not see her as limited to her five-foot-tall body.

To be honest, during the pandemic we didn't know if it would ever be possible to see Amma in person again. During this time, I often remembered Swamini Krishnamrita Prana's words from a question and answer session in the Kālī Temple. She spoke about the gift of longing for Amma and its power to deepen one's devotion. Our physical separation from Amma has clearly brought this gift of longing into our lives. We have also experienced that not being physically near Amma is not pleasant, but we understand it is her gift to us.

Surrender As Best We Can

In March 2020, we left Amritapuri just as the Covid pandemic was starting and traveled back home to Denmark. We had planned to retire and to live a simple life in a small house. We hoped to focus on sādhanā and sēvā, with frequent long stays in Amritapuri.

However, our plans were turned upside down when we experienced Amma's inner inspiration to buy a property, 'The Course and Holiday Centre, Blushojgaard,' which was close to our small summer house. After our decision to buy it, Amma came to each of us in our dreams and confirmed our decision. Today we run the place as a non-profit company, with the hope that it will soon be an official Amma Center. In our hearts, we already feel the center belongs to Amma. (In January 2024, Blushojgaard began the process of becoming an official Amma Center.)

We felt Amma's grace during every step of purchasing the property. All of the preparation, approval of documents, and transfer of money were fully in place when we moved in six weeks later on October 1, 2020. When we finished the process, our lawyer looked at us and said, "What has just happened here? It's simply not possible to get three property trades in place this fast." But, of course, with Amma's grace, it was possible!

We feel Amma's tangible help in everyday life at Blushojgaard. Let me share a few examples. The town of Ebeltoft, located 4.5 km away, has a large, well-functioning recycling station. When you visit the recycling center, you would think they had been trained by Amma's āśhram recycling team. At the Ebeltoft Recycling Center, you can get rid of sorted waste. The items that are still functional are stored in large containers, where local people can take them free of charge. The recycling site is a bit of a treasure chest for Blushojgaard, a sign of Denmark's abundance.

One day as we were upcycling some old fabric for curtains, we had trouble finding the right curtain tape to sew on. There are no shops selling such things nearby. A few days later at the recycling center, we saw a woman putting a large basket with a lid into one of the containers. When we lifted the lid and looked in the basket, it was filled with the exact specialized ribbon we needed to finish the curtains.

One day, when our mood was a little low, we found a small vase with the painted words: *Happiness is a choice*. We brought it back to the new center as a reminder of Amma's omnipresence and to remind ourselves of Amma's mantra: "Happiness is a decision."

May all beings everywhere be happy and at peace by Amma's grace.

11

From Darkness to Light

Karuna Irene - Spain

I come from a mostly atheist family, and I used to be very proud of this. I was fond of saying things like, "Religion is the opium of the people." (Karl Marx) or, "The only church that illuminates is the one that burns." (*Mago de Oz*, Spanish rock band).

One of my friends almost managed to convince me of the existence of God when I was twenty years old. Even though it had been months since my grandfather passed away, I still couldn't stop crying. I was full of anxiety and didn't understand what was happening to me. He was the first relative whose death I lived through. It left me hurt, angry, and sad.

My grandfather had taken on the role of a father in my life, and now I felt like an orphan. Many of my friends didn't understand why I was so upset. They often said things like, "He is in a better place," to which I always replied, "That is impossible! How can he be better off than he was with his friends, his family, and his cowboy movies? His life was full of laughter." Amma, I don't know where he is now, but please take care of him and my grandmother. They were great people who gave us all the love in the world; they did so much sēvā without even knowing that word existed.

One night when I was suffering a lot of anxiety and couldn't stop crying, one of my friends told me that my grandfather was with God. I didn't argue with her. Instead I curiously asked her many questions. We talked about God until I fell asleep. The next day I woke up feeling terrible again. Within a few days, I concluded that everything we had talked about was nonsense.

Now, however, I can say that I know that God exists. The lyrics of the bhajan *Mātā Rāṇi* comes closest to expressing the joy this brings:

> *The Empress of the Universe has showered her grace, all my wishes have come true. The Divine Mother heard my prayers, all my wishes have come true.*
>
> *She has cleared all my paths, desires that were blocked have been fulfilled. My Mother, my Mother has come to take my sorrows away, all my wishes have come true.*

***

I have known Amma for only a short time, but she has known me forever:

> *ōm viśhvamātrē namaḥ*
>
> Salutations to she who is the mother of the universe.
>
> (*Lalitā Sahasranāma* 934)

The first time I was in Amma's physical presence was in 2018. But as I look back on my life, I can see certain moments of mental clarity and turning points where I could have made dire decisions. Every time I was on the edge, something inside me said, "No." I can now recognize that this was Amma. There were times when I was in such bad mental shape that it seemed impossible for me to stop, but I did — that was Amma.

I didn't have a bad childhood, but I was very sensitive and had low self-esteem, which brought me a lot of suffering. My biological parents divorced when I was eight years old. My biological father didn't do things the right way. Amma, please help me to be at peace with him. My mother, on the other hand, was impeccable. She worked hard, she took care of me. What she couldn't do herself, my maternal grandparents did. I was raised with love.

By the time I was about fourteen years old, my parents had rebuilt their lives separately and had even gotten remarried. I lived with my mother and her new husband, who was the kind father anyone would be happy to have.

During adolescence, though, I began to think that I wasn't enough, that I wasn't valid, that I didn't deserve to be loved and that there was something wrong with me. There came a time when I didn't even want to live. Sometime later a psychologist diagnosed me with depression, anxiety, and anorexia with episodes of bulimia. Many people believe that anorexia is a disease born of vanity, that girls just want to feel pretty. The truth is that I didn't eat because I thought I deserved to suffer. I wanted to die. I just couldn't bear this inner torture anymore. Whereas Amma tells us to be brave and to make the decision to be happy no matter what, somehow I had made a firm decision to be sad and angry.

I started self-harming. I did it to feel something. I went from being a sensitive child to feeling completely empty inside. One day as I was about to self-harm, I heard a very strong voice in my head say, "What are you doing? Are you crazy? Stop this right now!" I didn't know it at the time, but now it's clear to me that this voice was Amma. The next day I talked with my mother, and we agreed that I would start going to a psychologist.

ōm sadgati-pradāyai namaḥ

Salutations to the one that leads us on the right path. (*L.S.* 201)

***

Everything went smoothly after that. I finished high school and went to the other side of Spain to go to university. I thought that I would feel more myself there, that studying would fill my intellectual restlessness. But it wasn't like that at all, because my concerns were more spiritual than worldly. I studied Comparative Literature, which introduced me to the *Mahābhārata* and the *Rāmāyaṇa*, India's two greatest epics. I loved them; they fascinated me. They contained stories of talking monkeys and magical weapons. Why wasn't there a movie about this? Do the Marvel people know these books exist? Although I may have been fascinated for the wrong reasons, it was an important first step.

That was the year my grandfather died. To deal with the pain, I started partying and drinking more than usual. I really lost my mind. I started to have episodes of persecution mania; I thought that someone was following me down every street. Once, I almost got hit by a car while trying to escape from someone who didn't exist. I hardly slept and hardly left my room. One night I went to buy some beer; alcohol helped me to sleep during the night. When I got to my room, a voice in my head yelled at me, "What are you doing? You used to drink to have fun, but now you're alone in your room. Stop!" Amma was definitely stopping me again. I was determined to destroy myself, but she was always there. I don't think there is a human way to thank you, Amma. It must be very exasperating being my mother, but I really appreciate you not giving me up for adoption.

I began to become aware of what was happening and started to take steps to overcome it.

ōm rakṣhākaryai namaḥ

Salutations to she who is the protector. (*L.S.* 317)

At that time, almost every night I went out someone offered me drugs, and I always said, "No." I survived several toxic relationships that could have ended very badly, but somehow I was able to get out of them at the right time. All this is only thanks to Amma.

In my junior year of college, I discovered that one of my classmates was being abused by her boyfriend. I managed to take her to live with me and made her file a complaint in court. These were very hard moments. From this experience, I have learned the importance of doing sēvā. When we do sēvā, we are not only helping another person, we are purifying our own mind as well. During those weeks I was so focused on helping my friend that there was no room in my mind for my own problems.

***

I finished university in 2018, and that summer, by Amma's grace, I ended up in Amritapuri. I arrived at night. I didn't know who Amma was. My traveling companions had told me about her, but I didn't understand. I thought that we would spend two weeks in the āśhram and that I would take time to sleep, go to the beach, read, and learn about meditation. It never crossed my mind that I had reached my real home.

> *ōm sukhapradāyai namaḥ*
>
> Salutations to she who grants happiness. (*L.S.* 192)

Soon after I arrived at the āśhram, when I was told I could get a hug, I loudly replied, "Yes, yes, yes." I wanted to leave the bags right there in the street and run to the hall, but my traveling companions made me settle down first. After my first darśhan, I went to my room and spent the whole night crying. I was angry that I'd had to queue for such a long time to have a stranger hug me for a few seconds. I called my boyfriend and told him that everyone here was crazy.

> *ōm karuṇā-rasa-sāgarāyai namaḥ*
>
> Salutations to she who is the ocean of compassion. (*L.S.* 326)

I put up as much resistance as I could and asked question after question: Why are most people wearing white? Why are some wearing red or yellow? Could I wear yellow? — it's the color that suits me best. Why were so many people called 'Swami'? Why is there no Wi-Fi? Why is everyone so focused on Amma's feet?

Slowly, though, I began doing sēvā, meeting people, and attending the programs. My resistance began decreasing. What helped me the most was singing bhajans, which is the spiritual practice that brings me closest to God. At first I put a lot of enthusiasm into singing along, maybe too much. I feel sorry for the people who sat around me in those days (and for their ears).

I started having favorite bhajans and reading their lyrics in my language. The meaning of the lyrics began arousing my curiosity about Indian culture and philosophy. This led me to research what I did not understand on the internet, and I began buying books in the āśhram. I bought them, but did not read them. Shopping is another one of my many vāsanās (latent tendencies).

A friend told me that ever since he met Amma, he only listens to bhajans. I thought he was crazy because I loved rock music and going to concerts. As it turned out, now I too am one of those crazy people.

Once all my barriers were down, and I was totally mesmerized by Amma, I began to pray. I repeatedly asked Amma not to leave me, now that I had found her without even knowing that I had been looking for her. One day during meditation, that prayer became so strong that I couldn't think of anything else. A moment of clarity came, and these words flooded my mind, "Irene, Amma is the kindest mother in the universe, and you are her daughter. Of course she will not abandon you."

While I was performing ārati[7] to Amma, I felt Amma looking at me, and it gave me a shiver and all my hairs stood on end. It confirmed my thoughts, and I have not been worried about being abandoned since then. I am sure that Amma knows each and every one of our thoughts — it's beautiful and, at the same time, terrifying.

***

Amma, forgive me for my thoughts. One that I regret is thinking about dinner while standing in line for darśhan. "Pasta? Pizza? Indian food? No, pizza for sure, with a lot of cheese. Oh God please let my pizza have lots of cheese, and let it be really warm." At that moment someone asked me my language[8]. I sank into Amma's embrace and realized what a fool I was for wasting my time thinking about dinner in the presence of the Divine Mother.

I would like to confess something else: I am envious of the children in the āśhram. How can those little creatures know so much? They approach Amma, take the microphone, and with very serious little faces they say, "Ōm Amṛitēśhvaryai Namaḥ. Today I would like to talk about verse x from chapter y of the *Bhagavad Gītā*." They go on to recite the verse in perfect Sanskrit. When I was their age, I was eating cereal while looking

---

[7] A traditional ritual involving the waving of a lighted lamp to the guru or deity.

[8] Before Amma's darśhan (embrace), an attendant asks your native language so Amma can whisper comforting words to you in your mother tongue.

at cartoons, wanting to become a Pokemon, and these kids can recite the scriptures from memory. My goodness, how much time I have wasted and continue to waste!

When I arrived here in Amritapuri I felt very lost in life, I didn't know what to do with my studies. Should I pursue a Master's degree? or another career? — so I went to an astrologer. During the session, she told me, "You have the power to heal with your words." I almost broke down right there! I had wanted to study psychology for years but didn't think I was capable of it. My astrology reading was in August 2018. By September, I was reenrolled in university as a psychology student. I hope to finish my studies soon and to specialize in eating disorders so that I can help people who suffer as I did.

***

I came back to the āśhram in March 2019 to spend two weeks here. My mother suggested the trip to me on a Tuesday, and by Friday I was already on the plane. At that moment, I was not well. Two months earlier I'd had a very painful breakup with my boyfriend, but I had not cried even once. Proudly, I said that I was fine, but it was obvious that I wasn't. So the first thing I asked Amma, while watching her in the Kālī Temple, was to help me cry — and she did.

After my darśhan that day, Amma smiled at me. She had a look of joy on her face, which I interpreted to mean, "How nice that you are back." As Amma looked at me, and I looked back at her, I started laughing, and she laughed too. That night my roommates woke me up when they came back to the room. They didn't realize I was awake. One told the other that I must be a very spiritual person because she had seen my darśhan, and it was obvious that Amma had recognized me. I took this as a sign that I made the right decision in coming back to the āśhram.

These two roommates took great care of me during that stay. From this I learned that Amma gives us what we need, not what we deserve. When we try to assess 'what we deserve,' I think our ego enters. In that darśhan I really needed a clear sign that I had made the right decision by coming to Amritapuri. I needed good friends, and Amma even put them in a room with me.

During that second trip I had another revelation. At that time I was wondering who Amma actually was. One day in the Kālī Temple during bhajans I thought, "Amma, you are God." She looked at me with a shrug of her shoulders and an expression that said, "Of course." I felt very foolish for not having seen this before.

ōm dēvyai namaḥ

Salutations to she who is the Goddess. (*The 108 Names of Amma,* 107)

I returned to Amritapuri for a third time in September 2019 and left in December, planning to return the following April, but the world had other plans. During the pandemic I got a little lost. There were periods when I watched the āśhram live stream and did the archana every day — and there were months when I didn't recite even one mantra. During that time, a friend inspired me, saying that even if we get side-tracked, we can always get back on track.

ōm dayā-mūrtyai namaḥ

Salutations to she who is the personification of compassion. (*L.S.* 581)

Amma emphasizes the importance of compassion. I believe that compassion should start with ourselves. There is no point in beating ourselves up for not doing enough sēvā or sādhanā. It's better to have an optimistic mood and commit ourselves that tomorrow we'll do better. We already encounter enough difficulties in the world without becoming our own worst enemy. If Amma loved us less when we don't do things right, I'm sure I wouldn't be here today.

> *ōm śhivāyai namaḥ*
>
> Salutations to the one who bestows all that is auspicious. (*L.S.* 53)

We must remind ourselves that Amma loves all of us, and so we must love and help others. In February 2022, when the war in Ukraine began and I saw how many people were suffering, I started to feel guilty for not doing anything. I began to pray, "Amma, give me the opportunity to help the refugees. Let me be an instrument in your hands."

> *ōm kāma-dāyinyai namaḥ*
>
> Salutations to she who grants all wishes. (*L.S.* 63)

Soon an NGO contacted my mother's company, which runs a hostel, proposing a refugee reception project. Of course we accepted. We worked for six months with them. It was physically, mentally, and emotionally exhausting. Unfortunately, what initially seemed like a great humanitarian project that could give hope to those fleeing the war turned into a trap. The NGO was only looking for financial gain, and its goal was to keep the refugees stranded in our hostel for as long as possible.

I worked in the kitchen. At first I didn't have much contact with the refugees. But since there was no one in the NGO who spoke English, they began asking me to translate. This is how I became aware of the deception and coercion. My mother and I became confidants of the refugees and helped them in any way possible. I tried my best to make the situation a sēvā, yet there were many situations where I felt completely useless.

Then I remembered Amma's words: "If you cannot give material support to those in need, give them a smile, a kind word and a compassionate look."

Ultimately, we managed to get almost all of the refugees to leave this NGO, so they could rebuild their lives. My mother continues to help those who are left and meets with them every week. These people have suffered a lot, and the authorities have not treated them very well. Amma, please take care of them.

Since returning to Amritapuri, I finished a panchakarma treatment (Ayurvedic rejuvenation system) and thanks to it, my health is improving. There are no words to thank the entire panchakarma team enough for all the love, affection and care they have shown me. Shortly after the treatment started, several people told me that panchakarma was very hard. I began to think, "What had I gotten myself into?" One morning, I shared my worries with one of the panchakarma doctors. She suggested I lay all my fears at Amma's feet. I went to the Kaḷari temple in the āśhram and did just that. All of my worries and anxiety about the treatment vanished.

> *ōm bhayāpahāyai namaḥ*
>
> Salutations to she who dispels fear. (*L.S.* 121)

Sometimes that's all it takes: a sincere prayer to the Divine Mother and the willingness to lay all our burdens at her feet.

Thank you, Amma, from the bottom of my heart, for everything you do for me.

12

A Mind that Cries for Kālī

Murali – India

We all tend to seek changeless joy from this changing, ephemeral world. In addition, we believe ourselves to be individual bodies with a mind. Contact with the world brings us varied experiences of pleasure and pain. We run towards pleasure and away from pain, which creates an endless cycle of cause and effect. This in essence is saṁsāra.

However, when we take refuge in Amma, a miracle happens. She not only alleviates our pain, but acts as the catalyst that can take this saṁsāric suffering and convert it into fuel to move ahead on the spiritual path. Often it is when I am at the pinnacle of such pain that my deepest calls to Amma have come. Most often, our sincere, intense cries to God arise in the darkness of such nights, and Amma answers those calls. In my case, she has always answered. Amma describes the role of pain on the spiritual path this way: "It is not that the pain calms or silences the mind, but in that pain, the bhāva (attitude and feeling) of prayer to God is stronger."

But, is such pain the only way to call out to God? The answer is complex, but somehow pain has a way of focusing the mind. In those moments, prompted by our suffering, all our other thoughts and desires cease. We have no other way out, but to surrender to the divine. In those moments, our pain becomes sublimated into prayer. So, today, I'd like to share some of my experiences and life lessons with Amma, my guiding light and protector, without whose direct interventions, I would not be sitting here today.

Once, there was a donkey who lived in a monastery. The donkey was bored of its life there and dreamed of traveling the world. One day, fed up with his monastic life, he went to his guru and said, “Master, I want to leave. I have much to enjoy and experience in the world outside.” The master knew that the donkey had a strong pull towards the world and that he would only learn through experience. The master agreed with a sigh and blessed the donkey, “May you have the strength to shake off all troubles, and may wisdom dawn in you.” The donkey prostrated and went on his way.

Soon the donkey and his owner were off taking long trips across the country. The donkey enjoyed all the various foods, sights, and experiences of the world. One day, as both of them were proceeding along a narrow country road, the donkey lost its footing and fell into an open pit. The owner peered down this deep pit and saw his donkey crying out from the bottom, “Master, save me, save me!” The man said, “Don’t worry donkey, I will find help and will rescue you.” He rushed off to the nearest village and brought back a group of villagers. The villagers dropped a rope down into the pit and tried their best to bring the donkey up. Unfortunately, the donkey was way too heavy for them to pull. He had gained a lot of weight from all the eating.

Finally, after much effort, the men gave up on the donkey, telling the traveler, “We have done our best, but we cannot save this donkey. Why don’t we just bury this poor donkey, and put him out of his misery. You can always buy yourself another donkey, can’t you?” The owner was reluctant, but thought, “The villagers are right. After all, what can be done now? This is his karma. I can go and buy another donkey tomorrow.” Saying this, all the men started shoveling soil on the poor donkey. The donkey screamed and kicked and lamented his fate. Suddenly, the donkey remembered the last words of his guru: “Shake off all troubles!" In his state of profound pain, he prayed to his master with all his heart, after all his life depended on it. He then started to shake off all the soil that fell on his back and furiously stamp on it. As the men kept shoveling more and more soil, he found that the layers of dirt under him piled up, bringing him closer and closer to the surface. With all the dirt beneath him, and his own tremendous effort, he was soon able to step out of the pit.

Through this painful experience, the donkey understood the real nature of the world and developed a deep dispassion towards it. Tears of gratitude filled his eyes when he realized that it was his master's all-knowing wisdom that finally saved and uplifted him. He soon returned to the monastery and fell at his master's feet, pleading for forgiveness for his mistake. His guru had converted the donkey's pain into pure dispassion.

In truth, I find that my own mind is like that of the donkey's in this story. Every time I react with anger, pride, attachment, disdain, greed and so on, I am taking a decision deep inside me to leave my master, Amma. Unlike the donkey, who was able to remember his guru's words when a challenge arose, I completely forget Amma's teachings when tests arise. This is why Amma stresses the importance of awareness in even the smallest of our words and actions. It is this very quality that helps us remember and apply Amma's teachings when crucial situations suddenly confront us in life.

***

When I am tested I tend to experience what Śhrī Kṛiṣhṇa refers to in the *Bhagavad Gītā* as, "smṛiti-bhraṁśhād buddhi-nāśhō" — loss of memory leading to destruction of intellect. (*B.G.* 2.63)

This loss of memory manifests as a forgetting of scriptural truths and the guru's words when trying situations arise. Let me share a story that illustrates this.

Amma stresses the importance of presence of mind in our daily lives, especially in our sēvā. My sēvā on the U.S. tour for many years was to make the batter for dosas and idlis (Indian savory snacks). One tour, in Santa Fe, after a long bus ride from Los Angeles, I started to grind a large batch of dosa batter. As the morning progressed I grew tired, and my sēvā supervisor asked me to take a break. I readily agreed and simply left, completely forgetting that a large batch of batter was being ground by a machine. I ate food, took a bath, and was midway through my archana, "ōm annadāyai namaḥ" — I bow to Devi who is the giver of food to all living beings — when I suddenly remembered about the thirty liters of batter I had abandoned. I sprinted down from my room to the kitchen and found that the machine had almost burnt out. The batter basically got cooked by the heat of the stone; all the water had evaporated. The whole batch was entirely ruined. I felt terrible! I had wasted so much of Amma's food. I started to scrape out the sticky mixture from the stone and scrubbed the machine and the walls around it, which were a mess. Dosa batter had splattered everywhere. What would have normally taken me fifteen minutes now took three hours to clean up.

In addition to this, I had to start making it from scratch again and had to finish that night. This meant that I would have to stay up very late and get no sleep on a travel day. This in itself would have served as a just punishment for my forgetfulness, but it seems Amma really wanted to drive the point home. While I was cleaning up my mess, a commotion arose in the kitchen. It was then that I found out that Amma would be coming to the program hall via the kitchen that day. My mess and I were directly in her path. Red faced and panicking, I started to scrub harder and faster. Perhaps, she would throw me off the tour or worse, assign me sēvā somewhere else; then I'd have to explain to everyone why I was fired from the kitchen!

A few minutes later, Amma came by. While everyone else was so happy, I was terrified. She glanced at me. There was no need for words. Nothing could describe that look. She knew what had happened. I knew that she knew. She knew that I knew that she knew. She looked at me with the most purposeful gaze, the most compassionate, empathetic smile. It reminded me once again of Mother's unconditional love, boundless forgiveness, and acceptance of our shortcomings.

***

To break the hard shell around my heart, life has sometimes presented me with insurmountable odds and pain. In this too I recognize only Amma's divine hand, because she had to make it clear to me that she is the only way out, that the objects and experiences of the world are limited. There was a lesson coming my way to show that pain is an integral part of every desire. It would not be an exaggeration to say that if it weren't for Amma's watchful eye, I would be languishing in a jail cell in the Middle East.

In the summer of 2008, while working for an airline in Dubai, I decided to make a large investment in a firm there. This was against the advice of an astrologer, who resolutely told me not to proceed with the investment. While he was saying this to me, my eyes fell on a somewhat familiar picture he had in his shirt pocket.

Pointing to the picture, I asked, "Is that Amma?"

"Yes," he replied, "I am a devotee of Mother. Do you know her?

"Yes, I have had Amma's darśhan," I said.

"Here, keep this picture for yourself," he replied, handing me Amma's picture. "Please don't proceed with this investment."

Can you guess what I did? I did not listen to him. I had seen my golden deer, as Sītā Dēvī had seen hers. Lacking life experience, and influenced by others around me, I went ahead and made the investment. Within six months, a global economic storm wiped out many financial businesses around the world. I, too, lost all of my money. Not only that, I had incurred a huge bank loan. At first, I was in denial. As the reality of the situation dawned on me, I realized my own stupidity and greed. My self-esteem and self-confidence plummeted. Almost immediately, I slipped into a state of depression. My days and nights were now filled with worry. How could I ever pay back the debt? The law of the land was that defaulting on a loan means jail time.

It was at this time that I went to see Big Swamiji (Swami Amritaswarupananda Puri) on his annual visit to Dubai. His presence as an emissary of the Divine Mother was invaluable. He offered strength and solace to many devotees going through the same economic turmoil I was. After satsang, Swamiji sang bhajans, and then sat at the edge of the stage to give prasād (blessed food). However, I took Swamiji's role as a representative of Amma quite literally. I was so craving for Amma's darśhan that I had somehow convinced myself that Swamiji was going to start hugging everyone there. It certainly looked like he was getting ready to do just that as he came to the edge of the stage. I was the first in line for prasād and approached him, knowing that there was an embrace coming. He looked at me, asked me my name and gave me prasād while saying, "Namaḥ Śhivāya." He angled his head to signal me to move on, so the next person in line could come forward. I was confused, almost flabbergasted, "Swamiji, *no hug*?" I blurted out. He looked at me, puzzled, and then burst out with loud laughter. He thought I was joking. When he saw my expression, he quickly realized that I was completely serious. After a moment of utter disbelief, he sensed my pain and gave me a very memorable Big Swami hug. I needed that so badly and burst out in tears. For me, this was not an ordinary event — it was Amma reaching out to me across the Arabian Sea. (Dear readers, please do not go to Big Swamiji for a hug. This was a unique moment that happened many years ago.)

My financial problem was still dire. Knowing my father's anxious nature, I had kept him in the dark about my financial situation, which dragged on for months. But my birthmother knew that something was not right. On one visit home, after giving me some words of encouragement, she gave me a copy of *The Gospel of Sri Ramakrishna*, which detailed the life story of the great master Sri Ramakrishna Paramahamsa. Sri Ramakrishna's yearning for Mother Kālī touched me deeply. His teachings about the need to renounce worldliness pointed towards a deep and profound truth. Up to this point, I was convinced that my suffering was because I had lost my life savings, which meant that I was an overwhelming failure. But the truth was far graver. The truth was that my mind had managed to embed the deeply false notion that 'I am this body.' It had convinced me that possessions and money are sources of security, that I am not complete in myself and that I have to have these things to feel fulfilled.

The question now was, how can I free myself from the prison of my own mind? How can I get a mind that craves God instead of the world and its false securities? Compared to this question, paying back a loan seemed quite paltry. Sri Ramakrishna had cried to Mother Kālī as if he could not live a single moment more without seeing her. In all these years of living on this planet, how many times have I even thought of God, let alone cried for God? And yet, here I was crying for things that are so transitory.

What a curse this was! Where will I ever find peace without a mind that cries for God like Sri Ramakrishna cried for Kālī. How can I become like that?

With such thoughts welling up inside day after day, I turned to the only person I knew to be Kālī herself in a human form. I went online and found out that Amma was about to go on her North America tour. Strangely, people at work had no problem with me taking a last minute vacation, and I booked a flight straight to Los Angeles for a full seven-day program. Even though I had met Amma in 1997, this was my first ever full-scale retreat. I wondered how I could ever ask Amma the questions that were consuming me.

Once at the program, I was given my sēvā assignment and was told to go to the hall to wait for Amma's arrival, which would be followed by meditation. After mediation, the moment I opened my eyes, Swami Purnamritanandaji appeared and asked me what my questions for Amma were. Apparently, the place I had chosen to sit was right in the middle of the question line, which I hadn't even known existed. Mother Kālī herself had opened the doors for me to ask the question of my heart, "Will Amma give me devotion like Sri Ramakrishna had for the Divine Mother." Amma looked at me and asked me to come for darśhan immediately. She then looked deeply into my eyes, with a compassionate and understanding smile and held my hands in hers. She slowly nodded as she examined me. There was a profound silence all around Amma. Nothing needed to be said. After this, before Amma exited the hall, she once again held my hand and kissed it. I received my mantra during that evening program while Amma was in Dēvī Bhāva, revealing her oneness with the Divine Mother. I felt like I had found a home amidst the turmoil of my worldly life.

I returned to Dubai and found that my life there was coming to an end. My company had abruptly closed down, and I was laid off. I flew to Amritapuri and gave a letter to Amma saying that I now had no way of settling my debts and would have to go to jail. Amma, who was engaged with another matter during my darśhan, did not physically read my letter then, or even look at me. Even though my intellect was racing and recognized this as a bad sign, deep inside I felt a calm resignation — my life was now literally in Amma's hands. She was my sole refuge.

I left Amritapuri and when I returned to Dubai, my phone rang. It was my father, who by the way still had no idea about this situation. Out of the blue, he said that he had managed to secure a buyer for one of his houses. He offered me a share of the money as my inheritance. Because my company had chosen to lay me off, I was also offered a generous severance package with six months' pay. By adding the two together, I was able to meet all my financial obligations. What had seemed impossible just two weeks earlier was all sorted out within a few days. By December 2010, I moved to Amritapuri, Amma's holy abode. Despite my arrogance, ignorance, and greed, Amma freed me from my worldly troubles, so that I could lead a life of spirituality with her. Amma, to this day, there is nothing that I can say or do that can express my gratitude for how you intervened in my life and saved me.

***

In her roles as mother and master surgeon, Amma showers us with an immeasurable amount of love and compassion. In fact, Amma says that she gives us anesthesia before she proceeds to remove impurities collected over numerous lifetimes. These very impurities prevent us from seeing the light within. In truth, the obstacles and pain we experience outside are only a tiny fraction of the mountain of latent negative tendencies and wounds we carry. However, when we have Amma in our lives, she tends to our inner wounds, while protecting us from the blows of the world, teaching us the lessons we need in order to grow. Without Amma's love, compassion, guidance, and grace, how can we even dream of overcoming these immense inner and outer obstacles?

Our own efforts in any endeavor in life are as feeble as an ant trying to cross the ocean. It is only through the power of God's grace that one can even accomplish seemingly insignificant tasks. As Amma says, "We need divine grace even to close our mouths after yawning." And this is especially true with our spiritual progress. If we wish to progress in scriptural study, contemplation, or meditation, we need Amma's touch of grace. We can write all the checks we want, but if the account holder does not sign off on it, that check is not worth the paper it is written on.

> *Amma, I have made so many mistakes and continue to fail you every day. You have showered so many blessings on me, but due to my mind's tendency to hold onto wrong notions, I have failed in reaching out and seeking refuge in your ever-open arms.*
>
> *I consequently suffer from my wrong understanding of the world, of people, and most importantly, of my own mind.*
>
> *Worthless as I am, I am still your child. You are there to pick me up and give me strength to go on each time I fall.*
>
> *Please Amma, forgive me for my errors, for doubting you, for allowing a part of my mind to even question and criticize you, for projecting my own faults onto you, for my failures to apply your teachings in situations, for my failures in aligning my thoughts, words, and actions with your teachings.*

I will try harder and, by your guidance and grace, I am able to surrender and merge in thy lotus feet.

As a baby holds the mother's sari while walking, let me also become a baby and hold on to you and lean on you and walk this arduous path.

Please never let me go Amma — never let me go.

I'd like to conclude with the second verse from Śhrī Ādi Śhaṅkarāchārya's *Bhavānī Aṣhṭakam*:

bhavābdhāv-apārē mahāduḥkha-bhīru
papāta prakāmī pralōbhī pramattaḥ
kusaṁsāra-pāśha-prabaddhaḥ sadāhaṁ
gatistvaṁ gatistvaṁ tvamēkā bhavāni

In this ocean of worldly existence which is endless, I am full of sorrow and full of fear.
I have fallen with excessive desires and greed, drunken and intoxicated,
Always tied in the bondage of this miserable saṁsāra (worldly existence),
You are my refuge, You alone are my refuge, oh Mother Bhavānī.

May all of humanity live in the same peace, tranquility, and joy that we enjoy in Amma's presence. As in Amritapuri, may everyone have food to eat. May all the children in this world be blessed with the same laughter and joy that we see in the āśhram children here. Like us, may everyone be blessed with a satguru, a true master, the only abode of real peace.

13

Amma the Master Gardener

Ananya Rueb - Germany

It was during Amma's 1997 Europe Tour when my mom first brought me to see Amma in Switzerland. I was two years old at that time. One of my first memories of Amma is the feeling of her hands under my arms as she lifted me up above her head and smiled so beautifully at me.

After that tour, my mom and I came to see Amma every year when she was in Europe. We always tried to attend as many tour stops as possible with the little money we had.

For as long as I can remember, Amma has been the most important thing in my life. Right from the beginning, I felt drawn towards her. From the time I was a toddler I felt connected to her, even though I couldn't talk to her. At the time, I spoke neither Malayalam nor English, but somehow she has always felt familiar and close to me.

I have many childhood memories of Amma, which I treasure like precious gemstones — like Amma piling mountains of candies in my lap when she hugged me, or her letting me spend thirty precious minutes snuggled next to her during morning meditation.

Seeing Amma on her Europe tour was always the highlight of my year. Not only did I love being around Amma, but I also treasured the opportunity to do sēvā. I loved helping to serve food most of all. I remember starting to look forward to seeing Amma two months before her visit each year. I also remember feeling sad beyond words when the last program was over.

School was not easy for me. For many years I was bullied by my classmates. The only light in those days was Amma's annual visit. It gave me the strength to keep on going, year after year. I have asked myself many times why I was bullied in school — I still don't know the reason. However, the experience has influenced how I interact with other people to this day. Because I know how it feels to be left behind, I make an extra effort to be friendly and welcoming to others. I actively try to get to know people who seem to be shy.

Recently, someone told me how much it meant to her that I took the initiative when we first met. This really touched me because I hadn't even noticed I had done so. It showed me that even small acts of kindness can bring happiness to others.

As a teenager, I once asked Amma what I could do to make the bullying stop. Amma suggested that I be very kind and give little presents to the other children. I tried following Amma's advice, but since I was very shy, it was hard for me to put her suggestion into action. While the situation with my classmates did improve, I never quite felt like I fit in.

As I grew older, I realized I was just drawn to different things than the other teenagers. I was never interested in getting drunk and partying all night long. I wanted to be with Amma, and my longing to spend more time with her continued to grow.

At the age of thirteen, while attending school during the week, I started babysitting and working in a store on Saturdays so I could be with Amma. My goal was to travel with Amma after finishing high school, and I saved every penny I could to make this dream come true. A year before my graduation, I asked Amma if I could travel with her for "at least one year" after graduation. Amma called me a "big baby," and agreed.

***

"At least one year" turned into six years. I had the opportunity to travel with Amma throughout India, Europe, and North America and was able to come to Amritapuri for a few weeks each year as well. In between, I took every job I could get in Germany. This included selling goods at Christmas markets, waitressing, cleaning in a psychiatric hospital, and working in an organic grocery store. I would be lying if I said I fully enjoyed these jobs. Nonetheless, I am grateful for the experiences and the money, which allowed me to spend so much time with Amma. One important thing I learned through all of these jobs was that no work is insignificant, and that the wealth of a person is not defined by their education.

This reminds me of a story from the *Rāmāyaṇa*, which was often told at the end of Amma's all night Dēvī Bhāva programs. The story is about a little squirrel, who helps build the bridge to Laṇka to rescue Sītā (Lord Rāma's wife) from Rāvaṇa (the demon king who had kidnapped her). The squirrel wants to help with the construction, but he feels small and insignificant compared to the strong army of monkeys who can lift huge boulders. However, the squirrel comes up with an idea. He decides to immerse himself in water and then roll around in sand. After each round, he climbs onto the bridgework and shakes the sand off his fur. He does this to help fill in the gaps between the rocks to make them more stable.

At first the squirrel thought, "I am so small and insignificant. What can I do?" But he found a meaningful way to contribute. The combination of heavy rocks and sticky sand made the bridge stable. This shows that no work is insignificant or meaningless, if performed with the right attitude. Amma says, "The amount of love, the amount of heart, which you pour into your work, makes it significant and beautiful." It is said that out of gratitude, Rāma stroked the exhausted squirrel with three fingers, and this is why we see three white stripes on the back of squirrels to this day.

While traveling with Amma, I felt like I was living my dream and wanted this way of life to continue forever. After four years of touring with Amma, though, my poor mom became very concerned that I would never go back to school and learn a profession. So, during the next Europe tour, my mom went to Amma and asked whether I should go to university. Amma agreed and told my mom to find me and bring me to her. I was doing sēvā at the Indian snacks stall at the time. When my mom came and told me what Amma had said I was completely shocked. What if Amma sent me away for studies? I did not want my dream of spending so much time with Amma to be over.

I went to the side of Amma's chair; she looked at me but didn't speak. I waited for more than two hours, but Amma still did not say a word to me. In my mind I remembered the silent deal I had made with Amma in my prayers. The deal was that as long as I could easily find a job and earn enough money to be with Amma, then continuing to travel with her was okay.

I wondered for a long time why Amma did not say anything to me at that time, and I came up with two possible answers — either I was not ready to accept Amma's answer, or Amma knew times would change soon enough.

***

When the pandemic struck, my dream-life of touring with Amma came to a sudden halt. At the time, I was working in an organic grocery store in Germany. I liked the work, and the shop owner had agreed to give me time off for all the tours I wanted to do with Amma. However, when Amma's U.S. tour got canceled and I didn't get my usual break from work, I realized that something in my life had to change.

Amma says, "Happiness is a decision. Whether we laugh or cry, days will pass by." I often contemplate these words. To be honest, I find it difficult to decide to be happy when I am sad or frustrated, so I try to make this decision by taking small steps. It's easier for me to think that Amma wants me to give my best in every situation. So instead of being frustrated doing the same job day after day, I thought of solutions to use my time wisely. One day I thought, "Why not take some courses at university and study for a semester? When Amma starts touring again, I will just pause my studies." Well, this one semester turned into two years. With Amma's grace I will have my Bachelor's degree in Biology by the end of next summer.

I chose biology because I love nature, and I want to do dharmic work. I do not want to earn my living in a way that harms people or nature. Not being able to ask Amma directly what to study, I once again made a silent deal with her in my prayers: as long as everything goes smoothly, I should continue studying biology. When a friend kindly offered to tell Amma about my studies, however, I was nervous. What if Amma was not happy with my choice? Later my friend told me that when he spoke to Amma concerning my studies, she refused to answer him, looking at him as if to say, "Why are you telling me this? I already know." My silent deal was confirmed.

The first few semesters of biology are packed with subjects like chemistry, physics, and math. These subjects were never my strong suit in school. Nevertheless, I committed to putting in as much effort as I could. I started getting up early every morning to prepare for my classes. I decided to attend every class and every single tutorial that was offered. Due to the pandemic, the first two semesters were all online. I was by myself with my computer all day long, but I didn't mind. Touring with Amma has taught me discipline.

When I felt tired in the mornings and didn't want to get up, I thought of challenging situations on the tours. I remembered how desperate for sleep I sometimes felt after long bus rides on the U.S. tours. After Dēvī Bhāva finished, we boarded the buses immediately. Sometimes we wouldn't reach the next stop until the middle of the night, after a sixteen-hour bus ride. Instead of going to sleep, my sēvā in 'Annapurna Snacks' included cutting vegetables soon after we arrived. By the time that was over, it was time to set up the snack shop. By the time that was finished, it was time to open for our first hungry customers. Even though I often felt like I had reached my limit after a long bus ride, my sēvā showed me that I am able to go far beyond what I think I can.

While away from Amma, I missed doing sēvā. It was then that I realized how much fulfillment it gave me to serve others and how it deepened my relationship with Amma. Amma says, "The opportunity to love and serve others should be seen as a rare gift, a blessing from God." In my morning meditations I used to pray to Amma to accept my studies as an offering. It motivated me to see my studies as more than just a means to get a good job; my education was a stepping stone to serving the world.

***

Throughout the past three years, there have been many situations in which I realized how much Amma's training on the tours has changed me. I will share one such experience that took place while participating in a mandatory internship in an organic chemistry lab. I was afraid of the chemicals we were using in the experiments. If handled in the wrong way, some of them could explode, or cause cancer, or badly burn the skin.

The situation reminded me of the San Ramon program during one of my first U.S. tours. On the second day of the retreat, Amma distributed prasād dinner to everyone. For this occasion, I was asked to help fry papadams (a crispy snack). I was instructed to count the number of papadams and felt very happy and confident performing this task. Usually, the frying takes many hours, but we worked fast and were done quite early. Somehow there weren't as many papadam filled boxes as usual, but nobody questioned it. The papadams ran out very early that night. I felt so ashamed! I just wanted to dig a hole and bury myself in it. My pride had kept me from asking someone else to double check my papadam count.

What felt so painful at the time has taught me a big lesson in humility and gratitude. The bighearted supervisor asked me to help again with the frying for the next summer tour. Luckily, everything went well that time.

When I was handling the chemicals in the lab, I remembered the papadam incident and understood it in a deeper way. I realized it had taught me the importance of awareness and teamwork, and to always ask someone to check my work. Instead of feeling sad about this mistake, I now feel blessed for the lesson it taught me.

During the last three years, I have felt close to Amma, but it was always right before exams that I felt her presence the most. I studied as much as I could before each exam. My goal was to give my very best, so I could say, "I have put forth my best effort, understanding that everything is not in my hands. The result is up to your grace alone Amma. Whatever happens will be best for me."

This reminds me of Amma's story about the man who gets invited to a job interview in a faraway city. Although he gets up early in the morning to reach the airport, upon arrival he might find that the plane cannot take off because of engine problems or bad weather. Even though the man made the best effort from his side, he ended up missing the interview because the factor of grace was not with him.

Contemplating this story helped me realize that I can only influence situations and their outcomes to a certain extent. This realization helped me to remain quite calm before and during exams. When my friends asked me how I managed to remain so calm, I shared Amma's story with them. Immediately I could see their faces relax. I was amazed.

Many years ago, Swami Shubamritananda-ji gave a talk along these same lines. He said that "no matter what you are doing, be aware that somebody is watching you." I never thought that I would one day be a role model of calm under pressure. Nonetheless, Swamiji's words inspired me to focus on giving my best while not harming others with my thoughts, words or actions.

***

Another way I stayed close to Amma during the pandemic was by spending time in nature. My partner and I look after a garden together. When we started gardening, the property consisted of fruit trees, nut trees, and a lot of grassland. Over the last few years, we have turned much of the grassland into vegetable beds. Every year, we are sure to keep one bed of flowers to feed the bees. We also leave piles of fallen leaves and piles of wood for insects and other animals like hedgehogs to enjoy. As time passes, more and more animals come to live there.

For many years I have heard Amma ask us to grow our own organic vegetables. Since my partner and I live in Germany, we have four seasons and with that, many opportunities to grow many different kinds of vegetables. We start in the spring by planting lettuce in our nursery at home. We grow many varieties of tomatoes, chilies, cabbage, beans, pumpkins, and zucchini from seed in our nursery. Before we transfer the baby plants into the garden beds, we prepare each bed with compost and horse manure. It is important for us to try to improve the fertility of the soil in a sustainable way.

Once the baby plants are in the beds, there is still work to do. The beds need to be weeded, the plants watered, and the army of snails shown their limits. Although this requires a lot of physical work, we love doing it. Working with nature helps us to calm our mind and brings us peace. During the summertime, we harvest veggies almost every day.

There were so many tomatoes this year that we filled pot after pot with tomato sauce, filling more than twenty jars. Each jar will provide for one meal during the winter. Right before we came to Amritapuri for this visit, we planted a few more veggies, like cabbage and leeks, that will be ripe in winter around Christmas time. We are trying our best to include at least a small amount of vegetables from our garden in all of our meals year-round, just like Amma suggests.

Amma says,

> "Everything in nature is a wonderful miracle. Isn't a little bird flying through the vast sky a miracle? Isn't a tiny fish swimming in the depths of the ocean a miracle? Unfortunately, people think that only if a fish flies through the sky can it be called a miracle!"

These words touch me profoundly. Indeed, everything in nature is a miracle! I love watching the cycles of nature and the perfection of the interactions that take place. When I spend time in nature, I feel my heart opening and my mind becoming calm and peaceful. Somehow nature puts things back into perspective and helps me to "see a frog as a frog and an elephant as an elephant." (Amma)

Frustrating situations become small and insignificant when I look at the vast sky or a beautiful flower. I experience this not just while sitting still, but also while actively gardening. I am fascinated by growing vegetables. Seeing a plant grow, taking care of it, and eventually harvesting it gives me such joy.

I have also noticed that my appreciation and gratitude for food has grown. I am so grateful for this experience and hope everyone gets the chance to grow their own veggies at least once. It is my prayer that more people take time to enjoy nature and her miracles. It is a powerful way to regain our love and respect for her.

***

I love to imagine Amma as a divine gardener and myself as a plant. Throughout my life, Amma has taken care of me and nurtured me. Thank you Amma! Just as a plant grows fruit and feeds others selflessly, I hope my actions will be of some benefit to the world too.

I pray that all of Amma's children may feel close to her in their heart, whether in her physical presence or not. May we all do our best to put Amma's recent Diwali reminder into practice, "Children, like any other decision, happiness is also a decision. Whatever happens in life, try to smile."

14

The Transformative Power of the Guru

Gangadhar Sahu – USA

I was born and brought up in the state of Odisha, known as the land of Lord Jagannāth. Back home in Odisha, most people limit their spiritual practices to visiting temples and idol worship. They are especially fond of Lord Jagannāth. The customs and culture of Odisha are very rich and full of festivals and celebrations. That was the way I connected to God in my childhood. There was no concept of needing a satguru for spiritual growth and upliftment.

I remained limited to that way of worship for many years, even after moving to the USA. I would go to temples on special occasions and perform rituals at home as part of my spiritual practices. Even though we lived close to Detroit, which Amma visited regularly for many years, we had never heard of Amma. I guess our time had not yet come.

Like every other parent, my wife, Madhusmita, and I were concerned about raising our children with proper values. We also wanted to keep them connected to Indian culture. Actually, our family's spiritual journey started when my son, Chandan was seven years old and my daughter, Ashley was two years old. We started taking them to the Chinmaya Mission in Chicago every week. Both of them participated in spiritual classes and *Bhagavad Gītā* chanting. They also memorized verses the way kids in Amritapuri do. While the kids were doing this, we adults participated in group discussions on spiritual topics. It was during one of these discussions that I heard about Amma for the first time. We were still not ready to meet her, so the search for a 'real master' went on.

In 2006, while visiting an Indian grocery store in Chicago, we saw a flier announcing Amma's visit. This time we were attracted like magnets and decided to meet her at her program. The whole family — my wife, myself, and our two children — made our way to the hotel. We were warmly welcomed and greeted by volunteers, given early tokens for darśhan and invited to sit in the front row. After some time, Amma entered the hall accompanied by blowing conches and the swāmīs' mantra chanting, and we saw her being welcomed with a traditional pāda pūjā.

Our first program happened to be the special Dēvī Bhāva program. Just before the curtains opened, Swami Amritaswarupananda sang *Jai Jai Sadguru Mahārāṇī*. The bhajan was so powerful and energetic that my heart melted. The tune resonated in my ears for a full week, twenty-four hours a day. I had been to many bhajan sessions in my life but had never experienced anything like it. All of the lyrics were displayed on screens, so we could sing along, become part of the music, and merge into it.

After Amma's satsang and bhajans, we went for darśhan. We didn't know what to expect. Amma's darśhan was unique. She hugged me and whispered, "*Mora suna pila*" into my ears, which means 'My darling son,' in Odiya, my mother tongue. As we sat near Amma after darśhan, I clearly remembered how Amma gave me a divine side-long glance, accompanied by the most beautiful smile, as if she had known me for a long time, and that she was happy that I had finally come to meet her. That divine glance and smile were so enchanting that it was the turning point in my life. From that day forward, profound positive changes started happening to our family. Our whole perspective on life, dealing with social pressure, and raising the kids changed. We began getting rid of negative qualities.

Sometime in 2007, we visited a temple in the suburbs where Amma had held her program when she first visited Chicago back in 1988. To our surprise, we found a large stack of old editions of *Matruvani* (Amma's monthly magazine) there. As I began reading, I learned about Amma's līlās (her divine plays), and how she had transformed many people's lives. With permission, I took all those old *Matruvanis* home and started reading them one by one. I was mesmerized and read almost all of them within a week. It was like a divine treasure for me.

The fact that she was a fisherman's daughter from a remote village in Kerala stunned me. In fact, she had only studied up to the fourth grade, and yet she was transforming so many lives. As she embraced each person that came to her, she listened to their problems and solved them with a few words, a mere touch, a glance, or by making a saṅkalpa — a divine resolve. She shared her devotees' happiness and sorrow, all while serving society with a vast array of institutions providing relief for the suffering. The list of her charities, and the aspects of society they touch, seemed endless. It was with this understanding that my love and connection with Amma started to blossom.

***

After meeting Amma, it became clear how important it is to have a satguru in our lives. Even avatārs, incarnations of God, like Lord Kṛiṣhṇa and Lord Rāma had gurus. In the *Mahābhārata*, Lord Kṛiṣhṇa and Arjuna are just good friends before the war, and Kṛiṣhṇa never acts like a guru. That is because Arjuna, the disciple, has yet to take birth. It is only when Arjuna is finally willing to admit he cannot solve his problems by himself and surrenders at Lord Kṛiṣhṇa's feet that Lord Kṛiṣhṇa manifests as the guru and guides Arjuna to victory.

Amma often refers to the story of Sage Dattātrēya who claimed that he had twenty-four gurus in nature, including air, water, fire, sky, etc., and that we have something to learn from each one of them. Out of ignorance, some people think that surrendering to a guru is akin to becoming a slave, but Amma says, "Even to learn to tie our shoes, we need someone to teach us."

Amma elaborates on this, saying:

> "The guru is the one who wakes us up from the sleep of ignorance and helps us realize our true nature. When we've forgotten a poem we learnt as a youngster, it all comes flooding back when someone recites the first few lines. Our current state of spiritual forgetfulness is like this. The guru's teachings hold the power to remind us and awaken us. Just as a filter purifies water, the guru purifies the disciple's mind, removing the ego."

Amma says everything in the universe is created by God with one exception, the ego. This is the only thing created by us. Because we created the ego, we fall slave to it at every turn. Surrendering to a guru's instructions is not slavery. Actually it is the way out of slavery; it brings us back to the path of supreme freedom and everlasting happiness. Amma does not force anything on us. She does not tell anybody to change their religion. Love is her religion. She accepts us the way we are and embraces everybody irrespective of their caste, religion, nation, or social status.

The following verse from the *Guru Gītā* perfectly sums up our great fortune at having Amma in our lives:

> *dhyānamūlaṁ gurōrmūrtiḥ*

pūjāmūlaṁ gurōḥ padam
mantramūlaṁ gurōr vākyaṁ
mōkṣhamūlaṁ gurōḥ kṛipā

The root of meditation is the form of the guru,
The root of worship is the feet of the guru,
The root of mantra is the word of the guru,
The root of liberation is the grace of the guru.

Guru Gītā, Verse 26

The story of Śhabarī in the *Rāmāyaṇa* perfectly illustrates the ideal relationship between a guru and a devotee. Śhabarī was a young woman, the daughter of a hunter, with a heart of pure gold. The great Mātaṅga Ṛiṣhi was her guru. At the time of his death, Sage Mātaṅga told Śhabarī that she would one day have the darśhan (vision) of Lord Rāma in physical form.

Many years passed by. Every day, the elderly Śhabarī would come out of her āśhram, with the help of a walking stick, and pluck berries for Rāma. She would pluck one, taste it and, if it was sweet, she would put it in her basket, discarding the bitter ones. She wanted to give the good berries to Rāma. She would decorate the āśhram with fresh flowers each morning thinking that Lord Rāma would visit her that day.

One fine day, Lord Rāma and Lakṣhmaṇa, Rāma's brother, came to her house. Her joy knew no bounds. Lord Rāma cherished the berries offered out of love and blessed her. Śhabarī lived the rest of her life in deep meditation and reached the heavenly abode. This story shows that the words of the guru never go unfulfilled and highlights the unflinching faith of Śhabarī in her guru's words. Like Śhabarī, we should always keep our house and mind clean in the hopes that Amma might visit at any time.

***

Before I met Amma, I never sang. However, with Amma's infinite grace, I started singing all around our house from the very first day I heard her bhajans. Slowly, we became branded the 'Amma people' in our community of Odiya friends. Any time we attended a function, we were greeted with, "Oh, the Amma people have come." We are really proud of that nickname that affirms our faith and connection to Amma.

As the years passed, we couldn't help but notice the transformational impact that Amma's infinite, unconditional love and grace were having in our home. I, for example, slowly developed an aversion to meat and became a complete vegetarian. The entire family did. Before meeting Amma, my wife and I were obsessed about our kids' grades. We wanted to make sure that they got 100 out of 100 on all of their school tests. A 98% was not acceptable. But after meeting Amma, our perception about raising children changed. We began focusing on their overall growth. We began to care more about raising nice, kind human beings with good values rather than being obsessed that our children should top every exam. We are very indebted to Amma for transforming and inspiring us to raise both of our kids well.

In our Odiya community, both of our children are role models for their friends. Many times, our community members ask what our secret is. We always say that whatever they are now is all because of Amma; they are Amma's children. Swami Amritaswarupananda Puri always says Amma is like a brake in the car. If a car doesn't have brakes, we know what will happen. When you are living without a satguru in your life, it is like driving a car without brakes. Our kids were raised with Amma's protective brakes.

***

In 2011 during her North America Tour, Amma visited Iowa before her stop in Chicago. The program in Chicago was set to begin immediately after the Iowa program. Our family went to attend the Dēvī Bhāva program in Iowa despite a heavy sēvā load in Chicago the very next day. We thought we could come back just after darśhan and do our sēvā at the Chicago venue.

We got early darśhan tokens, had darśhan, and Amma told us to sit beside her. Usually, people sit next to Amma for ten to fifteen minutes and then get up to give their spot to other devotees. However, as we were about to get up to leave the stage, Amma made a sad face and told us to keep sitting. This happened six times. Five hours passed before we were able to leave.

We started driving back to Chicago around 4:00 a.m. and found that a heavy rainstorm had passed through while we were sitting next to Amma. There were lots of broken trees on the highway. If we had left earlier, we would have driven right into this dangerous storm. Amma knew this and prevented it.

> *ōm sarvajñāyai namaḥ*
>
> Salutations to she who is omniscient. (*Lalitā Sahasranāma* 196)

Amma is that omniscient mother who does everything she can to protect her children from all troubles.

***

By Amma's grace, our lifestyle changed even more after the Chicago āśhram opened in 2012. Every Saturday, instead of going to parties, we would attend satsang at the āśhram. Our children looked forward to participating in Amrita Balakendra and AYUDH — the āśhram youth groups, where they learned to sing bhajans, chant archana, and contribute to the community. Going to the āśhram has become a regular part of our routine.

With Amma's grace, we moved to the Chicago āśhram in 2019. Very shortly after we moved in, the Covid pandemic struck. As the whole world was reeling in fear, we felt like we were in a safe haven. By Amma's grace, we have been living there ever since, surrounded by a beautiful, natural landscape and a wonderful community of spiritual brothers and sisters.

Out of her compassion, Amma takes on the role of a mother, a humanitarian, a friend, God or guru — whatever is required. Contemplating on what I can offer to Amma in return, I have taken inspiration from the following story from the Mahābhārata that illustrates this point:

Vidurānī, the wife of Vidura, was an ardent devotee of Lord Kṛiṣhṇa and always longed to have him visit her house. Since Vidura was not of royal birth, they were hesitant to invite him, but the Lord had other plans.

One day, Lord Kṛiṣhṇa visited the Kauravas in Hastināpur to try to avert the war. When Duryōdhana heard about this, he invited Lord Kṛiṣhṇa to join him for delicious food served on golden dishes. Lord Kṛiṣhṇa refused to go to Duryōdhana's palace for the feast, as the intention behind this invitation was unrighteous.

Instead, he visited Vidura's house uninvited. Lord Kṛiṣhṇa was famished and pleaded with Vidurānī to feed him. With lots of love, Vidurānī looked for something to feed Kṛiṣhṇa, but all she had was a banana. She offered him the banana, but in her ecstasy of love and devotion, she threw away the fruit and gave him the peel. Kṛiṣhṇa affectionately accepted the peel and relished it joyfully. It tasted sweeter to him than all the preparations and offerings made by Duryōdhana. When Vidura came home, he was shocked at what he saw and exclaimed, "Oh, Vidurānī! What are you doing?" Kṛiṣhṇa whispered to him not to speak, for Vidurānī was fully absorbed in transcendental love.

From this story, we can see that the Lord actually does not need anything from us, but he will accept anything that is offered out of love and with a pure heart, and he will relish it.

Amma encourages us to treat others with love and kindness as well saying, "Be like the honeybee who gathers only nectar wherever it goes. Seek the goodness that is found in everyone." She elaborates on this point explaining that when we point one finger at others, three fingers are pointing towards us. So before judging others, we should introspect and try to improve ourselves. We should be able to see goodness in everything. When we see an egg, think of the hen inside it. When we see a seed, think of the tree that it contains. When we see death, we should see the beauty of life. When we see the diversity in the world, Amma asks us to recognize the unity behind it all.

***

A week ago we flew from Chicago to Amritapuri via Delhi, and took a few days to visit Amrita Hospital in Faridabad, and to go to Vrindavan as well. When we visited Vrindavan, we were warned by local people to be careful about the monkeys. They are notorious for snatching eyeglasses and cell phones from people. I kept my phone in my pocket but held my glasses in my hand. Before entering the temple, one of the monkeys tried to snatch them from my hand. He was not successful, and I put the glasses in my pocket. Once inside the temple, I had to wear the glasses to have the darśhan of Lord Banke Bihari. I was overwhelmed by the darśhan and crowd. While exiting the temple, due to lack of awareness, I forgot to put my glasses in my pocket. The very moment I stepped out of the door, a monkey appeared, snatched my glasses, and climbed a tall pole. I did not know what to do.

One of the local people ran to get a juice box. All the while, the monkey was playing with my glasses, wearing them and trying to bend them. I prayed to Amma to get my glasses back safely, as I didn't have a spare pair and am completely dependent on them. Once the kind man returned with the juice box, the monkey took it, climbed back up the pole and dropped my glasses. As they hit the concrete below, one of the lenses came out of the frame. So, I was forced to wear one glass lens for some time. This incident taught me that I need to have more awareness and that anything can happen at any moment. Nothing is in our hands. Only her grace can guide us through the bumps on the road.

Since bhajans are the main source of my connection to Amma, I conclude with a stanza from *Ammē Ī Jīvaṇḍē*, one of my favorite bhajans as my closing prayer.

ammē ī jīvaṇḍē kaṇṇunīr oppuvān
ammē ī jīvannu śhānti nalkān
ammē jaganmayī aṅgallāt-illārum
nin pādalābham āṇātma-lābham

Mother, to wipe away my tears,
To grant peace to this embodied self,
O Mother, who has manifested as the universe,
There is none but you.
To reach your divine feet is the true fulfilment of life.

We can't even think of life without you, Amma — the bhajans, spiritual values, and wholesome āśhram life. We seek your grace that we may all serve you better, following the path of dharma with you ever in our minds.

15

Drawing My Beloved

Lasita – USA

One morning before going to work, I woke up remembering a dream. It was nighttime at the Amritapuri āśhram, and I was walking from my room to the Kālī Temple. No one else was around; all was still. On the ground were little lights, like the ones lit for Kārtika (Amma's monthly birth star celebration). I followed the lights into the temple and passed into the inner sanctum. Sitting before Kālī was Amma, lit by a single lamp. In that dream, I sat beside Amma, and we looked at Kālī together. I then performed pāda pūjā, gazing into Amma's eyes and at her lotus feet as I was pouring milk, ghee, honey, and rose water onto Amma's feet. As the dream ended, I lay my head in Amma's lap and fell asleep.

When I woke up, I was not in Amritapuri but back in the mundane daily routine of my life. I had to go to work to teach. So I got up, rushed to get ready, and taught History and English to my middle school students. I forgot about the dream.

A few months later, as I was sitting in the back of the hall at M.A. Center in San Ramon, I noticed the lyrics of a particular bhajan. They struck me deep in my heart, and I remembered my dream. The bhajan was *Akalattā-kōvilil*. I had never heard it sung before or since. The words were astonishingly similar to my dream:

> *In a temple far away, an eternal flame glowed from an oil lamp.*
>
> *Mother sat there, waiting with deep compassion*

to light the way for those wandering in the darkness of ignorance.

One day, as I passed that way in my aimless wandering,
the radiant one beckoned to me.

She opened the door of the sanctum sanctorum,
took sandalwood paste and gently smeared it on my forehead.

She sang songs of God as she embraced me with her soft hands,
and I drifted into sleep in her arms.

A new dream came and sat near me, whispering a great truth:

"Why do you cry? Are you not aware that you have reached the lotus feet of the Goddess of this universe?"

I awoke with a deep sigh and there before me,
I beheld her luminous, lotus-like face clearly.

I began crying tears of joy mixed with sadness. It felt as though Amma was directly saying to me through the bhajan, "Daughter, you're always with me, but you have to remember that and keep your heart open." I was struck with an immediate desire to draw what I had dreamt in the light of this bhajan. Thus began my journey to rediscover how art can become sādhanā, spiritual practice.

In fact, for several months leading up to this moment, I had been going through a difficult period feeling disconnected from Amma and neglecting my drawing sādhanā. But before I share more about that, let me explain how I met Amma. When I was a young child of four or five years old, I was invited to go with my best friend and her family to see Amma. I honestly don't remember much about that first visit besides loving the way Amma smelled and loving the rolling golden hills of San Ramon. I returned home to my parents and brother and excitedly shared about my experience. I guess something I said interested them. The next time Amma came to the United States, my whole family went to see her. Since then, we have all been coming for Amma's darśhan every year. My grandfather, lovingly known as "Tin-Barn-John", also became a devotee. His faith and dedication to sēvā are a great inspiration to me.

***

As a small child, I loved getting darśhan from Amma, eating the chocolates she gave me, and resting my head in her lap. I liked sitting on the pīṭham (seat) next to her. Amma braided my hair once, while a satsang was going on, and I still remember the gentle feeling of her divine hands in my hair. I loved touching her hand when she arrived or left the program hall and getting showered with flower petals at the end of Dēvī Bhāva. I also relish the memories of getting crispy papadam and ice cream from Amma during the retreats.

I loved Amma with all my heart. Whenever she left to continue her North America tour, I would be sad. After she was gone, I would continue on with my child's life, playing with my Amma doll and looking at the many pictures I had of her on my wall. It wasn't until I entered adolescence, and started becoming more self-aware, that I developed a bond with Amma that went beyond simply wanting to lie in her arms and eat chocolates. I began wanting to do sēvā all the time at Amma's programs. For several years I barely saw Amma during her programs because I would spend all day serving food in the San Ramon dining hall. Despite the heat of June, I loved the feeling of connectedness I had with Amma while doing sēvā. I would chant my mantra and smile as much as I could to bring joy to others. When Amma drove away from the program during the break, I would happily take the chocolate she handed me out of her car window, which she smilingly told us was for her "sēvā children."

It was during this time that I started to draw Amma. I drew Amma and the gods and goddesses constantly, so much so that my mom encouraged me to make a book to give to Amma the next time she came to the United States. Thus began my hobby of drawing as much as possible and giving those drawings to Amma every year. It felt extra special to create something just for Amma.

This went on for several years, but as I became a teenager, my mind became tumultuous. I began to experience the typical trials of a teenager growing up in the Bay Area in California. I became engulfed in māyā (delusion) and got involved in many petty dramas. I also began to struggle with mental illness.

I had always been an anxious child — I was constantly terrified that someone would come to my home and hurt my brothers and parents while they were sleeping. At night I would say elaborate prayers, asking Amma to protect all children, all animals, and all humans, and then I would make a special request to Amma to protect my family and my cats and dog. There were times when I would become so anxious and suffer such bad insomnia that I could only fall asleep by taking all of my Amma pictures and laying them in a circle around my bed. I suffered this mostly in silence, only sharing it with my inner Amma.

But now that I was older, the teen hormones and the complex social dynamics of an American high school took things to an entirely different level. I experienced severe depression, eating disorders, self-harm, and suicidal thoughts. These thoughts plagued me, and my mind became a very dark place. Unfortunately, unlike my younger self, I did not go to Amma for help. Instead, I simply let my mind take me deeper and deeper into darkness. I still loved Amma, but at that time, she felt distant. I knew that she was watching me, and I was sure she was disappointed in me.

I felt immense guilt because my spiritual journey had taken a back seat, replaced by a strong attachment to my phone, friends, people I dated, movies and TV. I had stopped chanting my mantra, which I had been chanting at least 108 times daily for several years since receiving it at the age of eleven. When I looked at Amma's photo, I felt disconnected from her. I knew that Amma came and kissed each of her children's foreheads every night, but instead of finding comfort in that, I just felt shame. I thought, "Amma must look at me and think, 'Wow, what a failure. I gave this girl so much, and she is doing nothing with it.'"

I let my mind become a tangle of pain, trauma, and sadness. My mood swings were intense, and I felt I had no control over my thoughts.

Amma says,

> "Our problem is that we identify with all the moods of the mind. When we are angry we become anger. It is the same with fear, excitement, anxiety, sorrow, and happiness. We become one with that emotion, whether it is positive or negative. We identify with the mask, but in reality none of these moods are really you. Your true nature is bliss."

***

As I got a little older, though, I was able to reestablish my strong connection with Amma, mostly through AYUDH (Amma's youth wing). Several peers who were long-time devotees encouraged me to join. They suggested that I come on retreat and tell Swami Dayamritananda Puri about my problems. I was nervous, as I had isolated myself from my āśhram peers for years. I was afraid I would be alone.

Instead, I was embraced by all and had a fantastic experience connecting with other people and thinking about Amma. During the Q&A sessions with Dayamrita Swamiji, I realized that other teenagers were dealing with the exact same struggles I was. We talked about how difficult it was to overcome peer pressure in American schools and how we often felt isolated in our peer groups. Realizing I was not alone was so powerful.

I firmly believe that Amma saved my life by bringing me to that AYUDH retreat. My suicidal ideation had become quite bad, and I had stopped eating and sleeping. Without Amma's subtle intervention in my life, I don't think I would be here today. Thank You, Amma!

When I next saw Amma on tour, I was so happy because I felt that my heart was once again connected to her. I told Amma about my desire to attend school near the San Ramon āśhram. She agreed. We talked about my studies, and I asked if I could go on tour with her once I was eighteen.

College began a new chapter in my relationship with Amma. I went on tour with her each summer and became part of the beautiful, sometimes crazy, Amma tour family. I began to live for those summers — the rest of the year was spent waiting for Amma to arrive again. I was not particularly good at spiritual practices. I tried to do archana every day, but mostly failed. I even stopped drawing and making art.

But when I would see Amma in Seattle at the beginning of each U.S. tour, that wondrous, indescribable feeling returned to my heart, every time. Seeing Amma's smiling face as she entered the hall was everything I wanted and needed. Every tour with Amma has been a highlight of my life. I am so grateful to Amma and my sēvā families ('Banana Leaf' coffee stand and darśhan sēvā on stage) for the many opportunities they have given me over the years.

Traveling with Amma and doing sēvā for her tours is an experience like nothing else. I learned so much about myself. I realized that I *loved* sleep more than anything, and I often had to fight against my feelings of self-pity and exhaustion. I also learned, as Amma says, that we are all role models for someone else. Because my sēvā involved being on stage, others were actually watching me. So I had to act properly and kindly and do my sēvā with great awareness. You never know how your behavior might influence someone else.

I still struggled with feelings of guilt and shame. I knew I could do better, but Amma was always so tender and gentle with me. I often came to her crying, and she would wipe my tears away and help me work through the intense issues I was having with my eating disorder.

Once, I wrote her a letter about how guilty I felt, and what a bad person I was, and how I was not selfless enough. Amma took some sandalwood paste and put it on my forehead, chin, cheeks, and nose, all the while saying, "Nice, nice, nice, nice." Amma knew I needed a gentle mother, and she took care of me in a way I didn't even know I needed.

The next turning point came after I offered my drawings (that had been inspired by my dream and the *Akalattā-kōvilil* bhajan) to Amma on Guru Pūrṇimā day on yet another U.S. tour. After finishing these illustrations and giving them to Amma I felt great peace.

It was at this time I realized that drawing helped me to focus intently on Amma, so I started working on drawing every one of Amma's 108 names. I didn't know it at the time, but Amma was gently tending and watering the seed within me that loved creating art for God.

***

Shortly after offering my art to Amma, Covid-19 arrived, and art became one of my lifelines. I had learned to draw digitally on an iPad right before Covid, so I began drawing on it constantly. I started illustrating the meaning of bhajans. When Amma began broadcasting programs online, she would often sing the exact bhajan I had drawn a few days before. This happened many times, and it felt like Amma was directly saying to me, "Daughter, you might be far away from me, but I know each and every one of your actions. I am with you."

During those early Covid days, I would draw pictures of young Amma doing her daily chores, and think of Kṛiṣhṇa. Like a small child, I would work in my parents' garden and pretend to be Amma and sing Kṛiṣhṇa bhajans as I worked. I tried to imagine that blissful state where everything is God. This period of drawing art for Amma was such a happy one for me. I felt intimately connected to Amma and the āśhram. I just loved thinking up new ideas for drawings.

Eventually, though, I found myself drifting into the dangerous territory of the ego. "Wow, you're doing a great job handling all this craziness with Covid," it said, "Good job!"

Unsurprisingly, I became complacent. I stopped my daily meditation and stopped attending the nightly ārati (ceremonial worship) on 'Zoom' that we held with a few other devotees from San Ramon. Slowly, I began to slip back into the dark hole of depression. I stopped drawing regularly, and even when I did draw, I felt no enthusiasm or connection to God.

Once again, I started to feel so far away from Amma. As 2020 ended, and it became clear Covid would not be gone anytime soon, I began to feel angry with Amma. I thought, "Why did she leave me here? Doesn't she know that I'm suffering?"

My mind was so full of darkness, self-pity, and ego that I couldn't see that I was not doing my part to stay connected with Amma. Amma always says that self-effort is essential if we want God's grace to flow to us. I was not putting in any effort, so how could I expect God's grace to reach me? Amma has repeatedly shown me that if I put in just a little effort, she will pull me into her arms. But I let myself forget this. I wasn't doing sēvā, I wasn't drawing for Amma, nor was I meditating.

Instead, I wallowed, watched TV, spent a lot of time online, and listened to audiobooks. I tried my best when I returned to my teaching job, but even in classrooms full of students, I felt disconnected. I no longer saw my work as sēvā. Instead, I saw it as a form of torture and got frustrated with things that would normally not bother me.

Honestly, I started to lose hope. I thought to myself, "Will I ever see Amma in person again? Will Covid ever end? Will I ever be allowed to enter India again? Will Amma ever be able to come back to the United States?" I don't know if I lost faith, but I definitely lost hope. I knew Amma could hear my thoughts, but I felt abandoned.

Here is some Amma wisdom that I wish I had followed during this dark time:

> "Don't feel sad that you cannot be as disciplined as you would like to be. Do what you can. Don't be sad about what you are not able to do. Don't push yourself too hard. Don't suppress or judge yourself. Give the body the food and sleep it needs. There is nothing wrong with that. But don't overly pamper yourself either. There may be lapses in your discipline. We may fall down. But we shouldn't allow it to make us feel frustrated. When you fall down, instead of lying there on the ground thinking

> how comfortable it is, remind yourself of your goal. Get back up and keep moving forward. Never accept defeat."

I had accepted defeat, which made me feel more hopeless. I had stopped watching Amma's webcast; it was too painful. It made me sad to see Amma when I couldn't be there. I withdrew into the hellscape of my mind, and my depression deepened. Eventually, I reached rock bottom.

By Amma's grace, I had the good sense to speak with Swami Dayamritananda Puri, admitting to him that I had been suffering in silence for almost a year. I told him that I desperately missed Amma and felt like everything would be okay if I could just be in her arms. He told me I needed to see Amma and talk to her in person if I could. With grace, I got some time off work and was able to come to see Amma in early 2022.

***

Honestly, I was terrified to go back to Amritapuri. I felt so ashamed of how I had spent the second half of the pandemic and was so scared that Amma would look at me and be angry or disappointed in me. When my mandatory quarantine for new arrivals was finally over, I had my first darśhan in over two years. Amma did the exact opposite of what I had feared.

It seems obvious that Amma would treat me with love, since Amma truly is an ocean of compassion. But I had created such a negative image of myself that I was somehow convinced that Amma would not want me anymore. Instead, she lovingly read my entire letter as she held me close, rubbing my back as I sobbed. She pinched my cheek and told me she wanted me to be happy. As I sat on the stage after my darśhan, I felt my heart begin to heal.

As I remember this darśhan, two of 108 Amma's divine names flood into my mind:

> *ōm tamaḥ-kliṣhṭa-manō-vṛiṣhṭa-svaprakāśha-śhubhāśhiṣhe namaḥ*
>
> Salutations to she who sheds the light of her blessings on the hearts of those suffering in the darkness of ignorance. (95)
>
> *ōm nijapuṇya-pradānānya-pāpādāna-chikīrṣhavē namaḥ*
>
> Salutations to she who is happy in exchanging her own merits with the demerits of others. (100)

Though my heart was still very battered and I still felt sad at times, seeing Amma again rekindled my urge to do sādhanā and sēvā, two things that had grounded me and kept me happy in the past. So when I returned from India, I started to draw again. Within a year, I finished the project that I had started in 2020, illustrating all 108 names of Amma.

***

I am so grateful to Amma for providing me with this tool to fight my negative tendencies. Making art is a beautiful way to focus entirely on God. When I'm drawing, I often feel myself completely engulfed in the image before me, leaving no room for depression, anger, and anxiety. I am also grateful that I live near the San Ramon āśhram and can do mail-order bookstore sēvā and regularly see my satsang family. These factors have helped me enormously in controlling my negative thoughts.

I will end with a quote from Amma, which reflects one of the lessons I most need to learn:

> "Our every thought and action has the power to bring light or darkness into the lives of many. So we have to be careful that our actions are the kind that bring joy and satisfaction to others. We shouldn't fall into a state of despair when we see the evil in the world. Nor should we allow the wrongs done by others to encourage us to do similar wrongs. Instead of cursing the darkness, let us try to kindle a small lamp."

I pray that we all find ways to feel connected to Amma, whether we are physically with her or far away. I pray that we all are brave in our spiritual journeys and always do our best to follow Amma's instructions. With Amma's grace, may we all become bright lights of love and light in the world.

16

Ultimate Compassion

Navin – Singapore

Over the last two-and-a-half years, there have been many talks wherein we have heard how people met Amma. Some met Amma through advertisements, some through friends and family, some were even born by Amma's grace via banana prasād[9]. Not me, though!

Before I got to know Amma, I was a 'goonda' (gangster). One day, I was meeting my friend, a renowned gangster and a wanted man. Suddenly, we were surrounded by a team of special squad police officers who arrested me and all my friends. At that moment, I knew that my wild days of doing as I pleased were over.

It so happened that the head of the squad was a long-time devotee of Amma. He threw all my friends in prison, but he saw something in me: a chance to reform. He gave me an ultimatum, saying, "You can choose, Navin. You can either go to prison for a long, long time, or you can do as I say and change your ways." Out of fear, I picked the second option.

His conditions were strict. Every Friday, I was to visit Lord Gaṇēśha with offerings at a temple near the police station. After the prayers, I had to deliver the prasād to him at the station. I was to be home by 9:00 p.m. sharp — not 8:59, not 9:01. To prove I was actually there, I had to answer his phone call on our landline. He was trying to instill discipline in me. Once,

[9] Sometimes when couples approach Amma asking for her blessing to conceive, Amma will give them a banana to eat that she has put her saṅkalpa (divine intention) in, for them to have a child.

when I asked him why I had to do all this, he held up a pair of prison shorts, and I found myself enlightened with no need to ask further questions!

It was not easy for me to obey him. Since the age of fifteen, I had fallen into bad company. The gang lifestyle gave me a sense of recognition and power. I was used to giving orders, not taking them, so I was always thinking of ways to get around his rules. One memorable day, I skipped the temple visit because I had woken up late and would not be able to make it on time. I went to the store, bought bananas, and tried to pass them off as temple prasād. But somehow, my guardian-police officer always caught me out. Yet, by Amma's grace, he never gave up on me.

That year, in 2009, the police officer forced me to attend Amma's Singapore program which was a three-day-long affair. I was interested because it was the weekend of my birthday and my first chance to have a night outing in a loooong time. When I laid eyes on Amma, my mind said, "Here is someone pretending to be a God-woman." Seeing all her devotees, my first thought was that I had somehow walked into an alternate universe where people are overcome with devotion and love for the lady in a white saree. I reckon that my entrance into Amma's program hall was like Dracula entering a church. It was all very strange to me, and seeing Amma hug people left me very skeptical. I spent the first two days watching people in simple white clothes intensely chanting their mantras with japa beads. I felt extremely out of place in such a devotionally charged atmosphere. Because Amma ended programs late at night, around 12:30 a.m. I began scheming to go to a nightclub for a birthday bash on the last night of the program.

I arrived for the third day of Amma's program with a huge wad of cash in my pocket, ready to slip away after midnight, thinking that Amma would finish at her usual time. Little did

I know that Amma would give Dēvī Bhāva darshan that night. I watched Amma like a hawk, waiting eagerly for even the slightest pause, hoping she would go to the bathroom or take a break from hugging the thousands of people who had come. To my horror, Amma didn't take any breaks. Even worse, she seemed to be taking her time with each person who approached her. As time went by, Amma seemed to become more vibrant and enthusiastic instead of more tired. People were falling asleep all around me and snoring, but not Amma. As Amma got more and more energetic, I got more and more dejected. My phone rang non-stop as all my friends kept calling me into the wee hours of the morning. Frustrated, I tried to escape the program hall a few times under the pretext of visiting the bathroom, but the determined police officer followed me even there. He didn't let me out of his sight.

Darśhan kept going: 1:00 a.m., 2:00 a.m., 3:00 a.m., and before I knew it, it was 9:00 a.m. the next day. By then, my friends had given up on me. By then, my irritation vanished and curiosity overtook me. I realized there must be something special about Amma. Who is this lady who does not even need a toilet break, food, water, or any other human necessity? She is sitting and hugging people for so many hours without even the slightest trace of tiredness on her face! People much younger than her had become exhausted. Finally, Amma called those who didn't have tokens for darśhan. The police officer handed me a mango and asked me to give it to Amma.

When I reached her, she beamed at me as though I was her long-lost child and exclaimed, "You have come at last!"

After that darśhan, something changed within me. I donated the entire wad of cash in my pocket, intended for partying, into Amma's donation box at the program. Thank you, Amma, for catching this child and taking him into your divine embrace on that fateful day. I know that it is purely Amma's will and grace that made that police officer bring me onto the path of devotion instead of to prison. I could have gone the same route as all my friends, but somehow Amma's will prevailed. Today, I fondly remember that police officer with gratitude and respect.

***

Amma's biggest lessons to me are probably summarized in this one verse from the archana:

> *ōm stēya-hiṁsā-surāpānā-dyaśhēṣhādharma-vidviṣhē namaḥ*
>
> Amma strongly disapproves of bad qualities such as stealing, injuring others, using intoxicants, etc. (*The 108 Names of Amma*, 75)

In this dark age of Kali Yuga, it's very common for people to throw away their values for instant gratification, small pleasures, or to force others to submit to their desires. This is what being in a gang is all about. I have lived that life and now, purely by God's grace, I can say that I am experiencing another life; a life that is grounded in values instead. We can see many youths today wanting to follow the path that I left, and I can say from the bottom of my heart that real, infinite pleasure only comes from the Divine Mother, and for that, we need to safeguard our values.

Amma has always told me never to touch intoxicants or be violent, both of which were hallmarks of my life as a gangster. It is not easy for someone like me to let go of anger or my attachment to intoxicants. Still, Amma has, over the years, protected me from the worst of my own actions with infinite patience and compassion, which is my saving grace. Amma herself has told me on many occasions that I was supposed to be serving prison time but that I've been protected by grace.

After I met Amma, I heard her mention in a satsang one day that many of her children do not have money for food or clothes, but others spend lavishly. I decided that I would save all the money I used to spend on intoxicants and give it to Amma so that she could use the money to help those in need. I began saving the money that I used to spend on cigarettes and intoxicants and kept it aside to give to Amma when I next visited Amritapuri. One day, I caved in to peer pressure and joined my friends for a round of drinks. I took seventy dollars from the money I had been saving for Amma and left my house feeling really guilty. I could not enjoy myself even when I joined my friends, as my conscience kept pricking me. I left the party early and drove back home.

On the way, an old woman flagged my car down and asked me for a lift to a nearby residence. I agreed. She was friendly and sweet to me. When I dropped her at her location, she took out exactly seventy dollars from her purse and said, "Use it wisely." Saying so, she gave me the dollar bills and left. I was stunned! I got out of my car and went in search of her, but it was as though she had vanished. I could not find her. I returned home and put the seventy dollars back into my savings box in front of Amma's picture. I made a promise to Amma that night, that I would never remove any money from there and would only add to it. After a few months, I went to Amritapuri and nervously gave Amma all the money. She gave me a tight, reassuring hug and exclaimed, "THIS IS MY SON!" I felt on top of the world.

To bullies what gives a sense of power, perhaps more than taking intoxicants, is actually leadership, achieved by controlling others. I realized, staying in Amritapuri, that Amma achieves the same goal of natural leadership, without forceful control. She has hundreds of thousands of followers, but they're all bound to Amma by love, friendship, and the other divine qualities that Amma embodies. I came to realize that Amma's methods of leading are much more effective, long-lasting, and enjoyable. Without realizing it, I began smiling at others more after living in the āśhram. Those with whom I once fought have turned into friends, as I took the time to understand people instead of being aggressive. Because of Amma's own love and patience toward me, this change took place within me. I developed the habit of smiling at people even when they were unfriendly to me.

One day, while on a visit to Singapore, I met someone from a rival gang. In the past, my first reaction would have been to start a fight. But that day, I smiled at him out of my newly formed habit. For a moment, he looked confused, but then he sheepishly smiled back at me. He then turned and walked away without starting any trouble. This may seem like a minor incident, but to me, this was life-changing and the biggest demonstration of how transformative Amma's love is.

On another occasion, I had been wearing a T-shirt with Amma's picture on it. I got into an argument with someone on the street, but then I apologized to him, remembering that aggression is not what Amma wants me to display. The man's response still rings in my mind today. He said, "I'm glad you apologized because you are wearing Amma on your T-shirt!" I now realize that all of Amma's children represent her in some way when we interact with others in the world. I try to be mindful that people are actually judging Amma through my own behavior, even when I'm not aware of it. Amma does not care about her own reputation; she is more interested in our inner transformation and well-being. To that end, Amma has been working on me tirelessly.

***

Amma's commitment to protecting me from myself, especially in the last few years, is astounding. I have no words for the immense motherly love, anger, irritation, and other wonderful emotions and expressions of tough love Amma has shown me. To me, these were all expressions of the relationship Amma has with her children, and how free she feels with me. Even when I rebelled against Amma's instructions to take the vaccines during the pandemic, Amma told me that I must continue to stay in the āśhram, as this place would protect me from my prison saṁskāras[10]. Although Amma threatened to make me leave many times, she never actually allowed me to. Even when I directly disobeyed Amma, she had nothing but patience with me.

In spite of Amma's best efforts to protect me, I was deeply committed to getting myself into trouble. Once, I got on a motorbike with two others. Riding triples is actually very dangerous, but I wanted to go for a joyride. We met with an accident and just as my face was about to hit the ground with what would have been fatal force, I felt a hand catch my face and bear my weight. In the daze that I was in, I had no idea whose hand it was. I assumed it was one of the other two boys I had been with, and later, I even thought I had imagined that catch. I sustained no serious injuries. Later, I happened to visit an astrologer. He told me that it was my guru who caught me and broke my fall that day. He advised me not to leave the safety of the āśhram compounds from then on.

For wrongdoers, there is no bigger reality check than knowing that the CCTV cameras are watching all our actions. For me, Amma is my own personal CCTV. Amma once said to

---

[10] Mental impressions from past lives that shape one's character and influence the circumstances one is bound to experience, according to the law of karma.

me, "My eyes are ever on you! I am watching everything you do." I have felt the truth of these statements many times. Once, during darśhan, Amma demanded that I turn out my pockets. I had never before been treated like a small boy. I was both exasperated and thrilled that Amma cared that much. Amma has even spanked me when she caught me red-handed doing things I should not have been doing!

During the pandemic, I would not attend Amma's evening programs. Instead I'd stay in my room and watch YouTube. But Amma made sure I came for bhajans and meditation regularly. Every day, she would scout the crowd to see if I was there, and if I wasn't, she'd ask a brahmachari to call me and find out where I was. I attended bhajans and meditation regularly for a while. After a while of policing me like this, Amma cut me some slack, and I relapsed into not coming again. Amma once told me that I'm like an elephant that takes a bath and then throws mud on its own head. Like that, I had seasons of being good and then going back to my old ways.

Eventually, the guilt of not attending Amma's programs ate at me, and I felt too ashamed to even go for the Tuesday prasād lunch or darśhan. One day, my friends here in the āśhram told me that Amma was making a list of those not coming for darśhan too, and that she planned to call out our names. In fear of becoming infamous again, I took a token and went for darśhan. The brahmachārīs next to Amma, who knew me and understood my feelings, told her about my sorrows. Amma asked, "Why do you feel ashamed?" I replied, "Amma, I have not been doing any sēvā or sādhanā, and I thought you would throw me out of the āśhram." Amma laughed and said, "If I were to throw people out of the āśhram who don't do those things, the āśhram would be empty!" Amma then reassured me. "You are a good boy now. You are not committing any crimes here.

You used to do many bad things, but now you're a good boy." That reassurance and certificate of good conduct from Amma was important to me, especially because I knew that Amma is watching me and is always with me.

***

Amma even dedicated a song to me during the pandemic. It was the bhajan, *Mātṛu-vātsalyattōḍ-enne*. This is the verse that resonated most with me:

> *manassinē ēnikkāyi sammānichcha śhēṣham amma*
> *kaṭakkaṇṇin samjña kōṇḍ-ōnn-aruḷiyallō*
> *chittamē ninakku pōkām saṁsārattil chennu vēṇḍum*
> *uttama-sukhaṅgaḷe nībhujichchu-koḷka*
>
> O Mother, after gifting me this mind, You, with just a fleeting side glance, seemed to command: "O mind, go forth into saṁsāra and partake of its finest pleasures."

Amma, you created us, your children, and then gifted us this mind. In my case, my mind has definitely been chasing great worldly pleasures. It is a lifetime's work to bring the mind under some semblance of control. In fact, in the *Bhagavad Gita*, Arjuna tells Lord Kṛiṣhṇa that the mind is harder to control than the wind (6.34). He describes the mind as turbulent, restless, strong, and stubborn. All of these words accurately represent my struggle with my own mind which is like a powerful monkey. I pray to Amma to get the grace of my own mind and to win over the vāsanās (latent tendencies) that have been plaguing me my entire life.

Amma's grace notwithstanding, Amma has often said that we need our own grace or "the grace of our own mind" to perform the right actions at the right time. Often, even though we know what the right thing to do is, we don't do it when it needs to be done. What is the use of such knowledge?

One day, while in India, I received the chance to use my knowledge at the right time. At that point, I had imbibed the idea that Amma is always watching me, sometimes even testing me. After many scoldings from Amma and interrogations about intoxicant abuse, I told myself that I'll be sure to act in the right manner. Someone tried to sell me some substances that would have been highly attractive to me before, but, somehow, I found the inner courage to say no. I felt I owed it to Amma, seeing her struggle to save me from bad company, from bad choices, and seeing her worry each time news hit the channels about young people like me being arrested. Amma would often ask me, "Did you see the news? Remember! Be careful!" At that moment, I felt so much joy and pride in myself for being able to say no.

Later that night, in a dream, Amma told me, "Son, I'm very happy." I want to tell everyone, especially the youth, watching this satsang one thing: Saying 'No' is never going to be as popular as saying 'Yes,' but we should learn to keep the company of those who applaud us for our ability to say yes and no at the right times. Those who only want us to say yes all the time aren't true well-wishers. Saying no is as important as saying yes — perhaps even more important — and it's a very useful lesson that Amma cultivated in me. I'm still learning when to say yes and no, as sometimes right and wrong are not so clear-cut in life.

Amma has not only taught me to use my mind the right way, but she also gave me many opportunities to refine the quality of my thoughts and speech by asking me to learn mantras and pūjā. These are things that maybe many of Amma's children take for granted because it comes easily to them, but for me, these are herculean tasks. It took me ages to learn to pronounce Amma's names in the archana without making mistakes. Due to my past actions, I have often felt that my memory and speech have been impaired somewhat, but thanks to Amma's instructions and grace, I now feel that I have regained some control over what I thought was lost to me forever. Amritapuri is a land of opportunities, healing, and growth for people like me. It was in Amritapuri that I learned most of the lessons I should have learned from an early age.

Another value Amma taught me was working with the spirit of sēvā or service. Previously, for me, having physical strength was an asset to look attractive, gain clout, and be intimidating. I would never take part in manual work. In fact, I have often looked down on it. But after coming here, I noticed how any sēvā becomes fun, like a festival, around Amma. The āśhram residents' attitude towards sēvā rubbed off on me. I am reminded of something that Amma often says about association. She says, if we venture into a perfume factory, whether or not we actually applied any perfume, we are bound to come out smelling like perfume. Similarly, the fragrance of the āśhram residents' sēvā-oriented lifestyle influenced me positively without any effort on my part.

I am grateful that Amma gives me chances to use my physical strength to perform various sēvā-related activities around the āśhram. Recently, Amma conducted an AmritaSREE program, and all the āśhram residents took part in it in the darśhan hall. We were distributing sarees essential food items, but my mind was wandering. "Hey Singapore!" Amma called out. "Pay attention!" She'd caught me giving items to the same people again and again. All our actions performed under Amma's watchful eye make us more alert and aware, which in turn makes our minds sharper and our actions more beneficial.

Amma, I am so grateful for the protection you give me, for the love you show me, for the nurturing you have given me, and for the lessons and values you have taught me. I am touched that you have treated me like your own son and that you never gave up on me, loving me with the tenacity that only mothers can muster. I can never repay you for everything you have done for me, but I know that you are my mother and have always been my mother in every lifetime. You are my only refuge. My humble prostrations at Amma's divine feet.

17

The Divine Connection Within

Gita Devi – Turkiye

'Connecting-the-dots' was one of my favorite childhood games. It is the game that almost all the kids in my country play when learning the alphabet. In the game, after all the dots are connected, the image of an animal comes to life through the drawn lines. For me, trying to guess the hidden image before drawing all the lines, was the best part of the game.

The last time I was home in Turkiye (Turkey) for a family visit, a 'connect-the-dots' game appeared in front of me. This time I had no interest at all in guessing the hidden image. This time the joy appeared between the dots; the lines now represented the thread of love that connects me to all. Amma says, "If we dive deep enough into ourselves, we will find the one thread of universal love that ties all beings together."

Verbal communication plays a significant role in most people's lives. I remember that during my childhood, it was much easier for me to communicate by just looking at someone without talking. It took me a long time to realize that not everyone experiences the world this way. For most people, a conversation is essential for communication to take place. There are very sharp memories in my mind in which I tried to imitate the way that people talked. Years passed like this.

In my second year of high school, the psychology department made us all take an inventory test to understand and clarify our communication style. Out of my group of ten really close friends, nine of us were classified as 'left-brained' — logical, structured, and analytical in their communication. I was the only one labeled 'right-brained,' meaning more creative, intuitive, and big-picture oriented. What a huge disappointment! All my effort at imitating people had been a complete waste of time. My brain was wired differently from theirs, which explained why I had to work so much harder to communicate the way they did.

The scriptural story of the tenth man perfectly mirrored my situation. For those who do not know the story, let me briefly retell it. On the way back from school, ten students wanted to cross a river. Once they had crossed, one of them decided to check to see if all of them had safely crossed. He counts his nine friends without remembering to count himself and declares that the 'tenth person' must have drowned, for he is not here. Another student starts to count in the same way and reaches the same number, nine. Eventually all ten students count and find there are only nine of them. They finally conclude that the tenth person is missing, and they start crying.

At that very moment, a wise person passes by. He asks the youngsters why they are all crying. They tell him their story: "Before crossing the river we were ten, but now we are only nine. One of us is missing, but we cannot figure out who that is." Then the wise person asks one of them to count again. The youngster counts all of his friends from one to nine and says, "I told you, there are only nine of us here." The wise man takes the boy's finger and makes him touch his own chest. "You are the tenth!" declares the sage. Finally, the boy understands with joy that *he himself* is the tenth man. Each of the young men count again in the same way and discover with delight that the tenth person has indeed been found. I am the living example of this story! I am the lady who had forgotten to count her real self.

***

Some years after my graduation from university, as I was driving my car home from work around midnight, I suddenly felt a deep emptiness within. The road lights disappeared. I seemed to be driving in the air, not on the road. In that emptiness and darkness, two questions appeared in my mind; "What am I doing? What is my time here on Earth for?"

It took me three years to be able to ask myself this question again boldly and seriously. That is why, whenever Amma says, "Be bold! Be courageous!" I feel like she is speaking directly to me. Sometimes, even though we know what is the right thing to do and what is wrong, the voices coming from outside become so prominent that we cannot hear the voice coming from within, the voice of our conscience.

When the fire of longing for truth becomes strong enough, it starts giving us the inner light to see the path and the courage to move forward. By 2014, I found myself at an āśhram in Madurai, India. It was then that my real journey, "the journey from myself to myself," as Rumi says, truly started.

Over the next several years, Mother India offered me the immense blessing to go through many sādhana (spiritual practice) programs and to serve in more than ten yoga teacher training courses. But, to be honest, I am not sure how much the teachings entered into me.

Worldly life provides us with many creative possibilities to escape from the things that we don't want to see, hear, or face. If you don't want to eat something, there are many other options. If you don't want to do something, the world gives you the choice to do something else.

But in most of the āśhrams I stayed at, this is not the case. Food is the same for all. If you want to go to the main hall, there is only one way to go. If you don't want to see someone, I am so sorry, you cannot escape seeing them. If you don't want to conform to the āśhram schedules, unless you have a proper reason, you are out of luck.

While worldly life encourages us to differentiate ourselves from others, āśhram life, or we can say spiritual life, teaches us the importance of simplicity, the power of togetherness, sameness, oneness. While differentiation increases attachments, the power of togetherness brings unconditional love.

More often than not, we mistake attachment for love. While attachment causes weakness, love brings forth strength and wisdom. Because we lack understanding, we often use the word love when we really mean attachment.

Let me share some of the differences I see between attachment and love. Attachment is rooted in selfishness, in the small "I," seeking personal happiness, while love is selfless, seeking the happiness of others. Attachment manifests as taking — it clings to people, things, or situations in order to gain something — whereas love gives and sacrifices. Attachment is conditional — a relationship lasts only as long as it serves one's purpose — but love is unconditional and never diminishes. Attachment comes from the mind and looks for happiness in the external world, whereas love arises from within. Attachment binds, but love sets free. And while attachment requires effort to sustain, love is effortless and natural — it is simply being.

Contemplating the meaning of true love — with Amma as a perfect, living example — has been an amazing experience, full of grace. Thank you, Amma!

When we are attached, we emotionally depend on external supports, like someone leaning on a walking stick. If our walking stick is taken away, we fall down. And as long as we walk while leaning on it, we live with the constant fear of losing it — because our ability to walk depends entirely on it. If the stick is lost, we feel that we cannot walk at all. This fear of loss brings sorrow even before anything is taken away. And when the loss finally does happen, we instinctively search for a replacement — another object we believe will give us the same happiness. And so the vicious circle begins.

So, do you think decisions made under this mental-emotional confusion can truly guide us to what is right? I must admit that in the short term, when guided by attachment, I sometimes attain limited happiness. In the long term, however, attachment always ends in pain. Remember, it took me three years to be able to speak aloud the question that troubled me within: "Why am I here, for what?" During this time, I kept spinning around in this vicious circle of temporary happiness that always led to suffering. Then Amma whispers again and again, "Be bold, my daughter! Be courageous!"

***

The last time I was back in Turkiye, I started helping out at a nearby veterinary clinic as daily sēvā. Normally the clinic was closed on weekends. But that weekend, there was an exception — a tiny puppy needed care; it was too small to stay in the shelter. Since I lived close by, they asked me to look after it, which meant I would need to check on it every three hours.

I instantly replied that I could not do it. It seemed like a complete waste of time. Checking in on the little puppy all weekend long just seemed like too much. Suddenly the same question once again flashed in my mind: "What am I doing? For what?" But this time, the vibration was totally different. I had been going through so many teachings, listening to Amma everyday, watching her, trying to remove my selfishness...and still, I was reacting in the same old way!? As soon as I noticed my wrong reaction, I called the vet back, apologized for my initial response and said, "Yes, of course I will help."

Spiritual life under the guidance of a satguru (true master) like Amma gives many opportunities to notice the walking sticks that we lean on for support, so we can be free of them. Instead of dependence and attachment, we begin to feel the joy of togetherness and oneness.

Just a couple of weeks ago in the Amritapuri āśhram, we all packed thousands of kilos of rice for Amma's AmritaSREE Project, a network of self-help groups aimed at empowering unemployed and economically vulnerable women by providing them with skills and vocational training. A few weeks before that, at Amma's Faridabad hospital, a construction site turned into an āśhram because of the love uniting us. We, meaning thousands of people from different backgrounds, different cultures, different ages and genders came together to say, "Healthcare for all!"

On the way back from Faridabad, during the lunch stop at the Ettimadai campus of Amrita University, one of our brothers shared the joy he experienced volunteering in Faridabad. He said, "When I say we made a difference, I am not just pointing at the familiar faces of the Amma family. We the workers, the suppliers, the daily visitors, the ones whom we are most probably not going to meet again, we, all together in harmony, put our effort to better the world we live in."

Amma says,

"Those who run after the external world will always experience nothing but chaos and confusion. Whereas those who go deeper, who inquire into its real nature, will certainly find that there is only harmony and oneness and no diversity at all."

***

Now I would like to tell you how I met Amma. I heard about Amma during my first journey to India. Although I did not hear much about Amma in the North, once I came to South India, it was much more common among foreign travelers to hear things like, "I will go to Amma soon," or, "I am just coming from Amma," or, "Have you had Amma's darśhan yet?"

In 2015, a friend, who was staying in Amritapuri said she could only meet me if I came to the āśhram. It was Christmas time. Compared to the small āśhram I had come from, Amma's āśhram was huge and so crowded. I remember the bhajans very clearly. Thousands of people were singing together; in between each song, the air was filled with the laughter of children playing. It felt as if fairy dust was floating above us during the singing, and gently dropping on our heads in the intervals in between songs.

After the bhajans, my friend dragged me to the side pathway where Amma walks to her room. As we stood there, my friend made me stretch out my arm as Amma passed. Amma looked like a doll dressed in white, with a precious smile on her face — and the way she walked! It was almost impossible not to smile while looking at her. As Amma passed by — carrying her enchanting fragrance — she smiled at me and touched my hand. This made the people around me, including my friend, so excited. I didn't understand why, it all seemed so normal.

The very next day, I received my first physical darśhan. It was also okay, perfectly normal. I left the āśhram soon after. The next week, on my day off, I again came to the āśhram, not to take Amma's darśhan, but just to sit and watch Amma as she hugged people. In each of Amma's actions, there was only the giving of love, no taking. She was the embodiment of giving itself, and she was not just hugging people. While hugging, she was also reading people's letters, wiping away tears, responding to phone calls, blessing archana books, kissing tree saplings (for blessing), giving instructions concerning her charitable institutions, and cracking jokes with the kids around her. She was doing all of this without claiming "I am doing all this," but with complete simplicity. Amma was like Dēvī — the Goddess — with ten hands. I was so impressed and inspired.

The next week, I came again. The time after that, in between two yoga teacher training courses, I asked permission from my manager for a short break and came here for a couple of days. I was not behaving like my normal self. Soon the judgment and self-blaming began. My thoughts started to confuse me. I began to wonder if what I was feeling could be real. I was sure I must be doing something wrong.

In the *Bhagavad Gītā*, Śhrī Kṛiṣhṇa says, "Your mind can be your best friend, or worst enemy." (6.5)

Unfortunately, my mind was becoming my biggest enemy, so I took a big step backward and did not come to Amritapuri for a while. During this time, I did not want to hear anything about Amma — nothing at all. Whenever I missed the āśhram, my mind responded with a list of petty things I disliked about Amritapuri.

In the end, I could not stay away. I remember the first moment I came back after that long break. As the rickshaw turned the corner into the āśhram, I took a deep breath, as if I had been holding my breath for a long time. Thank you, Amma, for not giving up on me! Please help me to control my thoughts.

***

In 2015, I was at Arunachala, staying at the āśhram of Ramana Maharshi. There is a belief that whatever you think while walking around the sacred mountain of Arunachala comes true. I remember a professor from Amma's university sharing a similar story. At that time, I was planning to take a three-year-long Vēdānta course in Rishikesh, but in the end I couldn't bring myself to tell my family this, and so the plan remained just a dream.

Time passed, and just before the pandemic, Amma opened a new door for me — to pursue a master's degree in philosophy at her university, which is one of the top higher-education institutions in India. My studies made me stay in Amma's presence, where I studied scriptures continuously for two-and-a-half years. Beside my formal university studies, I also attended Amma's second seat of learning — the āśhram — a place open to all, where we study and directly experience the scriptures under her divine guidance. Even now, she continues to graciously guide me in my PhD studies.

Last Guru Pūrnima, the holy day honoring the guru, I had to stay with my family in Turkiye to help with some issues back home. I knew this was the right thing to do, but also felt upset to be away from Amma. The night before Guru Pūrnima, I went to bed very sad. But in my dreams that night, I was in heaven on Earth and reached Amritapuri just in time for the celebrations. I put my luggage in my room, quickly changed, and went to the hall. There was a chair with my name written on it at the very front. As soon as I sat down, the music started. I woke up, filled with bliss, took my shower, and attended the celebration online with my birth mom.

Amma often says, "Suppose the left hand is injured. Does the right hand say, 'Oh, that is the left hand; it has nothing to do with me?'" Let me continue with this analogy a bit. Does the right hand turn back and hide itself or say, "Yes! Now it is my turn. I will be the only hand!" Of course not! On the contrary, the right hand immediately catches the left hand and holds it tightly. It tries to stop the bleeding and applies medicine if necessary. Do you know why? It is because the right hand does not see any difference between itself and the left hand.

I believe this is how our beloved Amma sees each one of us. She does not see any of us as different from herself. Our pain is her pain, our happiness is her happiness, our time is her time.

***

Let me conclude with a visualization. Please visualize a heavy, rainy day — a monsoon day when we cannot go outside. Eventually the rain stops and the sun peeks out from behind the clouds. A warm smile has appeared on some of your faces already. Now add a rainbow to your vision. A rich smell arises from the earth, as the sun dries up all traces of rain, giving us a warm hug. Finally, feel the touch of the rainbow. Feel the joy and bliss within.

Notice how the rainbow took all of our attention in this visualization. We completely forgot about the rain, the clouds, and the sun. But is it possible to think of a rainbow without these other elements? Can a rainbow exist without the rain? Does the rain get upset because the rainbow gets all the attention? Does the sun judge the rainbow for its colors, thinking it should be only one dazzling color? Does the rainbow feel proud for getting all the attention?

I don't think so. None of them can exist without the other. In the same way, none of us can exist without each other. I cannot exist without you; you cannot exist without me. We are all one.

We are all beads strung together on the same thread of Amma's love.

18

Pazham, Pappadam, Payasam

Param Gopalasamy – USA

Last Tuesday, I sat down with my prasād lunch blessed by Amma, and on the plate I saw my favorite combination — payasam, banana, and pappadam, which I love to mix together. For those who are unaware of this combination, mixing the payasam, banana, and pappadam together makes a wonderfully sweet-and-sour savory mix that has been passed down through generations. If you haven't tried it, definitely give it a go next Tuesday.

It struck me that this combination symbolizes a great spiritual truth. Our experiences and moments with Amma are the payasam, sweet pudding. The sweetness of these moments form the basis of our love and devotion to Amma. These moments are what help us form a deeper relationship with her. However, unlike payasam, which one tends to get tired of after a while, our moments with Amma always leave us wanting more, no matter how many we receive. Our experiences with Amma are like limitless, ever-tasty payasam.

The banana, the 'pazham,' keeps our mind focused on the present moment, as it is both sweet and sour. Often while we are enjoying the sweetness of the present moment, sourness enters in, as we drift into patterns of thinking about the past and dreaming (or fearing) the future.

The word 'pazham'[11] actually has a unique sourness to me. My full name is Parameshwar. Having grown up in the U.S., my

---

[11] 'Zha' is a syllable in Malayalam that makes a 'ra' sound without rolling the tongue, similar to American English pronunciation of 'ra'.

name was never pronounced correctly by anyone who was not Indian. So at the age of four, I decided to shorten it to Param. Even in kindergarten I knew that keeping my long name would make life much tougher than it needed to be. However, since most people in the U.S. are unable to roll their r's, my name was often pronounced, "Pazham." This wasn't a problem until I started doing the U.S. tour. Once my friends found out that 'pazham' meant banana in Malayalam, that was it for me. I was called "banana" or "banana boy" for years to come. Although I explained that they were pronouncing my name wrong, it fell on deaf ears.

When we eat something very sour, it affects our whole body, causing us to recoil. We are truly alive in that experience. This represents the wake-up-call we need to shake us out of our familiar patterns. It guides us back to the present moment.

Even while writing this satsang, I often thought about the future: "Will this be well received? Will people laugh? What will Amma think? What if 'Pazham, Pappadam, Payasam' becomes a widely used analogy within the āśhram?" All of these thoughts and more passed through my head during the process of writing, but then the sour reality of the target word count brought me back to the present moment.

The pappadam represents the lessons that life has in store for us. Now, you may be thinking, "The pappadam is singular, but the lessons are plural...so how does this part of the analogy make sense?" Well, when eating the pappadam, you always make sure to break it up, so that small pieces are evenly mixed throughout the food. In the same way that these salty pieces are harder than the other two ingredients, the lessons interspersed throughout our life with Amma are sometimes hard and difficult to digest. And while the sweetness of our experiences, payasam, and the sourness of staying in the present moment, pazham, is a good combination in itself, it is the saltiness of the pappadam, the lessons learned, that truly makes our life with Amma a flavorful masterpiece.

***

Amma has been a part of my life since I was five years old. By age six, my family had started doing many stops on the U.S. tour every summer. By age nine, we were doing the full U.S. tour. So when I was a kid, summer meant the joy of going on tour with Amma, being with my friends, and of not having to go to school.

Looking back on my U.S. tours, I can now see that it had all the elements of the pazham-pappadam-payasam combination. It brought sweet experiences with Amma and my friends, constant action to keep us rooted in the present, and the sweet-and-sour lessons that Amma taught us along the way.

Amma finds a way to teach us lessons in so many seemingly small moments; but in Amma's eyes, nothing is small or insignificant. As Amma always says, "If a vital screw of a plane is missing...the plane cannot take off. So nothing is small and insignificant."

During a tour many years ago, a devotee donated cookies to the tour staff. One of my closest friends and I were tasked with distributing these cookies. After we went from the kitchen to the staff room, and all around the hall giving out cookies, there were two left at the bottom of the bag. We figured this was the universe's way of rewarding us for our hard work.

However, right before enjoying our reward, we checked the ingredients and found out that my friend was allergic to one of the ingredients in the cookie. Still wanting a reward, we remembered we had seen a gumball machine in the hotel lobby. The price for one gumball was twenty-five cents. Our young entrepreneurial minds immediately went to work. We could sell the cookies. The price we settled on was twenty-five cents per cookie.

With this brilliant idea in mind, we charged around the Chicago Hilton Hotel offering, "Cookies for a quarter." After much effort, we finally stumbled across a tour staff member who offered us a quarter out of pity. He didn't want the cookie. Wanting to prove our business acumen by actually selling it, we forced the cookie into his hand and ran away. We headed straight to the vending machine to enjoy the fruits of our labor, a gumball. As things tend to do, this news got back to Amma.

We went to sleep that day, unaware of what was to come. The next day, as morning darśhan was about to end, my parents were called to the stage. Amma explained to them what we had done, and my parents gave me a nice scolding. My business partner and I were then told to wait by the elevator for Amma so that we could get our second round of scolding.

When she saw us, Amma laughed and invited us into the elevator with her. After we'd reached her floor, she playfully spanked us in front of everyone. Then she called us into her room to talk about the karmic weight that borrowing money brings with it. She explained how hard people in the world work for money, and how many people struggle to earn a comfortable living. Amma even told us, "If you ever need money, ask Amma for it." Even though it seemed like such a small incident, two children and a quarter, Amma taught us both a lifelong lesson about money, while giving us the unforgettable experience of being playfully spanked by her.

My tour friends and I did not have the same level of scriptural knowledge that Amma's kids in Amritapuri have today. With our batch, Amma emphasized sēvā. Most of our time on tour was spent serving others. I mostly worked in the bookstore, where I enjoyed memorizing all the numeric codes of the books and

CDs. This drew the amazed wonder of the tour staff, which did wonders for my budding ego. At the age of nine, my best friend and I moved on to full-time 'popcorn sēvā.'

By the end of every program, there was sure to be some popcorn on the floor and a batch we had burnt. We kept this popcorn in a bowl to be thrown out after the program. One day as Amma was walking back to her room, she glanced over at our popcorn stand. We were standing there, waiting to give Amma a bag of popcorn we had made specially for her. To our joy, Amma came and stopped right in front of our stand. Our joy quickly turned into fear, as we saw that Amma seemed a little upset. She was gazing at the bowl of popcorn we were going to throw out. "How can you waste this?" she asked. She started eating from the bowl. "Be more careful," she said, "so food isn't wasted." She started feeding us the good popcorn from the bag we had made for her. Again, this may seem like a small moment, but Amma used it to teach us a lifelong lesson to never waste food, while giving us an unforgettable memory of eating popcorn prasād from her hands.

***

Another part of working in the popcorn stand involved going out and selling popcorn to the people sitting in the dining hall or snack shop area. This was our least favorite part of the job. It involved leaving our friends to go interact with strangers, which could put us in socially awkward situations. On tour stops where new friends joined us, we would always delegate this work to them. When it was just the three of us, we would play a game to decide who would have to go. Many times, it was me. Looking back, this may have been Amma's way of teaching me to be more independent.

With each coming year, our team's enthusiasm for popcorn slowly dwindled. We had started off as cute nine-year-olds selling popcorn, but by the end we were gangly preteens hanging out with our feet up on the table. We seldom went out to sell popcorn. At the end of that year, we asked Amma how to improve the popcorn stand. We had started making parfaits earlier that year and were thinking about adding fries.

She responded that it was time for us to quit making popcorn and to move on to kitchen sēvā. I was clearly on an upward trajectory. I had moved from the bookstore, to popcorn, to dishwashing. If you told most thirteen-year-olds that their summers would be spent washing dishes for an average of fourteen hours a day, for two months, chances are they would not react positively. However, Amma had inculcated such a love for sēvā in all of us by that point that we couldn't wait to start. Amma ensured that my best friend and I were put in different departments, to keep us from goofing off, which was probably a good call.

A couple of years later at the Washington D.C. program, as I was moving a cart of dirty dishes back to the kitchen, my dad saw me and said, "Amma has said that we will all be moving to Amritapuri at the end of tour." To his surprise, my response was, "If Amma says so, then we'll do it." He had definitely expected more of a pushback from my side. If another fifteen-year-old living in the West had been told that he would be moving to a village in India, I'm pretty sure the response would have been quite different. But our experiences, after years of touring with Amma, had inculcated the quality of surrender to the guru's words.

To be fair, I had no idea what I was getting into. I thought school in India would be very similar to the U.S., but I was in for a very salty pappadam. My first impression of the āśhram was, “Wow, this is like the U.S. tour, but all the time!” Amma was giving darśhan, bhajans were going on, nearly everyone I knew from the tour was there, this was going to be an absolute breeze.

School threw a bit of a wrinkle into this experience. I had to adapt to wearing a school uniform, speaking in Malayalam, and interacting with teachers and my fellow students in a completely different way. It wasn’t too long before I started dreaming about life outside the āśhram and working in the world to earn money. This desire became stronger with each passing year. When I finally headed off to college in Bangalore, and started to get a taste of the world, I couldn’t get enough. In fact, I failed a class in my third semester due to lack of attendance. My parents asked Amma if I could come back to the Amritapuri campus. From then on, although I still managed to cut class, I never dipped below the minimum requirement.

In fact, the semester I failed, my attendance was 78% just two points below the minimum requirement of 80%. The very next year the minimum requirement was lowered to 75%. My initial reaction was annoyance, “Couldn’t they have done that a year earlier, so I wouldn’t have failed?” However, this may have been Amma’s way of bringing me back to her, as I was starting to stray further off the spiritual path.

***

After I completed my engineering degree, I did an MBA in Mumbai. Unfortunately, the desire to experience the world to the fullest had yet not left me. If anything, it had gotten stronger. The payasam of experiencing life with Amma was dwindling and the pazham of living in the present moment was nearly gone. My mind was purely fixated on the future, so the pappadam of learning lessons from life’s experiences was fading away as well.

I started to work in Bangalore, and after nine months, I got an opportunity to move back to the U.S. After my MBA, Amma was pushing me to go back to the U.S. and work there. I was always unsure as to why. So in June 2020, I moved back to the U.S. and started to experience the freedom that I had always longed for. I enjoyed times with my friends, had a couple of girlfriends, and lived my late adolescent dreams out to full effect. However, after a couple of years, I started to realize the emptiness of material life. Everyone without a spiritual background seemed to be searching for meaning in materialism. Since such a life has no inherent meaning, it becomes a fruitless search. In fact, when I would go to be with my friends in the Amma community, my more worldly friends would say things like, "I'm jealous of the community that you have. I wish I had a chance to volunteer and serve like that."

After moving into my first apartment and getting a new car, I was happy for a while. But as I sat in my apartment, the thought hit me, "This is all that material life will give me for the rest of my life. If I choose this path, it will just be moving from a big apartment to a big house, from a nice car to a nicer car...incrementally, until I die." This extremely sobering thought made me reconsider my material goals. Later that year my dad called me and said, "Professional life in the West will have its benefits and its trappings to keep you there, but you have Amma. You don't need to fall down the same trap that I did when I was your age. See how you can align your life with Amma." His words really hit me hard.

Over the next few months, I started to attend more programs in the D.C. āśhram with Br. Ramanandamrita-ji. I even toured with him on the East Coast. Having this regular connection with chanting, meditation, and bhajans felt right, so I decided to move to the D.C. āśhram. I wanted to take a conscious step to keep Amma at the center of my life, even while working in the world. A couple of months ago, the move happened without any external pressure from my parents. It came from my own head and heart. I knew deep down that I would only feel content by aligning my life as closely with Amma as possible. Living in the D.C. āśhram with Ramanandamrita-ji was the perfect way to do so. Amma has seen me go through so many different phases in my relationship with spirituality, all the while molding me into someone who has willingly chosen to move back to an āśhram. I never could have imagined myself doing this in my early twenties.

When we see Amma's example in front of us at all times, and then watch our own paltry minds that falter over so many different desires, it can be easy to feel unworthy or undeserving of Amma's love. However, treading down this path of self-hatred is not productive to our spiritual growth in any way. Growth only happens through love.

A few months ago, as a brahmachāriṇī was giving a satsang, Amma interjected. She said how much she valued the brahmachāriṇī's innocence. Amma spoke at length about how special this quality in the brahmachāriṇī was. Upon hearing this, I immediately thought to myself, "There's no way Amma would say this about me, I lost my innocence a long time ago."

The next day when I was at the coconut stand, getting a coconut, one of the brahmachārīs suddenly looked at me and said, "You know what's special about you, Param? You have that innocence about you." In Malayalam, this word is 'niṣhkaḷaṅkata,' which is the exact word Amma had repeated multiple times the day before to describe the brahmachāriṇī. Nobody has ever used that word to describe me in my life, and I am sure Amma materialized this word to shake me out of my funk. It was her way of telling me to move forward with a positive attitude.

Seeing ourselves as less than others, or thinking that we are incapable of achieving spiritual progress, is not humility. It only hinders our spiritual journey.

***

I will be going back to the U.S. tomorrow and feel happy to be heading to the D.C. āśhram. I always feel Amma's presence with me there. The payasam, pazham, and pappadam are all available to me back home too. The difference is, back at the D.C. āśhram, the payasam does not take the form of direct experiences with Amma, but of indirect experiences during programs and tours. The pazham is the daily prayer and work involved in setting up the programs, which keeps us in the present. The pappadam are the lessons we learn through our interactions with all of our brothers and sisters along the way.

I have always been too lazy to read the *Awaken Children* books on my own, but the D.C. āśhram has given me the opportunity to listen to a passage from them every evening during evening prayer. I now look forward to those readings and would like to conclude this satsang with a quote from Amma's *Awaken Children, Volume 6* that particularly inspires me:

> "Children, it is easy to say impossible to anything asked of you. It takes no effort, just a few movements of the tongue. Is anything possible as far as you are concerned? This word impossible is a curse on mankind. Try to remove the curse, work hard, and you will see that nothing is impossible."

The *Guru Gītā* from the *Skanda Purāṇa* best expresses for me the grace of having Amma in our lives:

> *ajñāna-timirāndhasya jñānāñjana-śhalākayā*
> *chakṣhur unmīlitaṁ yēna tasmai śhrī-guravē namaḥ*

> Salutations to the guru who removes the darkness of ignorance from our blind eyes by applying the cleanser of the light of knowledge, by which our eyes are opened.

May Amma's grace help us to open our eyes to the light of knowledge and awaken the power within us that can surmount any seemingly impossible situation.

19

Surrender and Grace

Elizabeth Madhurima – USA

I was born less than a year after Amma, and I have been blessed to live all this time under her motherly wings. I met Amma in 2000 and have seen her on tour in California every year since then, until Covid arrived. From 2020 until now, our connection has continued through the grace of the live streaming programs.

This is my very first visit to Amma's earthly abode, Amritapuri. In this satsang, I will share how Amma overcame my indifference and drew me to her. I will also talk about how she tames the mind and opens the heart.

Delay Before Meeting Amma

I met Amma in November 2000, when she held her programs in San Rafael, California, rather than at the San Ramon āśhram. San Ramon was quite a distance from my home, but San Rafael was not far from a place where I sometimes worked. As it turned out, I was due to work there during Amma's visit.

I'd had many opportunities to meet Amma before this. From the early 1990's, I knew several people, including my future husband, who had met her at various locations in the San Francisco Bay Area. One friend excitedly announced, "Amma is coming! Amma is coming!" each time her tour dates were posted. Each time I remained indifferent, thinking, "I am not looking for a new teacher." But when I learned that she was coming to San Rafael, close to where I would be working, I said to myself, "How close does she have to come before I go to see her?!"

The moment I crossed the threshold of the large doors into the conference center, even before I could see where she was, I felt a wave of energy in my heart and tears spontaneously came to my eyes. Immediately, I knew she was the real deal — not 'just another spiritual teacher with an ego and an agenda.' Beyond any doubt, I knew that Amma was 'clean,' and that she had no ulterior motives and did not want anything from me.

It brings tears to my eyes when I think about the lengths to which she went, and the patience she has for this slow and meandering child.

Endearing Experiences

In June 2019, Amma blessed me with endearing experiences in San Ramon, and I started feeling closer to her. During one darśhan, I received a prasād (blessed) apple from her. I looked at it and wondered, "What does this mean? What do I do with it?" After contemplating, it came to me, "Eat it." The apple was for eating — not staring at or saving. This led to another realization, that I should "Live life. Life is for living."

On another occasion, I had a spontaneous desire to be near Amma's feet. Somehow, I was allowed to sit near her while she was giving darśhan. I was sitting on the floor right next to the corner of her chair. To my right were the people passing the prasād items Amma gives to each devotee after their embrace. To my left were people waiting in the darśhan line as they approached Amma. The darśhan assistants were also standing nearby. Somehow, I found room on the floor and was able to sit with my legs folded without being jostled or disturbed. I have heard that mahātmas can bend and stretch time. This experience made me wonder if Amma could also bend and stretch space!

I was close to her feet and able to look up and watch her. I was touched by the enormity of her care and compassion, as she gave her attention to one person after another, always with so much love.

I spent time looking for Amma's darling divine toes. Sometimes they are covered by her garment. Although I'm a Westerner, I have heard of the power of the guru's feet to dissolve the ego, and I was drawn to them. However, I did not try to touch her, as I did not want to interfere with darśhan — or be asked to leave! I sat there for five, then ten minutes. I thought someone would come at some point and ask me to leave — but no one came.

I continued sitting by her feet. Fifteen minutes passed, then twenty, and still no one asked me to go. After thirty minutes, I only got up because I had a darśhan token and it was time for me to join the darśhan line! How had I been allowed to stay so long without a stage pass? I had never seen this — only grace!

Going to India: Amma Plants a Seed

Before 2019, I had no interest in visiting Amritapuri. I was satisfied that I had Amma in my life and looked forward to her regular visits to San Ramon every year on tour. I also believed that she was available within my heart at any time, and that I did not need to go any place special to see her.

When Amma's November tour dates were announced, I learned she would not be coming to San Ramon as usual, but instead would hold her programs in Hollywood. I promptly booked plane tickets and registered for a hotel room for the duration of her stay. I did not want to miss seeing her in November and have to wait until she returned the following June. Little did I know then that, due to the Covid pandemic, she would not return any time soon. I am ever grateful I made the decision to go to Hollywood when I did!

During her visit in November 2019, the idea dawned on me to go to India. This was remarkable after years of indifference to the idea of going. At first, I thought that I had the idea, that it was my idea. But as my sense of doership gave way to witness awareness, I realized it was Amma's thought, a seed she had planted in me.

First Step: Asking Amma

I wanted to ask Amma before proceeding, but wasn't sure how. When I told another devotee I had a question for Amma, she said, "You know, you can ask Amma yourself — in English." She explained I could do it when I went for darśhan, without an interpreter. This was news to me!

At my next darśhan, when I was held in Amma's arms, she began whispering, "Daughter. Daughter. Daughter," in my ear. I picked up my head, leaned back so I could face her, and said, "Can I come to Amritapuri next year?" Without skipping a beat, she said, "Yes," and pulled my head back to her chest and continued chanting, "Daughter. Daughter. Daughter," in my ear. It was over in a flash. I had my answer.

Planning for 2020: Silent Retreats

I set my sights on going to Amritapuri in 2020, intending to participate in the month long silent retreat offered in late summer. Completion of at least one week long silent retreat was a prerequisite. I began looking for a week long program I could complete as early as possible. As it turned out, one was scheduled the following February, in Hawaii. This all came out of the blue and would definitely be a stretch.

Over the years I have taken many retreats, but usually within driving distance of home. This retreat would require a plane trip that would burn a lot of fossil fuel. However, I was born in Hawaii, and the retreat site on the North Shore of Oahu was close to where I lived as a baby. I had not returned there in decades, and the prospect called to me. I registered for the retreat.

The week long retreat was momentous. It included a lot of tapas (spiritual practices/austerities) in an idyllic tropical setting with two of Amma's long time monastic disciples. We were blessed to meditate at the nearby ocean several times, and joyfully participated in beach cleaning sēvā together.

During a check-in with the retreat coordinator, I said I was born in the Islands and had lived close to a nearby beach as an infant. I asked if it might be possible to go there. Out of Mother's infinite compassion, our last beach cleaning sēvā was scheduled at that very beach. I was moved to tears to return there.

Before the end of the retreat, one of the swāmīs performed an early morning hōma (fire ceremony). This special blessing at my birthplace was especially meaningful.

Some doors open only briefly. I am deeply grateful that I was alert and attentive and took the opportunity to attend the February 2020 retreat. Such grace!

Bringing Awareness Into the Present Moment

This trip to Amritapuri has been an ongoing exercise in bringing conscious awareness into the present moment. I have encountered many circumstances and events that have broken me out of my comfort zone and kept me on my toes.

After nearly two days of travel, compounded by very little sleep, I found myself in the position of an international visitor, far from my familiar continent, time zone, climate, language, and customs. My senses were bombarded with much that is new and different, all in a very short time. It was a lot to take in. In hindsight, I see this was part of Amma's masterful process of short-circuiting my mind and bringing me fully into the present moment.

Operating on little sleep has been a frequent occurrence since reaching Amritapuri. I could be mistaken, but my theory is that less sleep is yet another way Amma works to dismantle the iron grip of my mind. This may not apply to others, but it also happens to me when Amma comes to California on tour.

The high heat and humidity have been very difficult for my body. As a point of reference, at the time of writing this, it is 29°C/85°F here in Amritapuri, while it is 2°C/36°F at home. I overheard a comment that it has been, "cooler than normal" during this period. If so, I am grateful for any little grace afforded during my stay!

After one week, my body was showing distinct signs of distress. I thought I might have to leave the silent retreat for medical care. Fortunately, one of the instructors helped me identify the issue, (being overheated), and helped me figure out how to adapt. I was encouraged to drink more water, use a damp cloth to wipe and cool myself, wear more light-weight clothes, and avoid the heat of spicy Indian food — even though it was very tasty. After making these changes, I was better able to cope with the heat.

Taming the Mind

As we know, the mind can be an enemy or a friend for the sādhak or spiritual aspirant. The difference depends on personal effort plus the inscrutable factor of grace. My mind tends to be very unruly. Slowly and patiently Amma has been helping me tame it, so we can retrain it into a humble servant.

Amma has numerous ways to help quiet the mind. She may change the way for us to reach the stage to offer ārati (a special ceremonial worship done by devotees), or the way by which we receive the prasād lunch, or she may change the schedule or eligibility for all kinds of activities. This creates opportunities to give up attachments to having things done a certain way or at a certain time, and return to loving acceptance.

For example, during my stay I also wanted to participate in the ārati, but it took three different scheduling attempts before arriving at the actual date to do it. At first, an ārati date was not available until just after my scheduled departure. This helped me clarify my priorities, and I postponed my departure. My ārati date changed two more times. Each change was an opportunity to practice even-mindedness, non-attachment, and surrender.

Finding a Sari for Ārati

For a woman, a big part of ārati involves wearing a traditional Indian sari — something I had never done. There was the option to wear simple white, but I felt that wearing a sari was like preparing for a wedding, and fitting for this momentous occasion. I contemplated my intention for doing ārati, and my feeling was simply this: to love and adore Amma.

There was so much grace supporting my preparations. Without me asking, an Amma sister offered to loan me a blue sari. She showed it to me and it was beautiful. However, I did not see myself wearing blue, so I decided to look further. I continued contemplating what color to wear. One night, the color came to me — yellow-green with gold.

I went to look at prasād saris and saw shelves filled high with them. The one on which I first laid eyes exactly matched the color I had envisioned. Not only did I effortlessly find the color I was looking for, but it also fit my budget beautifully. I felt so much grace!

Extending My Stay

Amma took care of every detail of my trip. This included determining how long to stay at Amritapuri and when to return home. It took this child a total of three attempts to attune to Amma and get it right.

I originally booked my plane ticket in July. My plan was to attend the silent retreat in October, and allow myself a few days before and after.

Soon after my arrival, I realized I had not given myself enough time to acclimate to Amritapuri or integrate after an intensive monthlong retreat, let alone explore and enjoy the āśhram. I extended my stay by a week and a half.

After the silent retreat ended, I found out about doing ārati. This inspired me to extend my stay again. I was trying for another two weeks, but that would put me at the peak of Thanksgiving holiday travel in the U.S., when airfares spiked to double and triple my original fare. After the holiday, fares would drop back down.

That's when I thought, "If I extend a bit longer, I can have time to give a satsang." I changed my return flight once more. My return date finally felt right.

As if to confirm this feeling, Amma had a little surprise in store for me. When I proceeded to make the change on the airline website, expecting to have to pay a significant change fee, I swiftly received confirmation that my changes had been made, and that 'this change is free of charge.' Only grace!

Giving Thanks

I would like to thank Amma for her solicitous care, guidance and protection for this small child. Words do not suffice, and yet I thank Amma for melting the ego and opening the heart with her boundless love and compassion. Indeed, I pray for this boon for all my Amma brothers and sisters.

Departure and Separation: A Closing Prayer

My departure from Amritapuri is fast approaching, and I have been feeling sad at the prospect of physical separation from Amma. Yet I see she has planted many seeds of devotion in the garden of this heart, and they have happily taken root and begun to sprout. I pray that these sprouts become sturdy and strong and that I become firmly established in Amma. May we all become firmly established in Amma!

20

Impossible Is Nothing

Aiknaath – United Kingdom

Amma has taught me three lessons on my journey to being here today. The first lesson is surrender — and how, once we surrender to Amma, we realize she is always with us. The second lesson is that with Amma's grace, nothing is impossible. The third precious lesson she has given me is to know the value of family.

Lesson 1: Surrender

I want everyone to think back to March 2020, when this unknown destructive element, this virus, spread across the world. I was a final-year medical student back then, and I remember having to make calls to families explaining that their grandparent, mother, father, son, or daughter would likely not survive their admission to the hospital. It was easy for me to question Amma during this time — to ask why she put me on this path and what I had done to deserve being there.

Amma has placed me in many such trying circumstances that have taught me to have complete faith in her, and I'd like to share one such story today. I call it: 'How I Got Arrested in Barcelona Trying to Do Sēvā for Amma.'

Now, not many people know the full story of how I got arrested — not even my family. (So Mum, Dad, Revathi Didi, and Kurunandan Bhai...please cover your ears.)

Over the years, I have been blessed with the sēvā of helping coordinate projects for AYUDH Europe, the youth branch of Embracing the World (Amma's global network of charitable projects). Just as borders were reopening across the globe after Covid, I was asked to go to Spain to work on a project. People could travel, but you needed a reason to travel, including documents and approvals to justify your trip.

I was very careful before traveling. I took two Covid tests, filled in all the forms, and got a letter from AYUDH explaining why I was traveling. I also contacted the Spanish embassy to ensure that I had all the right documents.

On the day of my trip, I had a terrible day. In the morning, my alarm didn't go off; I ran to work with a half-packed suitcase and got caught in the rain. I hadn't brushed my teeth, showered, or eaten. Work was difficult; there were lots of emergencies, and I ended up leaving two hours late.

When I got to the train station, my train had been canceled, so I took the bus. I kid you not — the bus broke down! So I took a cab. When I got to the airport, the airline said my flight was fully booked, and they had to put me on the last flight of the day! This entire time I was totally fine, I mean everyone has one of these days, right?

So I finally caught my flight and arrived in Barcelona. I got to the immigration counter and showed them my documents. The immigration officer turned to me and said, "That all looks good, but where is your humanitarian/charity approval form?" To this, I replied that I only had an email from the embassy. The officer said that would probably be okay but he had to run it by his supervisor. At this point, I was thinking, "Ahh, I'll be fine. Amma will take care of it."

The officer returned with two armed immigration officers. These officers escorted me to the back of the airport, sat me down in a room, and asked what I was doing, who I was with, etc. I explained to the officer my intentions, and he said that in theory, my coming was okay, but since I didn't have the necessary forms I'd have to talk to the chief immigration officer. The only problem was that he wasn't there, so I would have to spend the night in jail, and he would talk to me the following day.

I said no problem and thought in my head that it would be a funny story to tell Amma later.

They take me to the back, search my bag and take away my toothbrush, hairbrush, and food as it could be dangerous. Bearing in mind I still haven't showered or brushed my teeth, at this point, they must have thought I was a homeless person! So I sleep in my little cell overnight and pray to Amma, saying that I trust her, and I know it will be okay.

The next morning, they take me to another room, where they introduce me to the chief immigration officer. The chief officer turns to me and, pointing to a woman present, says, "This is your lawyer. You will need to have a formal legal interview before we send you home."

The woman turns to me and starts speaking to me...in Spanish! Now, I know a little bit of Spanish, and what I'm pretty sure I hear is: "You're going to jail in Spain. You will be fined, and you will have more hearings."

Now I'm really scared. In my head, I'm thinking: "Oh my God, oh my God, Amma! I'm going to get arrested properly now, I'm not going to be a doctor. My parents are going to kill me! I'm going to have to join a prison gang! What do I do, Amma? What do I do???"

The chief immigration officer started asking me questions, and I explained why I was there. He asked if I had any more proof . "No," I replied. My lawyer, in an attempt to help, took out her phone and searched for my name.

The first Google search result came with a photo of me and an article about my experiences with Amma, my work with AYUDH, and a conference I went to for Amma at the United Nations. The chief officer asked:

"Do you know this saint?"

I said, "Well, a little bit."

He turned to the other officers, and they took my phone. They kept reading and looking at me, reading and looking at me. Eventually, they went to the next room and returned with my passport.

The officer said: "You're a very lucky man," and stamped my passport. "You're free to go."

Ever since this event, I have no doubt that Amma is somewhere out there, watching me, looking out for me, and in this case, probably laughing at me. Why Amma decided to have me arrested to teach me this lesson, I don't know. I would have much preferred a phone call or something!

Anyway, for me, this lesson of surrender has permeated my life as a doctor. I now know that as long as I keep trying, as long as I keep maintaining my surrender to dharma (doing my duty earnestly), Amma will guide me through the darkest times.

***

During medical school, I was a bit crazy for Amma. During one of Amma's Europe tours, I felt the need to see Amma as much as possible. I used to go to the hospital during the week and as soon as I would finish, I would take the first flight to Amma's program and the last possible flight home, even if it meant coming back to the hospital still in the sēvā clothes I had been wearing, helping my father in the tour kitchen. I smelled so badly of oil that some of my friends thought I was working the late shift serving fast food at KFC.

During this time I was a little sneaky. Before I would leave a program, I would always come to Amma and say, "Amma, I don't know if I can come to the next program, can I get darśhan?" and Amma would usually say yes. One night in Barcelona, I said to Amma:

"Amma I'm not sure if I can come to Finland, can I get darśhan?"

Amma looked at me with a smile and said, "I'll see you next week."

As Amma predicted, the next week arrived, and I made it to the program in Finland. But I arrived just as Amma was leaving the hall after the first day of darśhan. I was disappointed but thought I'd see her the following day.

You might guess what happened the next day. It was a super busy program, so I went to the kitchen to do sēvā until the late afternoon. Afterwards, when I tried to step into the hall, someone grabbed me and asked me to do a special errand, and by the time that was done, I'd missed Amma again. No matter how hard I tried to see Amma, someone would always pull me away.

On the night of Dēvī Bhāva, after I had been working the entire day doing sēvā, my dad came to me and asked if I could get a document from his room. As soon as I got there and started looking for the document, I sat down, and fell fast asleep!

I woke up the next day with ten missed calls and tons of WhatsApp messages. When I spoke to my dad, he told me that nobody could find me, even though a search party had been dispatched. He also explained that unfortunately, Amma had once again already left the hall.

I was sad, but had to get back to work, so I booked a cab to the airport. When we arrived, there was a white car in front of us, blocking the way to the entrance. The driver honked his horn to get the car to move, and I said not to worry, that I could walk. As I got out of the car and walked past the beautiful white car in front of us, I peeked inside: it was Amma! Immediately, without thinking, I opened the door and helped Amma out of the car. As she walked into the airport, I somehow ended up holding her bags, and before I knew it, was walking right behind her through the private security station.

On the other side of security, Amma was about to go up the stairs to the preflight lounge, where many devotees and swāmīs were waiting for her. But Amma being Amma, stopped at the base of the stairs and decided to take a seat nearby. Immediately, all of the devotees and swāmīs ran downstairs and swarmed around her.

I took some of the bags and placed them off to the side. When I turned around, I saw Amma surrounded by a sea of devotees. She began looking around as if she were searching for something. Finally, she saw me in the distance and signaled for me to come over to her.

"Son, where have you been?" Amma said as she beckoned me over. "I've been waiting for you!"

I hurriedly climbed over the group of devotees and sat on the floor right next to her chair. I sat there for a full hour as she gave satsang. Truthfully, I can't remember what she said; I spent the whole time just in bliss.

Lesson 2: Impossible Is Nothing

The second lesson Amma taught me is that nothing is impossible with her grace. This story is about how I became a doctor in the first place.

When I was seventeen, I came to Amma to ask her what I should study at university. I had never even considered asking her about studying medicine. In fact, it was the very last thing I had thought of doing. Typically, in the UK, becoming a doctor takes years of preparation. You're expected to tell the interviewer that you held a scalpel as a baby and dreamed of standing at the operating table. You need top grades, hospital experience, references, an entrance exam, and a personal letter to the university.

I had spent the last few years growing to love chemistry, mathematics, and physics. I was headed in the direction of chemical engineering. In fact, I hadn't even studied human biology! In my own mind, I felt like I was coming to ask Amma for her blessing to become a chemical engineer.

As I approached the front of the darśhan line and saw Amma's face, all thoughts left my mind. Instead of asking for a blessing, I asked Amma *what* I should study at university.

Amma looked at me, smiled, and said: "Why not medicine?"

In that blissful moment of being with Amma, I said: "Yeah, okay, medicine! I'll do that — that's a great idea."

As I left the line, it dawned on me what had just happened.

"Medicine? What?!" I thought to myself. I had just agreed to a decades-long — or rather, lifelong — career. I hadn't studied biology, I hadn't worked in a hospital, and I didn't have a CV! To make matters worse, the deadline for university applications was the following week! I panicked and went to my dad.

"Son, what are you worried about?" he said. "Amma is with you. And remember? She already told you: impossible is nothing!"

That's when I remembered the time I went to darśhan wearing a T-shirt that read: '*Impossible is Nothing.*' I was six years old. Amma smiled and pointed at the T-shirt:

"I like that," she said.

"Amma, for you, nothing is impossible," I replied.

"No, son — 'impossible is nothing' for *you*!"

At that young age, I didn't think anything of it; I was just excited that Amma had empowered me to pursue my dreams of becoming Batman or Superman. But now, my dad was reminding me that maybe she had been seeing beyond my boyhood dreams. I knew I had to give it a go — so I got to work.

I spoke to one of the tour doctors to get some work experience, booked the final slot for the entrance exams (the very next Friday evening!), and met with my principal. When I told him I wanted to be a doctor, he more or less said I was crazy. I should have submitted everything well in advance — the deadline was only a week away. It was impossible.

But I told him I was going to try anyway. He just shrugged and warned me not to be disappointed. Even my friends urged me not to pursue it, but I quietly ignored them all.

As I began to write my admission letter, I looked at the qualities and conditions required to become a doctor, and I realized that Amma had, in fact, been training me for it my entire life.

Through sēvā, Amma taught me selflessness and hard work. Through the tours, she showed me what it was like to work with a team and take on leadership roles. Through her unconditional love for all, she taught me the values of kindness, compassion, and care for others.

I did the work experience, submitted the application, and took the exam. To my surprise, months later, I received multiple offers from universities to attend their medical schools!

This story is not to sing my own praises for getting into medical school at the last minute. And to be clear, I don't recommend doing what I did — please take your time with the process!

I share this story simply as a testament to the fact that Amma always has a plan for us. Even when things seem impossible, with her grace, there is always a way.

Lesson 3: The Value of Family

The final lesson Amma taught me during the pandemic was about the grace I received from her devotees spread across the globe.

Like I mentioned earlier, the pandemic was truly difficult. I spent months consoling the sick and calling families to come see their dying relatives. Some days were so busy and awful that I would come home and do nothing but cry. I would look at Amma's photo and ask her why she had put me on this path.

And to make it worse, I couldn't even see her! At some point during the pandemic, I hadn't seen my family in months, my girlfriend in over a year, and Amma in years. I felt abandoned — like Amma had gone back to the āśhram and left me all alone in the UK. I even grew angry with my own brother, who was sitting in the āśhram so close to Amma, while I was struggling out in the world.

On one particularly difficult day, Swami Shubamritananda Puri called me.

He said: "Dr. Aiknaath, how are you? How's the job?"

I told Swamiji everything was okay, but I think he knew it wasn't. He asked about AYUDH and why I wasn't as involved as before. I explained to Swamiji that being a doctor was all-consuming and I didn't have time to do AYUDH sēvā like I used to.

Swamiji said he understood, but lovingly encouraged me by saying that Amma was asking us to try our best to continue her AYUDH work even if she isn't physically present.

"Okay Swamiji," I said. "I will try."

Some time later, I came to my first AYUDH meeting in what felt like ages. I thought I would just say a few words and then quietly disappear, but the moment I arrived, my heart melted.

I saw this group of young Amma devotees still showing up with enthusiasm and joy, despite not having seen Amma for years. They had so many project ideas and were eager to continue serving Amma no matter what. They were truly embodying the values of kindness, compassion, and dedication.

For the first time in over a year, I felt Amma's love. And in that moment, I realized I had been a fool. I had forgotten Amma transcends the physical plane. I didn't need to see her in person to feel her love.

I remember this experience every time we come together to serve Amma. We often say things like, "Brother (or *chetan*), can you come here?" or, "Sister (*chechi*), can you help me?"

To an outsider, this might seem like a mere formality. But to me, it's something much deeper. Just as we call Amma the Divine Mother, we are all her divine children. And I am truly blessed and privileged to be able to say that I am a little brother to so many divine brothers and sisters.

Of course, just like any family, we have fun, but we also fight! Amma continues to scold us and teach us lessons. But once we realize that Amma is always with us, when we surrender to her and work and love each other as a family, "Impossible is nothing!"

I dedicate this satsang not just to Amma, but to my family — my divine extended family — without whom I would not have made it through the pandemic or be here today.

I'll end with one last story, a small anecdote my father used to tell me: When I was six months old and hadn't said my first words yet, my father and mother were worried. That year in November, Amma was passing through Europe on her way back to India. My father brought me in my stroller to meet her at the airport. As Amma walked down the corridor, she stopped and looked at me.

At that very moment, I put my hands together and said, "Jai Ma!" Amma then put her hands together and said, "Jai Ma," back to me.

Throughout my life — whenever I've operated on a patient, consulted with a patient, or taken an exam or test — I've always ended by saying, "Jai Ma." (Victory to the Divine Mother!)

So now, I ask all of you to conclude my satsang with me, and chant:

Jai Ma!

21

The Hammer of Love

Anandi – France

Recently our beloved Amma said that we should not move while she is tuning us. I started reflecting on this and found that I have been "moving" quite a lot, trying to escape the hammer of love that she is using to help me. Sometimes I do this consciously, and sometimes unconsciously.

In this satsang, I will share about how Amma has influenced me and transformed my health, romantic life, and professional life. These three areas have always been most challenging for me, even to this day. They have been the playground of my ego, ignorance, and arrogance towards God. Please don't judge me too harshly. I'm only a lost child, searching for home.

To give you an idea of my background, I was born in Germany, and grew up in France and Mali (West Africa). Growing up, I traveled so much that I don't really have a hometown.

I discovered spirituality in Laos, became a dancer in Japan, and a yoginī (spiritual practitioner) in India. My passport is issued by France. If you were to ask about my ethnic background, it's a mix of Italian, Algerian, Swiss, German, French, Greek, Lebanese, and Gypsy.

I've been told that I asked about God for the first time when I was seven. The story goes that I read the Koran, the Bible, and the Torah and declared: "I choose the path of love and will follow it my way!" I asked never to be baptized again. It was not until I came to Amma that I came to know my own true name, Anandi.

Living in the West was a challenge that I was totally ill-suited for. Instead of a nice suburban house, my favorite places have always been graveyards and deserts. My hobbies include drawing under tables, walking along river beds, and reading books all night long. I often chat with cows, birds, trees, stones, and even objects — but rarely humans. My confidant growing up was my rabbit, and my mentors were the sky and the ocean.

My education took place during the course of my travels, and it mainly came from ancestral cultures. When I landed in Paris at the age of fifteen, in the midst of so-called modern society, I was traumatized.

By the age of twenty-seven I was living two lives. During the day, I was an interior designer for a luxury brand, wearing fashionable clothes and high heels. I was in a relationship with a computer software developer, who worked for a huge bank. This life matched society's expectations but did not match with my beliefs or my heart.

At night and on my days off I was a fervent anarchist and activist. I participated in social, ecological, and artistic projects like the rehabilitation of child soldiers, bee conservation, and art workshops to help people become aware of their own value and talents.

At the time, I was divided and busy fighting against myself and the world. At some point I started searching for a way to die. I played a lot with death but it never accepted me. Back then, I drank, smoked, and consumed every artificial pleasure I could find.

One day in 2012, I scolded the rising sun: "That's enough! I can't continue like this. You have to do something!" I guess the sun god complained about my behavior to Amma because that very day someone said to me, "You should meet that lady who is healing people with magical hugs."

I thought, "Magical hugs? Great! Let me give it a try."

It is said that "the master appears to the disciple when she is ready." The problem was that I was enslaved by my anarchist mindset. My basic tenet was, "No God, no master." And yet, Amma came all the way down to my level to meet me where I was.

Amma chose to embrace this angry scorpion. As Amma often says, "It is the nature of the scorpion to sting the sage, but it is the nature of the sage to save the scorpion from the river where it is drowning."

Amma often says that change can only happen through experience; I guess that's why she made my first darśhan an intense one. It was a profound experience that brought about a huge change within me. When I approached Amma for that first embrace, I felt as if I were being pushed into the void. Her fragrance and the melody of her voice blew me into an ecstatic state. It was like bathing in heaven, like being a fetus in the womb, like being a star during the Big Bang. Suddenly it was over, and I was thrown back into the cold. I felt like a fish struggling out of water, or a baby taken out of the Matrix[12]. I couldn't breathe, I couldn't see, I couldn't even walk properly.

Away from Amma's embrace, I took refuge in the soundscape — the bhajans. As I sat there, I experienced the greatest feeling of separation that I had ever known in my life. When I finally came back to my body, twelve hours had passed. My memory was blank. All that remained was a strong feeling of the infinite ocean and a vast, silent desert within. Amma had rebooted me completely.

---

[12] In the film *The Matrix*, people live in a simulated reality (called the Matrix) without knowing it until they are "unplugged" into the real world.

First Tuning: Letting Go of Attachment to the Body

I left Paris on my thirtieth birthday in 2015 and arrived in Amritapuri in 2016. This is when Amma, the great spiritual master, began tuning me.

After I had arrived in Amritapuri and received darśhan, I began experiencing incredible headaches, throat pain, and blood loss. I was bleeding a lot, which was really scary. I wanted to run away. This marked my first attempt to escape from Amma's hammerblows of love. I ignored my symptoms and acted as if there was no problem with my health, but internally, I was frightened.

Because I was studying Ayurveda at Amma's college at the time, it didn't take too long before one of my teachers noticed something was wrong. The team sent me to the gynecologist, who said, "Your body is on fire!" She gave me an Ayurvedic treatment to cool me down. I went to Amma and said, "I don't want you to do the job for me, but please explain what is happening and what I have to do."

Amma replied, "You are a healer, but you have to heal yourself first. Go for a scan of your ovaries."

Again I tried to escape the hammerblow of Amma's love. I didn't go for the scan and continued my Ayurvedic training. As soon as I stopped the Ayurvedic treatment, my fever spiked. Somehow, I received my certificate and turned my attention back to my own health.

Finally surrendering, I checked into a hospital during a visa run and asked for an ovary scan. The gynecologist was surprised by my specific request.

"Shouldn't we talk about your symptoms first?" he asked. After an hour-long conversation, he finally agreed to do the scan. As he sat in front of the screen, his face turned pale. He asked, "Are you ready for surgery tomorrow morning?"

The success of my Ayurvedic treatment coupled with surgery proves the truth of Amma's words: "Combining Ayurveda and allopathy is the future of medicine."

When I came back to Amritapuri after the surgery, I started a new round of Ayurvedic treatment. I was very weak. When life-threatening experiences come, you don't need books on impermanence to understand how precious human existence is. I slowly recovered thanks to Amma's darśhan, Dr. Sushila's guidance, and the loving care of the panchakarma team. The sacred waters of the Amritapuri swimming pool, along with the purifying pūjās (worship ceremonies) and hōmas (fire rituals) conducted at the Kaḷari temple, also supported my healing process.

One night, Kālī, the fierce aspect of the Divine Mother, appeared in my dream and told me to make a doll of her. Of course, by Amma's grace, a puppet-making workshop appeared out of thin air.

As I got to work on the doll, I forgot all about my pain and became fully focused on Kālī alone. As I continued making the doll, happiness started to blossom. I was internally guided by Amma's inner voice through each step of the process and externally guided by one of my Amma-devotee sister's expertise. She was constantly popping up at the door with a huge smile, asking, "Kālī okay? Show! Show!" A few weeks later I brought my Kālī doll to Amma and got a unique family darśhan! Since then, I have not had to think about ovarian cancer again.

Second Tuning: Cutting the Attachment of Worldly Love

Once, I foolishly went up to Amma asking, "Amma, can I become a renunciate?" while simultaneously thinking, "If you do say yes, please give me a spiritual partner too!"

She mischievously replied, "Yes, if you like." Her response opened up a process for me to discover what it truly means to renounce. Amma designed a perfect līlā (divine play) for me to learn about men.

Amma says, "There is no problem with seeing the divine in the beloved one. The problem is that the present generation is constantly changing from one partner to another. They have no endurance." I tried to trick Amma's tuning hammer by asserting, "Ok then let's find *the* one."

I started scanning each and every man in the āśhram. (I beg your pardon for that, guys.) It began to drive me crazy. Seeking a partner became a kind of sickness. Even my sādhanā (spiritual practice) was polluted by my search. I was restless and hopeless, fully trapped in and by my delusion.

At the beginning of each new relationship, I asked Amma to bless us during darśhan. How many embraces did I waste? Each time I went up with another guy, she scanned me from head to foot and stared at me as if I were offending her. Her facial expression was clearly saying, "Are you talking to me? It's not possible you are asking me this again."

What nonsense I had fallen into! I was so ignorant about who Amma truly is. With endless compassion, Amma continued tuning me, even though I was the blindest of the blind ones. Her grace works like Ayurveda. She doesn't bother much about the symptoms; she goes straight to the source of the problem.

For my thirty-fifth birthday, I received a WhatsApp message from a man I had never been able to forget. He has been sitting in the seat of my heart since I was thirteen years old. By this time, I hadn't seen him in seventeen years. Our love story was the kind that inspires books and movies, and apparently it wasn't finished.

Amma says that to dig into the past is to bring up a lot of pain. Of course, I didn't want to hear these words at that time. I was sincerely convinced that I needed to be in a relationship to feel complete. So, I packed up all my belongings in my newly-bought āśhram flat and went to Amma for a blessing!

Amma knew that I was yet again running away from her tuning, but she let me go ahead, saying, "You go, you try." How beautiful is our Amma! She fulfills our desires to help us get rid of them through experience. I arrived in Switzerland full of expectations, projections, hopes, and ignorance!

We both worked very hard. Step by step, the attachment decreased and unconditional love grew. We both discovered that we were acting out a script, which was not what we wanted at all. Society, the educational system, our families, and so many layers of conditioning had been manipulating us. We were slowly able to listen to our hearts and to see beyond our egos. The truth suddenly dawned in us. We discovered that neither of us had a calling for family life. Thanks to him, I came to understand that my desire to be a couple was a mirage, an old pattern stuck in my cellular memory. He taught me about self-contentment and emotional independence. Eventually, we decided to break up. Ironically, we loved each other more after separating than we ever did when we were together.

At the time, I was struggling with money. I told him I was thinking of using the last of my savings. He strongly opposed this idea saying, "No way, that money is for your life with Amma! Let me take care of worldly affairs. You take care of our souls." His words stunned me into silence.

Amma says that worldly love is like two blind people coming together. From experience, I now know that is absolutely true. With Amma's grace, we did walk a few steps away from the darkness towards the light.

***

Here is a small poem I wrote about Amma's guidance:

My Mother is like Fire
You can't approach Her

But once in a while
My Mother is like Water
Inviting everyone to bath in Her

The most often
My Mother is like Earth
Healing all the wounds in your heart

Sometimes also
My Mother is like Air
Storming in your worldly affair

Endlessly
My Mother is like Space
Pervading the vastest inner peace

She burns the Ego
She waters the Faith
She grows the Strength
She blows the Doubt

She is the Ultimate Truth.

Third Tuning: Attachment to the Doership Illusion.
Desires are like illusions, as soon as one disappears another appears. For me, the illusion of being the doer is the most difficult attachment to dissolve. For so long I've been planning for the future, making decisions, anticipating, and optimizing. This makes complete surrender to the guru a huge challenge for the body and mind.

Perhaps because I am an artist, I identify more with my ego than others do. Because we artists "create" things, we can easily forget that we are only passing on things that come from the self. We are actually not creating at all, we are merely channeling. As Amma says, "Art is God's beauty manifested in the form of music, painting, dance and so forth." She also said, "The beauty of your words, the charm in your actions, the allure of your movements...all depend on the amount of silence you create within," and that "whatever may be your offering to God, what pleases him most is the attitude of your heart behind the offering."

For a long time I was attached to Butoh, a Japanese dance form. In fact, I was so attached to it that no silence could expand in me. I was a good performer, but my attitude and my heart behind the scenes were ugly. So, Amma graciously sent another hammerblow of love. As I was performing on a huge stage in Paris, I got badly injured. My right leg remained paralyzed for three full days. Did this slow me down and make me humble? Nope.

After surgery, I received the next hammerblow, my body wouldn't move at all. Dancing was now completely out of the question. It was during this time that silence began to dawn within.

After I healed, out of compassion, Amma fulfilled my desire "to dance in front of thousands of people" during the 2020 New Year's Eve Cultural Program. That night, twenty-seven women and I performed the 'Bhakti Lotus Dance' on the main stage in the āśhram. (Maybe you remember the white painted faces, the wild wind-like dance, and the white flowers lovingly thrown on Amma.)

My hope was to offer white flowers of peace to the world, but also to show my dance to my Amma and to be recognized as a "wonderful artist." Hidden behind my love were pride, desire for fame, and arrogance.

What could Amma do but turn the rehearsals into three weeks of constant struggle? She wanted to be sure I would finally learn the lesson. After weeks of fighting, crying, and finally surrendering, the show came off successfully. This time, I was finally able to experience that I was not the doer! I never felt like showing off again after that performance.

***

The dance with Amma continues, now in the form of dot-drawing. This artform has helped me to connect my innocent inner child. Actually, dot drawing is an ancient ancestral art, originally used in Buddhist rituals to protect the warriors fighting in the three worlds. It is a deeply sacred healing tool.

Long after Amma told me that I am a healer, I finally understood that it is Amma who is doing the healing through the art she manifests using Anandi's body. My attitude towards making art has totally changed. It has become a sēvā, a sādhanā, an offering.

Amma,

May I always be the pen in Your hand.

May I always manifest Your Love and Your Light.

May I go nowhere but pass on the guidance from the Non-manifested Land.

May I be nothing but always smell the Fragrance of Surya Atman.

Recently, a devotee sister told me, "If you can replace all your worldly attachments with attachment for the guru you will be doing well." I suspect that Amma is helping me with this and that on the day of my first darśhan, Amma made a resolve that I will never move away from her as I had abandoned my own self at the time. I believe this because I'm starting to consider the āśhram as the guru's body, my one and only home.

Amma says that if we do our twenty percent, she will manage the remaining eighty percent. But we have to do our part by trusting the process, cultivating our divine inner qualities, and surrendering fully to her.

In ten years, Amma completely renewed my being. Through disease, she renewed the divine feminine within me; through the love story, she renewed the balance between the male and female principles within me; and through art, she renewed my connection with my life's calling.

Amma's hammer of love is turning attachments into ashes, primordial silence becoming the only melody left in my heart. Endless Gratitude to you, Amma.

22

The Light of the Guru

Ramanpreet – USA

wāhēguru jī kā khālsā
wāhēguru jī kī fateh

Purity belongs to the great guru.
Victory to the great guru.

This is a common Sikh greeting, which describes the greatness of the guru. The guru holds the power to eliminate the darkness from our mind and turn it into the light of God. We are only victorious if we learn, love, and follow the guru's instructions, if we see God in all. Any victory we attain, over our senses, over this illusionary world called māyā, belongs to the guru.

I was born and raised in a Sikh family. We were first introduced to Amma by my father-in-law. He was a pious soul and longed for a living guru in his life. His search culminated with him meeting Amma for the first time in New Delhi in 1999. After meeting Amma, he brought back some of her books and read them through and through. I remember him saying, "Amma is coming to Chicago in July. You should go meet her. She is at the same level as Guru Nanak Devji." In his view, Amma's teachings are the same as those of *Guru Granth Sahib*, but "spoken in simpler words to suit the present context." I will be honest, my husband, Raman, readily agreed to go; I just tagged along.

After reaching the program venue, we saw a huge crowd. I was a bit hesitant to wait so long, as I was carrying our first child, Amrit, at the time. My joy knew no bounds when we were asked, "First time meeting Amma?" I beamed from ear to ear, and said, "Yes!" I was excited by the possibility of having an early darśhan.

After our darśhan, we got lost in the world and did not attend the monthly satsangs. We weren't sure how well we would be received as Sikhs and our child was only an infant. Then one day, out of the blue, Balan Uncle called us and said, "You should come to the monthly satsangs. It is ok for you to bring the baby. Kids are most welcome." As some of you may know, for many, many years Balan Uncle and Lakshmi Aunty lovingly hosted monthly Amma satsangs in the basement of their Chicago home. Thus started our journey towards Amma. We have never felt out of place in the Amma community because we are Sikhs.

Life was going well, and then the thought of having a second child started creeping up. We weren't sure what to do. So, in our next darśhan, we asked Amma. You can guess her answer. She said, "Whatever you decide, Amma is with you." We both walked out of the darśhan hall more confused than ever. We were expecting a yes or no, but Amma wants us to develop our power of discrimination and decision making.

Being Sikhs, we do not really believe in astrology or birth charts. However, as we were walking out of the hall, we saw Amma's jyōtiṣh table where the aśhram astrologers were giving astrology readings. I remember asking Raman if we should get Amrit's horoscope drawn up? He is a good husband and said, "Sure, dear."

The first thing the astrologer told us was, "There will be about a four-and-a-half year age gap between this child and his sibling. Our son Amrit was about three-years-old at the time. Mysterious indeed are her ways to answer our prayers.

My first child was born through a painful C-section. I really hoped I wouldn't have to go through another painful experience like that with the second child. I did whatever I could to stay healthy, like walking four to five miles a day and doing squats. As the due date came closer, my anxiety increased. After an ultrasound in the last week of my pregnancy, the doctor declared, "The baby is over eight pounds. I cannot let you get any bigger. Please prepare for a C-section tomorrow." My heart sank. This wasn't what I had expected. Raman, however, is always positive. The next morning, I got up and poured my heart out to our Amma. Amma always does what is right for us. It is we who need to have the faith and patience to understand this eternal truth.

When the doctor helped deliver Amrita, the umbilical cord was wrapped around her neck several times. The baby hadn't been getting any oxygen for God knows how long. They had to call a neonatologist to check on her. The surgeon later told my husband, "You are lucky we did a C-section or else you would have had to choose between your wife and the child." Amrita turned out to weigh only five pounds. It is here that Amma's mysterious protective grace manifested. By some miracle, our daughter somehow appeared larger in the scan than she actually was. It is thanks to this illusion that I had the C-section and Amrita is a healthy eighteen-year-old today. Only Amma knows how bad it could have been had she not been there protecting us.

It was this incident that finally led me to have full faith in Amma. Amma is a true guru who constantly showers her blessings on all. Amma is so humble. If she were to make us count the number of times she has helped us or been there for us, we would all be her staunch devotees. But she is Amma, the epitome of humility, helping us in countless ways we never even see.

***

Let me narrate another incident. On my last Australia tour with Amma, the head of the 'safety team' most compassionately invited me to join his team. Yes, you heard it right, I was invited to work on the safety team.

One evening in Melbourne, as Swami Amritaswarupananda-ji was giving a talk seated next to Amma, and I was dutifully standing in attendance next to the stage door, I fainted. All attention turned towards me. This was a very embarrassing turn of events. A doctor friend who was traveling with me heard the commotion and ran over to check on me. As I regained consciousness, my first thought was, "I hope I don't get fired." My friend later told me that Amma said, "Don't worry. She is okay."

Before going to Australia, I had been having some health issues. My doctor was recommending surgery, but I kept postponing it, not taking it seriously. The next day, I went for darśhan and requested Amma's guidance. Amma said, "Talk to the doctor, and do what he says."

I kept pushing this incident to the back of my mind until things took a turn in June 2020. My doctor was quite concerned at this point and referred me to an oncology surgeon. Usually, people have to wait for months to get an appointment with this surgeon. But, in my case, Amma's grace was at work in this undeserving daughter's life. Due to some cancellations, I got an appointment within a week, and within another week, I was scheduled for surgery. We could not believe the speed at which things were moving. Raman and I decided not to tell any of our friends or family as it was at the peak of the Covid pandemic, and we did not want them to worry.

However, about four days before my surgery, a very close friend of mine from the Chicago āśhram called and said, "Kyon Preet kya chal rahaa hai?" (Preet, what's going on?)

I replied, "Nothing. Life is just going on as usual."

To this my friend responded, "Something is happening with you. I feel like Amma wants me to tell you, 'Don't worry. Everything will be ok.'"

If this is not Amma's grace reminding us that she is with us always, then what else is?

Because of Covid, Raman had to drop me off for surgery. He was not allowed to enter the hospital or stay overnight as a caretaker. As fate would have it, my surgery took much longer than the expected two hours. The next morning, when the surgeon came to check on me, I thanked him saying, "I heard the surgery was complicated and took a really long time."

To this he responded, "Don't thank me. Go to the church you believe in and thank that God. The surgery was unbelievably complicated. I kept wanting to give up, but some power kept me going."

As many of you know, in America, doctors almost never speak like this. Being Amma's children, we all know what that power is.

In *Guru Granth Sahib*, Guru Arjan Dev-ji writes:

> *I have met a perfect true guru, who has taken me under his circle of protection. Hot winds cannot touch me. The guru is showering me with mercy and has become my help and support. O Lord, O great guru, I am making mistakes with every breath of mine. I can never be released if you keep an account of my misdeeds. Please be merciful and forgive me. Carry me across this ocean, without counting my misdeeds.*
>
> (Ang 819 by Fifth Guru, Guru Arjan Dev-ji)

In the Gurbani, which literally means 'that which has come out of the guru's mouth', the greatness of the guru is mentioned over and over again: "Even if a hundred moons were to rise, and a thousand suns were to appear, without a guru, there would be pitch darkness." (Ang 463 by Second Guru, Guru Angad Dev-ji)

In Sikhism, we find countless verses which talk about the importance of the guru in our life. It is very clearly stated in our tradition that it is impossible for a seeker to overcome the ego without the grace of a guru.

***

As Amma's children, I have always wondered, if we truly realize how lucky we are to have Amma in our lives.

Let me share a śhabad (sacred hymn) by Sri Guru Ram Dasji, who explains in simple terms how fortunate we are to have Amma with us:

> *That land, where my true guru comes and sits, becomes green and fertile. Those beings who go and behold my true guru are rejuvenated. Blessed, blessed is the father; blessed, blessed is the family; blessed, blessed is the mother, who gave birth to the guru.*
>
> *Blessed, blessed is the guru, who worships and adores the name of the Lord; the guru saves not only himself, but also emancipates those who come seeking refuge in him. O Lord, please be kind, and unite me with the true guru, so that I may wash the guru's feet and be emancipated.*
>
> (Fourth Guru, Guru Ram Das-ji in Raag Gauri)

Countless are the comparisons between Amma's teachings and those of the Sikh gurus, but my little mind is akin to a fish trying to swim to the depths of the ocean. Who am I to draw such comparisons?

In Amma's book titled, *Eternal Wisdom, Volume 1*, Amma says, "Instead of going after pleasures, understand the goal of life and live for that. Lead a simple life. Give to others what is left after meeting your own needs. Live without causing harm to others."

This is in total alignment with the three core tenets of Sikhism as taught by Sri Guru Nanak Dev-ji: 'Kirat Karni' — live honestly; 'Naam Japna' — focus on God and chant your mantra; 'Vand Chakna' — share with your community and give to charity.

We all know how hard Amma has been working for women's equality and upliftment. Indian society has traditionally been quite biased towards males. Satgurus (true masters) like Amma and Guru Nanak Dev-ji have always believed in equality. Personally, I do believe in women's equality; however, I do not believe in women's dominance. Yes, there is a difference, but the pendulum seems to keep swinging from one side to the other.

Back in 1469, when Guru Nanak Dev-ji decided to come and bless this world, there was significant societal discrimination based on caste, creed, and sex. Even at that time, Sri Guru Nanak Dev-ji preached women's equality.

Let me share the following verse in which he speaks about this equality between the sexes: "In a woman, a man is conceived and born. To a woman he is engaged and married. Woman becomes his friend; through woman, the future generations come. When his woman dies, he seeks another woman; he is bound to a woman. From her, kings are born. From woman, woman is born; without woman, there would be no one at all. So why think of her as lesser?" (Ang 473).

In Sikhism we believe that even though we were blessed with ten different gurus, the light is the same in all of them. I see the same light in Amma, which shines with infinite compassion towards all of us. Please listen to an incident that took place during the lifetime of the Third Sikh Guru, Sri Guru Amar Das-ji, that highlights this quality of compassion.

Once a boy named Prema was born after a lot of prayers and penance done by his parents. However, his mother died in childbirth and soon after he lost his father. Growing up, he fell into bad company. His property and money were devoured by evil people, and, to crown his troubles, he became prey to a virulent form of leprosy. His condition was pathetic. He was thrown out of the village.

In the same way we see buses full of devotees coming to Amritapuri, in those days groups of people used to gather and travel to go meet the guru, who was residing in a place called Goindwal at the time.

One day some Sikh devotees met Prema, the leper, on their way. Following their guru's teachings of compassion, they wrapped him in a cloth and carried him to Goindwal. On reaching the holy city, the Sikhs left Prema at the gates, for they weren't sure if Guru Amar Das-ji would like to see the leper. However, when the Sikhs reached the guru's quarters, he asked them, "Where is my son whom you have carried all this way? Why did you leave him outside?"

The guru sent for Prema at once. Seeing the boy afflicted with leprosy he bent down, and wrapped him in his own blanket. Then he gave him a bath with his own hands, cleaning him with the water from the holy tank. After a while, he asked his Sikh devotees to remove the blanket from Prema's body. When they did, they were astonished to see that Prema's body was now clean and healthy, instead of bearing the marks of the disease as before. Prema fell at the guru's feet and began crying. The guru lifted him gently and gave him his blessings.

Guru Amar Das-ji declared, "From today Prema is my son, and his new name is Murari."

A few hundred years later, this incident repeated itself when our Amma cured Dattan the leper out of her infinite compassion.

***

Before I conclude, I would like to recite one of my favorite śhabads, which I try to sing to Amma most mornings. I have added two words at the very beginning:

Dear Amma, You are wise.
You are eternal and unchanging.
You are my social class and honor.
You are unmoving — and firm.

How can I be worried when You
have taken me under Your wings?
By Your grace, I have found peace and happiness.
You are like an ocean full of pearls and rubies.
I am like a swan in the ocean.

We are constantly receiving endless bounties,
and You do not hesitate or get tired of giving.
You are my parent, and I am Your little child,
who is receiving kheer (sweet pudding) from you.
I play with You, and You caress me in every way.

Knowing that You are there for me, I enjoy this life.
O ocean of excellence, You are perfect, perfectly
all-pervading.
I cannot describe the bliss I will feel
when I will merge in you one day
and will remain eternally merged. (Ang 884)

23

The Journey to Her Feet

Vishnu – USA

In 2004, as I was receiving a hug from Amma in the Kālī Temple, I spontaneously asked her, "Who is Amma?"

Amma spontaneously hit me back with a rhetorical question, "Who is breathing inside you?" I immediately took a deep breath, and Amma laughed. Amma's question triggered a long process of contemplation within me. Whenever I have a difficult task, whenever I have to interact with someone, whenever anything in life happens that makes me question myself — I remember her words: "Who is breathing inside you?"

Amma imparts the highest levels of Vedantic teachings through seemingly simple statements. Isn't that wondrous!

We're so happy and joyous in Amma's presence. Any task seems easily doable; no task is insurmountable. For example, Dēvī Bhāva is over in Chicago and we have to drive 1,000 miles in a single day for the next stop in Boston? No problem.

But how do we sustain the same euphoric feeling while performing our everyday actions? We've got to connect to Amma's grace. We've got to connect to that which is ever-flowing, and experience Amma's presence within us.

When I was young, Amma shared a funny story that really spoke to me:

> A vacuum cleaner salesman once knocked on a grandmother's door. The grandmother opened the door, and before she could open her mouth, the man started his sales pitch. He said, "Ma'am, this is an out-of-the-world, superb DustBuster 3000. It'll ultra-clean any

> stain and leave your floors spotless." Sensing that the grandmother was going to interrupt him, the salesman enthusiastically continued, "If the DustBuster 3000 does not do its job properly, I will gladly eat manure."
>
> He sprung into action, nudged the grandmother, let himself into the house, and immediately poured a bag of dirt onto the grandmother's pristinely, clean carpet. Before the grandmother could say a single word, he took out the DustBuster 3000, set it on the mound of dirt, and then went around looking for the electrical socket. He looked around, but couldn't spot one. With a very puzzled look, he said, "Ma'am, this vacuum cleaner needs electricity to run. Where can I plug it in?" Amused, the grandmother said, "So, sorry. This house is still under construction. The electrical wiring hasn't been completed yet." We can all guess what followed next.

The salesman in this story had an excellent vacuum cleaner to sell, but there was no outlet. The flow of electricity is blocked unless an electrical socket is available. It's the same way with Amma's ever-flowing grace. If we keep our hearts open, we can always connect with it.

As we grow with Amma, the wealth we gain from listening to her stories keeps increasing — even when they're repeated in satsangs. The spiritual messages behind her stories are planted within as we listen and continue to grow each time we hear them. This is such a unique approach to giving guidance. I'm so grateful for this.

Once, as I was standing next to Amma during darśhan, she turned to me and said, "Son, when you see me hug each devotee, you are wishing that you were the one being hugged."

She was absolutely right. When we see Amma giving darśhan, don't we all wish that we were the one in Amma's warm divine embrace? Every word of the guru is significant. This moment was a teaching about oneness. Amma continued, "Son, instead of wishing you were the devotee in my arms, think that you *are* the devotee being hugged by me."

***

There are so many funny incidents that happen in Amma's presence. Amma's laugh is so hearty, so infectious that just seeing Amma laugh makes us laugh too.

This reminds me of an experience. When I was a child, my baby teeth would somehow always fall out during Amma's U.S. tours. Every time a tooth fell out, I would show it to Amma. Now I can't remember the reason, but at the time this seemed very important! After a couple of tours, Amma told me, "Save every tooth that falls out, string them all together in a mala, wear it, and then show it to Amma." Amma started saying this very seriously, then broke out into a hearty laugh.

Amma responds so spontaneously to our love! During the second day of the June retreat in San Ramon, when I was only three years old, Amma fed all of the little kids on tour a papadam. After Amma had fed all of us, she sat down to look at the artwork several of us had drawn. My dad was holding me on his shoulders, so I could have a better view. I noticed that Amma had fed everyone with papadam but that Amma herself hadn't taken a bite of one. I spotted a big bowl of papadams right there on the table, and on my father's cue, I took one to feed to Amma. As I stretched out my arms towards Amma, to my great delight, Amma got up from her chair, bit the papad, and started eating it. She shined a divine, out-of-the-world smile at me.

One day at Amma's San Ramon program, I made a clay model of Lord Śhrī Kṛiṣhṇa. When we went for darśhan, I showed it to Amma. Amma looked back at me quizzically and asked where Kṛiṣhṇa's lotus feet were. I answered that I had forgotten to mold Kṛiṣhṇa's feet because the Kṛiṣhṇa Bhava photo I had based the model on didn't show them. To my surprise, Amma took the clay model from my hands, molded Kṛiṣhṇa's lotus feet, and gave it back to me. In that moment, Amma taught me that surrender to the lotus feet of the Lord is the most important thing in life. Our feet take us to places, so it only makes sense that the Lord's feet will move us forward on the path. Ultimately, surrendering to the lotus feet of the Lord signifies that we want the Lord to lead us forward to the ultimate goal.

I remember how Swamiji eloquently stressed the importance of holding on to Amma's lotus feet during an early morning satsang. He eloquently suggested that we place one hand under Amma's feet, and place the other hand on top of it. This way, we won't be able to run away because Amma's foot will be pinning one of our hands to the floor.

***

In 2019, after a very busy semester at school, I was desperate to see Amma. She was touring Europe then. So I decided on the spot — I'm going to go. I booked my tickets at the last minute, slept in the Computer Science building at school, and woke up early the next morning to get the first flight I could out of the airport.

Except, I forgot a few things — a change of clothes, a toothbrush, socks, a jacket, and a blanket. Actually, I forgot everything and anything I might need for a trip to a new country during wintertime halfway around the world! I didn't even take a backpack with me. The only things I had were the clothes I was wearing, my wallet and my passport! My mom had actually reminded me to take at least a few clothes, but I was too rushed.

Once I landed in Barcelona, Amma took care of everything. A devotee graciously picked me up from the airport. I spent most of the day helping the kitchen crew unpack and then sped back to the airport to await Amma's arrival from Helsinki. When she arrived, Amma came over to me and asked, "O, so you are here?"

"YES!" I replied excitedly.

Then, something strange began to happen. From the moment Amma came into the hall, she didn't look at me or speak to me even once. From my side, I tried, I really tried everything I could: I stood at all the strategic places I could think of – next to her car, right by the entrance to the hall, at the bottom of the stage stairs. During bhajans, I sat right in full view of Amma, but that didn't work either. As my cousin and friends all got high fives from Amma, there was absolutely nothing for me.

You know, this is probably one of the funniest things that has ever happened to me in Amma's presence! It's amazing that we can be in Amma's direct line of vision, but Amma will shift her eyes to someone hundreds of feet away and smile at them. Our strategies to get Amma's attention are sometimes completely futile.

Not willing to give up, I came up with a plan. I decided to go into sēvā mode. I must have spent 14-16 hours every day helping in the dishwashing tent. As we all know, Amma says dishwashing is better than doing pāda pūjā.

But it didn't work; Amma continued the silent treatment. Even so, Amma took care of everything for me. One example of this still makes me shiver when I remember it. The nights on tour were freezing. Once, when I woke up in the middle of the night, I found that the person next to me had spread most of his own blanket on me. This person must have been cold himself. The self-sacrifice of this devotee is something I'll never forget.

I also made a ton of Spanish and French friends in the dish-washing tent. We'd casually call out "¡Vale!" (Spanish for "OK!") whenever we met. I casually mentioned to a few friends from Amritapuri and to Shubamritananda Swami that I had forgotten to bring any bags. They were kind of shocked. One of them gave me an extra blanket, so I wouldn't have to share anymore. But I made sure not to tell Dayamritananda Swami, or else I'd never live this down back home in San Ramon. It would have made me the subject of endless ribbing and joking. What happens in Barcelona stays in Barcelona.

Amma was still ignoring me. By this point I was starting to think that I must've done something quite terrible. By now it was Dēvī Bhāva night. Unable to take the silent treatment any longer, I took the chance to apologize to Amma during Swami Amritatmananda's bhajan set. Longing to receive a loving look from Amma, I sang *Abhayam Abhayam Ammā*, which has the line, "Forgive all the mistakes that this ignorant servant has committed."

I went up on the stage a few hours later as darśhan was coming to an end. As soon as I walked onto the stage, Amma turned and gave me the biggest smile. It was the same smile she had shone on me when I was a little three-year-old boy, holding out the papadam for her to eat. It was that immortal smile that is etched into all of our memories — the one that thrills us to the soul.

That night, Amma was wearing a pinkish-red silk sari, adorned with three garlands and a glistening crown. She had given darśhan to thousands of devotees, who had completely filled an entire stadium. Looking back, that smile probably lasted just a few milliseconds, yet those few moments felt like the highlight of the whole trip. My dishwashing effort had been worth it. "Abhayam Abhayam Ammā..." — Protect me, O Mother; I take refuge in you — you are my lifesaver. If such a situation ever happens again, I know I would gladly offer my time in sēvā once more. My heart was content — Amma had smiled, and I could return home in peace.

Except the show wasn't over yet. As I waited nearby for Amma to finish Dēvī Bhāva, at around 10 a.m., for some reason I walked to the back of the hall. I was walking on clouds by this point, ready to tuck beneath my brand new blanket and sleep for the rest of the day.

Instead, as Amma was exiting the hall, She stopped right in front of me, threw her hands up in the air, and said, "*Enna da* (Hey there), you came here without any clothes?"

"Yes," I replied.

"No toothbrush?" Amma asked.

"They gave me one on the plane," I replied.

"No soap?" she continued.

"Yeah... no soap," I said sheepishly.

"No nail cutters?" she asked in disbelief.

"Nope," I replied.

Hmm, I guess my friends couldn't keep it a secret!

Amma continued, "Shraddha is really important. And, don't they say cleanliness is next to godliness? Being clean on the outside is as important as being clean on the inside."

Amma then instructed a few people nearby to take me to a store to buy everything I needed. What followed was a simple shopping trip, but it was filled with so much bliss, because Amma had made it her assignment for us.

The next day, I showed up with fresh clothes and got a huge thumbs up from Amma. Amma took the time to inspect my nails, hair, and clothing and said, "Very good". In fact, today

I'm actually wearing the same shirt I bought on that memorable day. It's clean and washed, of course. Don't worry.

Throughout the U.S. tour that followed Amma continued sharing this incident with everyone around her. During this trip though, I've come with a whole suitcase full of clean clothes, along with shampoo, towels, and soap. You name it; I've brought it!

In this world of impermanence and fleeting moments, what more can we ask for than the assurance that the Divine Mother herself, our best friend Amma, is thinking of us?

***

I want to conclude with a very recent experience. This was the most challenging situation I've been in so far. Surrender was the only way forward. We can plan whatever we want, but Amma writes the masterplan.

The 2019 U.S. Tour had just finished, and I was in a big rush to get back to school. You all know how it feels the day after a tour ends. It's very emotionally charged because you're not going to see Amma for several months. You fondly remember the Guru Purnima celebrations in Toronto, the Dēvī Bhāva darśhan and singing your heart out to *Amma Amma Tāye*, as we all cry and the curtains close. You also remember that after days or weeks of living in Vaikuṇṭha, the literal residence of the supreme consciousness, you now have to return to the world. It can be a scary thought.

After the tour was finished, as my parents and I were waiting at Toronto airport, I was restless to get on my flight. At the same time I was imagining the scene around Amma, who was leaving for Japan that day. Suddenly, an announcement rang out in the airport, "Thunder storms in Detroit! All flights that connect to the East Coast are canceled."

We were stuck in Toronto. By this point, I was feeling devastated. My whole plan of getting back home as soon as possible had failed. There was nothing for us to do in Toronto, since we thought Amma had already left.

Within seconds of the announcement, huge lines flooded the ticket counters. We too were struggling to get onto another flight, hoping something might be available for the next day. Hotels were getting booked up as airplanes sat lifeless on the tarmac.

During the chaos, I knew there was nothing that I could do. My only choice was to surrender to the situation and bear the pain of separation from Amma, while waiting for flights to resume.

A text message flashed on my phone, "Amma is at the Toronto āśhram!" The message that came quickly after that was almost unbelievable, "Amma will be distributing prasad to all devotees and tour staff soon!"

What can I say? What a blessing that all the flights were canceled. We ran to baggage claim, picked up our suitcases and raced in an Uber to the Toronto āśhram. The evening that followed was so unforgettable. Amma's very presence put a spring into our step, destroying any heaviness in our hearts, and making all of us feel so very joyful.

ammaye kaṇḍu ñān ānandaṁ koṇḍu ñān
uṇmayil ellāṁ maṛannirunnu
ā naruṁ puñchiri pāl nukarnnīḍavē
ānanda-nirvṛiti ārāṭayā

I saw the holy mother and was immersed in bliss, I lost myself in pure existence.
When one drinks in that nectarine milk of Amma's smile, will one not lose oneself in ecstasy?

Ammaye Kaṇḍu Ñān

Amma sang all our favorite bhajans, gave us a delicious dinner, and looked at each one of us with such love. As for our accommodations for the night, well Amma took care of that too. The Toronto devotees let us stay in the āśhram for the night. We woke to the chirping of the āśhram birds the next morning and flew back to San Ramon, completely enveloped in the safe haven of Amma's divine embrace.

kātinnu kātāyi manassin manassāyi
kaṇṇinnu kaṇṇāy vilasunnōṛammē
prāṇannu prāṇan nī tanneyallō
jīvannu jīvan ninn-uṇmayallō

O Amma who shines as the Ear of the ear, Mind of the mind, and Eye of the eye

You are the Life of life, and you are verily the Life of the living.

Kātinnu Kātāyi

With every word that we speak, may Amma be our driving force. May we be able to let go and open our hearts. May we bring our minds and hearts together, and enrich the world by bringing about change in ourselves. May we work in the world as Amma's instruments of love and service.

24

Seeing with Amma's Eyes

Shanthi Minor - Canada

My yoga teachers in Thailand introduced me to spirituality, woke me up, and showed me how to feel good without drugs or alcohol. After my training in Thailand ended, I traveled by train throughout much of India and settled in Rishikesh to learn haṭha yōga and prāṇāyama with a real yōgī, a man in his eighties who could stand on his head! Within a few weeks, I had developed a taste for the peace and bliss of sādhanā (spiritual practice). I left my bad habits behind and began living a yogic lifestyle. This regular sādhanā awakened my faith in God.

Although I grew up Christian, as an adult I rejected my childhood faith and considered myself agnostic. I thought that we don't really know if God exists or not, and it seemed to me that faith was an irrational, blind belief system. But now after a few weeks of sādhanā, I just knew God existed. It wasn't a decision, it was a sudden, spontaneous shift. God's peace and bliss began to resonate so deeply that I never looked back.

After reading Swami Paramahansa Yogananda's *Autobiography of a Yogi*, I yearned to become even closer to God. The marvelous tales resonated with truth and opened my mind and heart. It felt natural to begin praying to Yoganandaji for guidance and to begin to follow his teachings. But I was deeply disturbed by one thing. Yogananda repeatedly mentions that there are three things that are the most auspicious for a soul to have: a human birth, desire for self-realization, and a living master. I prayed to him to take me to such a living guru, but I didn't believe that anyone as great as Yogananda could be alive in this age.

I wanted to return to India, not to travel, but to stay in an āśhram and do sādhanā. My flight was booked, and just before leaving for India, I went to visit my parents for Christmas. While at my parents' I read one of my mom's books about traveling alone in India as a woman. There was a page-long section in it about Amma and Amritapuri. As soon as I read it, I knew I was going there. I looked up Amma's website, and within two weeks I had arrived. Mysteriously, years later I read and reread that same book, but as hard as I looked I could not find the write-up about Amma again.

It can be difficult to explain experiences like this to others. They can easily dismiss them, saying, "Maybe you were looking through a different book," or "Maybe your memory is a bit off." Amma comes to us intuitively — through our inner voice of conscience, a gut feeling, or dreams. She has ways of showing us her omniscience. Every experience in life with Amma is deeply personal, always corresponding to my thoughts and deepest needs. I think I've only barely realized the significance of some of these moments, as new layers of meaning sometimes surface only years later.

***

I arrived in Amritapuri with my former boyfriend just a few days before my twenty-fifth birthday, in 2009. Amma was away on tour in Trivandrum, and I had this impulse to clean, clean, clean — to do lots of cleaning sēvā before Amma arrived. It seemed important. I think I was trying to cleanse my soul by scrubbing the kitchen floor in the Western Café. I was bewildered that I felt this way, but it felt right to prepare myself for meeting Amma.

When Amma returned, and I had darśhan, I didn't feel much at first but prayed to Amma to be able to experience the devotion that I saw in all those around me. It looked interesting!

I heard a voice in my head saying, "Stay, be patient, and things will happen."

My boyfriend and I signed up to join the South India tour. The night before we were to leave, I saw him in a smaller line near the main darśhan line. He called out to me: "Amma's giving mantras tonight!" I asked him how it worked. He explained to me he had just come from a meeting where he had been guided to choose his mantra, so Amma could initiate him. The meeting was over, but I didn't want to miss my chance.

My boyfriend had a neat typewritten slip of paper indicating the type of mantra he would like to receive from Amma. So I ripped off a sheet of paper from my notebook and handwrote the same thing that was on his paper. At the end of darśhan Amma gave both of us mantras! I was happy that my little plan worked, but then came the doubts. After all, this mantra is something we are to chant for the rest of our lives. It's supposed to lead us to liberation! I was now worried that I had somehow messed up my entire future by not going through the correct procedure. Now I would be stuck with the wrong mantra for the rest of my life! I went on tour but couldn't stop thinking about the mantra. I wanted to confess my mistake to Amma, so she could give me the right mantra.

During the first chai stop, we gathered around Amma, and she asked us a question. Looking straight at me, she held out the microphone. "No, no, no, not me," I said, waving my hands. I had nothing to say. Why was Amma handing me the microphone? Amma made a face that seemed to say, "Come on..." and held the mic out for me again. "No!" I said again. Amma sighed and passed the microphone to someone else. As soon as Amma looked away, I remembered my doubt about my mantra. "She knows my question!" I realized. "She was trying to give me the chance to ask it! And now I've lost my chance!" I felt deeply frustrated with myself. I looked at Amma and spoke to her in my head: "I think my doubt is silly, and I don't want to waste anyone else's time. Please just answer me in a dream." I was testing Amma. Somehow I expected Amma to just do as I asked, if she was able.

That night, I dreamt of Amma holding a microphone in her hand. She handed me the mic, just as she had done in real life. Again, I said, "No, no, no..." and waved my hands to refuse. She sighed, making the same face she had at the chai stop hours earlier. Then she handed me the mic again — but this time I remembered what I had to tell her.

Amma patiently listened to my whole story. When I finished speaking, an image flashed in my mind, and I understood two points of view simultaneously. From the limited perspective, I saw a car cut in front of a truck with a big birthday cake in the back. The truck swerved to avoid hitting the car, and cake fell out and splattered on the ground. The slippery cake led to other cars skidding and crashing into each other.

From the cosmic perspective, those accidents were destined to happen. That cake was going to fall no matter what; that car and truck were going to crash no matter what. It was inevitable. I instantly understood that our human perception of cause and effect is not the true reason things happen. From our limited viewpoint, we can't see the full picture — the cosmic order of things. With this stunning realization, I woke up, full of gratitude for my mantra initiation, orchestrated in Amma's own mysterious, beautiful way.

***

Everything I'm sharing comes from this limited viewpoint of cause and effect: that because I met my yoga teachers in Thailand, I stopped my bad habits; that because I read about

Amma in a book, I came to Amritapuri; and that because I didn't follow the rules, I got the wrong mantra. All this storytelling is fun, but in the big picture, the forces of karma and grace are at work behind the scenes, orchestrating the mysterious events that need to happen for us to wake up to our true selves.

In those days, I enjoyed so much bliss with Amma that I thought I was truly in heaven. I was in my full-blown honeymoon phase. When I went back home, I took great care not to waste a single penny, so I could stay in Amritapuri for as long as possible when I returned. When I finally did return to Amritapuri in January 2010, I had a new goal — to go on the U.S. tour with Amma. Financially it looked impossible, and I was told that it was very difficult to be accepted as tour staff in the U.S. By April my money had already run out, so I decided to max out my credit card and buy western-style Indian clothes to sell back home in Canada.

I was down to my last dollars but somehow had a strong intuition to delay my flight by just ten days. My rational mind protested, "You've already been here four months. What more could happen in ten days?" But there was no charge to change my plane ticket, so there was nothing stopping me. I felt like I was making a leap of faith and that Amma would catch me. I just had to jump. During those ten extra days, I unexpectedly received financial grace that was enough to pay for a plane ticket and all the retreats on the U.S. tour.

During that time I became friends with a great devotee, Purnima, a woman in a wheelchair who follows Amma everywhere in the world. I began to help her with her daily needs and committed to traveling with her as her only helper through the U.S. tour. Amma's grace continued. In the few weeks I was back in Canada, I had sold so many clothes and worked so many odd jobs that I had enough money for basic meals, gas, and shared hotel rooms. I ate very little, barely slept, did sēvā almost constantly, and was in bliss for nearly the entire tour.

During the tour, I felt blessed to connect with a spiritual big sister who mentored me throughout the tour. The few difficult moments I experienced became deeply powerful learning experiences. By helping my friend in the wheelchair, Amma taught me so much about true devotion and the grace that comes from doing sēvā and sādhanā. Despite her challenges, this devotee would always arrive at the morning program before it began at 10:00 a.m. — even after staying in the hall until the previous night's evening program ended around 3:00 a.m. Her example taught me that I could manage with less sleep and still feel amazing by Amma's grace. Amma showered so much grace upon me, showing me that she knew my thoughts and needs better than even I did, and that she was there for me, time and again.

On tour, Amma takes any small talent we have and helps us use it to our greatest potential! I met so many wonderful musicians on tour who invited me to play violin with them for Amma. Sometimes I played with so many different groups in so many different cities that I felt like I was touring with a band. At one stop I was invited to play solo violin, but I was shaking so much from all the śhakti (divine energy) that I didn't think I would actually be able to play. When it was my turn to play, I just prayed to Amma, "I'll go up there, but Amma please play through me. On my own, I can't do anything!" I stood on stage playing behind Amma who was giving darśhan. She turned around in her chair and looked straight into my eyes for the whole song. The music flowed through me. I had no idea what I was doing, I just gazed back at Amma as my hands, arms, and fingers moved. O Amma, you taught me how to let the divine flow through me in music — to step aside and be an instrument. I pray to always be an instrument of your grace.

***

After the tour ended, I returned home to Canada, where my immediate goal was to return to Amritapuri and to stay as long as possible. That year was tough. I was working five or more jobs at the same time and doing three hours of sādhanā every day. I longed for Amma, and often thought of leaving to be with her for a short while, thinking I was in control of my destiny.

During this time of longing, while remembering Amma at the end of Dēvī Bhāva, the following lines came to me accompanied by a melody:

Beauty incarnate you stand
Rose petals fluttering from your hands
Love incarnate you hold
The whole world in your hands

And me, I'm just sitting here,
With tears streaming down my vision
Wondering how I could be so blessed to be
Just sitting here, with tears streaming down my vision
Wondering how I could be so blessed to be
To be

Cause Everything, everything, everything, everything
That you do is beautiful.

While living and working in Canada, I met my partner and fell in love. My desire for longterm āśhram life had shifted, but I still came to Amritapuri. He joined me later, and for several months we enjoyed the grace of Amma's darśhan. For the new year, we left Amritapuri to travel throughout India together. I have learned and grown so much from this relationship.

As my journey continued, I grew tired of working so many different jobs that felt disconnected from my spiritual life. I prayed to Amma for work that would be of service to others and still allow me to spend time with Amma regularly. I ended up becoming a massage therapist, and with Amma's enthusiastic approval, I am continuing my studies to become an osteopath.

My six years of studies were very difficult. I was in school full time, working as much as possible to pay for my schooling. I battled with symptoms of burnout for the last two years of school, and I didn't know from one month to the next if I could afford to continue school. I prayed to Amma and she gave me the strength to succeed during those challenging years. I kept making just enough money to be able to continue studying and also to see Amma in Toronto and Boston.

Now I have a successful private practice and am able to make my own schedule for spending time with Amma. Although my running after the glittering seashells of worldly attractions has made my visits less frequent, I pray that Amma always stays in my mind and heart.

***

One of the most profound lessons in understanding the nature of my mind and how opening my heart to Amma's love can transform any moment into an experience of love happened during a program in Toronto. As usual, I was busy running around with a number of sēvā tasks, when I noticed my mind was being extra judgmental and critical of every person that I saw. My mind could definitely judge and criticize others on a normal day, but to the extent that it was happening now was actually absurd. I remember literally looking at an innocent devotee serving lunch and thinking "Oh, nice smile, but so phony. I'm sure you're counting all the karma points you're getting doing this easy sēvā".

I was literally driving myself crazy with all this negative mental chatter. At the same time, I realized it was all my own projections being thrown onto others. Still I couldn't stop. I prayed to Amma to help me control my negative mind as it was creating a living hell for me. It was taking every bit of my concentration just to behave like a decent human being.

Soon after, I was doing sēvā on stage, seating devotees near Amma after they received darśhan, when I saw one of the people I had mentally criticized go up for darśhan. I had seen this person angrily scolding someone earlier and was feeling judgemental and superior. But as this person went up for darśhan, she was glowing with beautiful child-like joy. I saw the sea of smiling faces around Amma. They all seemed to have left their worries and negative thoughts behind to embrace this precious moment with Amma. A spontaneous prayer came to my mind: "I want to see people like you do, Amma."

At that instant, Amma looked at me with a heart-stopping smile and nodded approvingly. Amma had been busy doing so many things during darśhan that I figured she wasn't paying attention to me. But she doesn't miss a beat with any of us. After I collected myself from the surprise of that blissful moment, I looked around the room and was stunned to see nothing but beautiful, loving people everywhere. Each person I saw was so beautiful inside and out — full of joy, hopes, good intentions, innocence, and love. My heart melted at each face I saw. I saw their goodness, and that goodness brought out the love in me. I was so shocked by the contrast of seeing everyone as bad to seeing everyone as love that I became utterly convinced that I create my own heaven or hell with my thoughts.

I once read a beautiful Amma quote just before going to sleep: "Children, Amma is always with you. Each time you think of her, Amma can clearly see your faces. Every night when Amma lies down to rest, Amma goes out to all her children all over the world. Amma's children are her swans, and like a shepherd Amma checks on them and brings any straying swans back to her fold. You are baby birds, and Amma is keeping you under her wing."

As I drifted off to sleep I thought, "But you don't come to me, Amma." That night I dreamt that after Amma finished darśhan, she somehow slipped out a side door. Nobody could see her but me, and I followed her. We walked out of the hotel hand-in-hand. We visited St. Joseph's Oratory in Montreal and looked out into the night sky. I told Amma my deepest secrets and worries, and she held me and listened as we laughed. I felt nothing but love. It was as if we had spent days together.

Eventually we ended up back at the door leading into the hotel. Amma looked at me, waiting for me to speak before leaving. I knew that once she walked through that door she would no longer be just mine; she would be everyone's again. I felt such gratitude for the gift of this precious time alone with her, but I also understood that so many others needed her too. I nodded to Amma. I was ready for her to go back to serve all her children.

She opened the door, walked in and was immediately surrounded by devotees who had been searching everywhere for her. From their perspective, it was clear she'd only been gone a few minutes. Amma turned and smiled at me once more before being swept away by the crowd.

I woke up remembering the quote I had read before falling asleep — and the doubt I'd had about it. I cried and cried at Amma's mercy for visiting "little me" and giving me such a full gift in the world of dreams.

I pray to Amma: may Amma bless our minds, our hearts, and our hands — so we may see the goodness in all beings, so we may serve others joyfully, and so, by her grace, we may merge in her divine form.

Amma, may we all become so small that we slip between your beautiful toes, and so vast that we merge into your infinite form.

25

Golden Memories

Ramana Erickson – USA

That I ever met Amma in the first place was a miracle. To explain, I have to give a little background. I grew up in various āśhrams both in the United States and India from the age of nine continuously until I was twenty-one. When people ask how that came about, I tell them it is because of the Beatles. By 1967 when I was five years old, the Beatles had brought both Indian music and spiritual culture into mainstream popular culture in the United States. Yoga studios and āśhrams flourished across the country, and my mother started practicing haṭha yōga āsanas. By the time I was nine, she became deeply interested in the wider philosophical aspects of yōga. We soon moved to an āśhram located in the foothills of the Sierra Nevada mountains in Northern California.

When I was a teenager, my mother became a devotee of a different guru, so I spent my high school years in an āśhram in Northern India, where I immersed myself in the study of Yogāsana, Yōga philosophy, Vēdānta (non-dual philosophy), Kashmir Shaivism, Sanskrit — especially Vedic chanting, Hindi, bhajan singing, harmonium playing, and tabla (Indian drums). Unfortunately, by the time I left that āśhram at the age of twenty-one, that guru had passed away amidst a flurry of scandals. I soon realized that the person who had previously been God on Earth to me was deeply flawed. I felt I had been duped and became bitter and resentful. I foolishly turned my back on Sanātana Dharma and vowed to never get involved in it again.

Instead, in 1983 I moved to New York City, and then to Los Angeles, in the hope of becoming a famous actor. In 1988 while living in Los Angeles, with my illustrious acting career going nowhere fast, my mother called me to happily inform me that she had a new guru and, as my birthday was approaching, she urged me to come to Northern California to see her for my birthday and meet her new guru. She sent me a photo of Amma. I laughed when I saw it. I thought, "Another phony trying to dupe people." However, my mother could be very persistent and insistent, and her wish ultimately prevailed.

On June 4, 1988, the day before my twenty-sixth birthday, I drove up to Miranda, California to Amma's retreat site, nestled amidst a beautiful redwood forest. Arriving in the early afternoon, I entered the main hall where around 100 people were gathered. They were all sitting on the floor around Amma's chair watching her give darśhan. I looked around at the people gathered there and nearly turned around and left. I recognized a large number of them as devotees of the guru I had left five years before. I thought to myself, "Oh God no, not again!"

I stood in the back of the hall observing Amma's hug, with negative thoughts whirling through my mind. Because of the small number of people, each darśhan lasted about five minutes. Amma would give an initial hug, then put your head in her lap and rub your back, then raise you up and put sandal paste at the point between the eyes while gazing into your eyes. She would end with one last long hug before moving on to the next person. I wasn't planning on joining the darśhan line. However, my mother badgered me until I finally said, "Ok, I'll do this for you as a present to you on my birthday."

I got in the darśhan line, and slowly slid to the front just behind my sister, Veena, who had decided to come up and meet Amma once she heard I was going too. From the moment I'd entered the darśhan line, the ferocity of my negative thoughts increased exponentially, "Oh God, this is so embarrassing, getting hugged in front of all these people, so many of whom I know...I can't wait to leave...This is awful!" I then devised the plan that when it was my turn, I'd tell Amma, "Thanks for making my mother so happy... See ya later!" We made it to the front of the line, and while my sister was being hugged, it suddenly occurred to me that perhaps Amma couldn't speak English. I assumed that if she didn't speak English, she would certainly know Hindi. So when it came my turn for a hug, my very first words to Amma were, "Aap ko Hindi aati hai?" which means, "Do you speak Hindi?"

Amma replied, "Hindi?" She laughed and threw my head down in her lap!

What transpired next took me completely by surprise. The litany of negative thoughts suddenly just stopped. They weren't replaced by positive thoughts...there was just silence. Amma raised me up and with her index finger put sandalwood paste between my eyes and gazed into them. I felt this intense, tangible transfer of energy like an explosion coming from Amma's fingers into the depths of my being. At the same time, a deep, wordless recognition that this divine being in front of me was intimately in touch with the ultimate truth arose within me. I was completely flabbergasted. It was like I had been slapped across the face with an invisible spiritual cricket bat. I found myself sitting next to Amma's chair, out of my body, watching myself ask Amma what sādhanā she recommended that I do.

I stayed for Dēvī Bhāva that evening, utterly mesmerized by Amma, leaving her on the morning of my twenty-sixth birthday. I didn't see Amma again during the 1988 U.S. Tour, but soon after that first meeting, I said goodbye to my acting career and moved to the San Francisco Bay Area. I wanted to be near the fledgling Amma satsang community that had formed there. I devoured Amma's bhajan cassettes – bewitched by her voice whose raspy, plaintive cry for the divine touched me to the core. I learned many of the bhajans on harmonium, and listened intently to the tablas, learning new tālams (rhythms) I hadn't previously known.

***

One evening, a friend who had turned her house in Berkeley into an informal Amma center, showed the video of Amma healing Dattan, the man suffering from leprosy, by licking his wounds.

When I saw that, I thought to myself either Amma is completely insane, or else is the greatest saint the world has ever seen. I decided I had to see her in her own home. This desire to see Amma in Amritapuri was intensified by the realization that Amma would soon become immensely popular. If I wanted to catch seeing her at the end of the "old days," I needed to get to Amritapuri as soon as possible. In November 1988, I found myself on a plane bound for Kochi. It turns out there were about fifteen others on that flight bound for Amritapuri too – that was the largest mass influx of foreigners that the āśhram had ever seen.

When our group arrived at the āśhram, I was greeted by Big Swamiji (Swami Amritaswarupananda Puri) who showed me to my spot in the men's dorm above the Kālī Temple. At that time only the main hall and adjacent upstairs balcony rooms had been completed. The floor above that was still under construction. On the Kālī Temple floor, a huge pile of sand had been off-loaded, sitting there like a miniature mountain.

At that time, the āśhram consisted of the unfinished Kālī Temple building, the Kaḷari (small original temple), Amma's birth house, Amma's simple apartment, rows of thatched huts housing the brahmachārīs and brahmachāriṇīs (celibate disciples), and a larger thatched hut that served as the darśhan hall. Amma was still giving Dēvī Bhāva darśhan in the Kaḷari every Tuesday, Thursday, and Sunday night.

When I was child, the first guru I had been with named me Venu when I was ten. The next guru I was with gave me the name Ramana when I was fifteen. However, now that I was with Amma, I thought, new guru, new me! I need a clean break from the past, and what better way to do that than to get a new name from Amma! I also figured that at that point I had only spent a total of one day with Amma in America. I had never told her my name, so she must not know it. It was the perfect time for a fresh start.

One day while walking, I saw Amma sitting in the sand near the Kālī Temple. Around eight local devotees were sitting in the sand forming a circle around Amma. When Amma saw me, she gestured that I should join the circle. Amma and the devotees continued their conversation in Malayalam (Amma's native language). As it was completely unintelligible to me, I began to daydream about what was foremost in my mind – getting a new name from Amma. I thought, "What if Amma gives me a new name right now!" Then my ego kicked in... I thought, "Instead of a simple name like Venu or Ramana, how great would it be if Amma gave me a really long, complicated, impressive Sanskrit name." I thought of wonderful names... How about Pratyabhignahridayeshwaramritananda! Yes, splendid! My delusional reverie suddenly ended. One-by-one Amma sat and stared intently into the face of each one of us sitting in the circle around her. When she got to my face, she smiled like the rising sun, raised her eyebrows and said, "Ramana!"

One night in the deepest, quietest part of the night, I was awakened by Amma's voice ringing out from the unfinished floor above the Kālī Temple dorm. Intrigued, I went upstairs to find Amma alone, leaning against one of the unfinished pillars. There were no walls yet. Amma was facing the ocean. As the moon was not out, the sky was a blaze of stars. Amma was holding her hands out towards the ocean, singing the hauntingly beautiful, *Sṛishtiyum Nīyē* bhajan, directing it to the Divine Mother as prakṛiti (nature), oblivious to all else. It is a scene I'll never forget.

Soon I moved from the dorm to a smaller room. One night at around two o'clock in the morning, there was a knock on the door. In a sleepy daze, I opened the door. The brahmachārī in charge of āśhram construction informed me that there was an urgent need for 'sand sifting' the giant sand pile in the center of the Kālī Temple, as another load of 'unsifted' sand was due to arrive in a few hours. Therefore, the existing sand needed to be sifted immediately. Could I please help now? After he said this, there was a long pause...He stared at me; I stared back dubiously at him. Finally he broke the silence with the magical words, "I'll bring chai." An instant transformation overtook me. I enthusiastically replied, "Ok! Just wait a minute, I'll change into my work clothes!"

Sand sifting is an interesting process. One person dumps a shovelful of sand onto a wooden-framed fine-mesh metal screen. The wooden frame is suspended in the air by ropes on one end. A person on the other end holds the wooden frame by its handles and vigorously shakes it back and forth. The finer sand falls through the mesh and is thereby separated from the larger particles that are tossed aside off the screen onto a separate pile. This finer sand is suitable for making concrete.

As my friend Eric and I were sifting away, Amma appeared. Eric and I stopped what we were doing and greeted Amma with folded hands. Amma went right over to me with her arms outstretched indicating a hug. I backed away in horror. I was a dripping mass of sand-caked sweat. Undaunted, Amma moved on toward me. I said, "Amma, no! I'm too sweaty!" Completely ignoring my protestations, Amma hugged me whispering, "Ma, Ma, Ma" in my ear. When she released me, she took both of her hands, wiped the sweat off my forehead, then ran her hands over her own hair saying, "the sweat of selfless service is like prasād (a blessed offering) for Amma."

Amma hugged Eric and then took the handles of the sand sifter from me. Eric started shoveling sand onto the sifter, and Amma started vigorously sifting. Amma did this for a full ten minutes before handing the sifter back to me. I was amazed at her untiring strength. I have often thought of Amma standing there sifting away with such strength and confidence, and it occurred to me what a great metaphor it is for what she does with each one of us.

We are the piles of sand on the screen, which Amma vigorously sifts through the fine mesh so that the large-particle-dross of ego, negative emotions, and likes and dislikes are separated out and tossed aside, while our finer, divine selves fall humbly through the mesh, making us suitable for use in the service of others. Soon after sifting sēvā, I was informed that Amma would be leaving Amritapuri for her first North India tour. I happily signed on for it. We departed on a December day in 1988.

***

The transportation for this tour consisted of one mid-sized Swaraj-Mazda bus that was designed to hold twenty to thirty people, and one small yellow car. A far cry from today's caravans of sixteen huge buses. There were at least sixty of us in that bus, including most of the fifteen foreigners who had been on my flight. It was very cramped, but Amma traveled with us most of the time, so we were happy. Long sections of continuous driving were broken up by swims with Amma at every river we came across, during which Amma lovingly washed our faces with soap, and served food and chai in a nearby field or by the side of the road.

Every day as we traveled, one of the brahmachārīs would lead the rest of us in the recitation of the Śhrī *Lalitāsahasranāma* (The 1000 Names of the Divine Mother). The brahmachārī would call, and we would respond with, "ōm parāśhaktyai namaḥ" — Salutations to the Goddess who is the supreme power. One day Amma decided to lead the chanting. Amma leading the Lalithasahasranāma was a wondrous sight to behold. She began singing each name, and with each name that she uttered, she became more ecstatic. The more ecstatic she became, the faster she started repeating the names until we barely had enough time to chant the response. Then Amma would get stuck on one name and repeat it over and over and over, faster and faster until suddenly with a cry and a laugh of pure bliss, she would throw her arms up in the air, then collapse in a heap, leaning against the wall of the bus, completely lost to this world.

Without batting an eye, Big Swamiji would take over the recitation for a few minutes, until Amma would finally return to waking consciousness and take over the lead again. This pattern — of getting stuck on one name, repeating it over and over, and culminating in Amma, crying out, laughing, and soaring to the heights of samādhi (union with the infinite) slumped against the side of the bus, then coming back down to our world, then leading the names again — happened over and over. The 1000th name was finally reached; the blissful archana had taken well over two hours to complete!

As the days of our northern journey continued, the Swaraj-Mazda bus became less and less of a friend. As you can see, I am not a small person, and I became convinced the

Swaraj-Mazda was built with people half my size in mind. My feet couldn't move, my knees were permanently smashed into the back of the seat in front of me, and half of my back stuck out into the aisle. I was in constant pain that kept me ever awake, even when we were traveling in the wee hours of the morning. I would look around the bus enviously, watching everyone around me, seemingly fast asleep. At first, I cursed the Swaraj-Mazda that I had nicknamed "the iron maiden" after an ancient European coffin-like box used to punish people. However, today I think back on that bus very fondly. Had the pain it induced not kept me awake, I would never have witnessed Amma literally saving the lives of everyone on the bus.

We were driving in the very late part of the night, perhaps around two in the morning. I was in my usual seat in the very back of the bus. The back row of seats sat higher than the others because the entire row was set on top of the back wheel hubs. As with many buses, the main seating area in the Swaraj-Mazda was set higher than where the driver sits. Because the driver sits in this lower position closer to the road, it's hard to see him from the main seating area.

Amma was seated in one of the front rows, just behind the raised row of backward-facing brahmachārīs. So that Amma could lie down, two brahmachāriṇīs gave up their seats and sat on the floor. From my higher vantage point, I had a birdseye view over the whole bus and could see everything, including Amma lying down on her side in front. Though the lower part of the front windshield of the bus was blocked from my view, I could see out the top part of the windshield, looking over the tops of the heads of the front-row brahmachārīs.

I was almost delirious with exhaustion; however my pain was such that I could not sleep. As we drove on, I saw something that I knew wasn't right, but my sleep-deprived brain was operating very slowly. After a second, I realized that there were the bright lights and blaring horn of an oncoming truck closing quickly in on us. Our driver had fallen asleep at the wheel, and our bus had drifted into the opposite lane, putting us on course for a head-on collision with the truck. I was just about to yell out when Amma shot up into a sitting position and yelled out the name of our driver at the top of her lungs. He and everyone else instantly woke up. He pulled hard on the steering wheel taking the bus off the road and onto the sloped shoulder as the truck blasted by within inches of us, horn screaming. With everyone now wide awake asking each other, "What happened," the driver brought us lumbering back up onto the road. Without another word, Amma lay back down and went back to 'sleep.'

***

Eventually, we reached Mathura, where I was blessed to witness Amma taking the darśhan of baby Kṛiṣhṇa in the huge temple that marks the place of his birth. What happened after Amma had taken darśhan was truly remarkable. When Amma exited the temple and was walking towards the stairs, a small group of six or seven simple Kṛiṣhṇa devotees were singing bhajans in front of the temple, accompanying themselves with harmonium, dholak (a drum), and kaimani (hand cymbals). Amma stood in front of the group to listen to their bhajan. Big Swamiji stood next to her, and the rest of us stood to the side, watching Amma listen to their bhajans. Suddenly, there was only what I can call a shift in the atmosphere. The air became thick and intense with spiritual power. I looked at Amma. The way she was standing was somehow different, and when I looked at her face, it was completely different, with an expression on it that I had only seen before in Swami Paramatmanandaji's old video footage of Amma in Kṛiṣhṇa Bhāva (mood of Kṛiṣhṇa).

Amma had spontaneously manifested Kṛishṇa Bhāva! The most extraordinary thing was that the little band of simple bhajan singers, without ever having met Amma before, without ever having heard about her, without ever having said a single word to her recognized what had happened, recognized exactly who was standing before them. They went completely crazy, bringing their bhajan to a frenzied, exultant, expression of pure joy and devotion to welcome their Lord. One old man jumped up and started dancing wildly in front of Amma in an ecstatic state. Overwhelmed, Big Swamiji burst into tears while Kṛishṇa-Amma listened with that serene Kṛishṇa smile on her face. Then, as quickly as it began, the atmosphere shifted and the intensity seemed to lessen. Amma looked like Amma again, and without a word our entire group made its way back to the bus.

Continuing on to Haridwar, Amma finally reached the banks of the Ganges River for the first time. Amma entered the cold, clear, fast-moving, waters of the sacred river, quickly holding on to a steel post that had been pounded into the river bottom to keep devotees from being swept away by the strong current.

The rest of us entered the water after Amma. Wanting to perform a great feat of tapas (austerity), I made a silent vow that I wouldn't leave the water until Amma did. This was a big mistake because after entering the holy Ganga, Amma closed her eyes and was soon completely lost to this world. After quite a long time, Amma's attendant somehow managed to pull Amma's body from the river to the riverbank. All the while, Amma's mind remained absorbed in super consciousness. By then I was frozen to the bone, and gratefully left the river, changing quickly into dry clothes. Some of us went over and held our shawls up over Amma's reclined body on the riverbank to protect her from the sun. She remained deep in samādhi. Big Swamiji started singing a bhajan to try to bring Amma back to waking consciousness, and we all joined in. When this didn't work, some householder women shooed us away so that they could change Amma's wet clothes, after which they gently placed Amma into the yellow car. We all returned to the bus. Later, after Amma had finally come down from her exalted state, she was asked about her experience. The story that got back to us was this: once Amma entered the water and held onto the iron post, she looked to the banks of the river and with her wide-open spiritual eye could see all of the great saints and sages who had through the centuries done tapasya (acts of austerity) on those shores. Seeing that, her mind soared, dissolving into the supreme.

***

Amma is the Great Mystery. The only way to know Amma is to become Amma. Until then, we can experience only facets of the gem that is Amma. For this occasion, I endeavored to open a window into a time long past to shed light on certain Amma facets — Amma the all-knowing mother protectress; Amma the ultimate sēvite; Amma as Kṛiṣhṇa; and Amma the ecstatic bhakta. But Amma's facets are infinite and range from simple village girl to Amma Ph.D., CEO, and Chancellor of universities, colleges, and hospitals... on and on, ad infinitum. Perhaps most importantly for us is Amma the satguru — the one who expertly guides us to the true self. What a precious gift is guru's grace. We can have all worldly success, even fly to Mars, but without a foundation in guru's grace, any outer achievement pales into insignificance. The great Ādi Śhaṅkara beautifully expresses this when he sings in his *Gurvaṣhṭakam*:

śharīraṁ surūpaṁ tathā vā kalatraṁ
yaśhaśhrchāru chitraṁ dhanaṁ mērutulyaṁ
gurōraṅghripadmē manaśhrchēna lagnaṁ
tataḥ kiṁ tataḥ kiṁ tataḥ kiṁ tataḥ kiṁ

"One's physique may be superb, one's consort likewise, one's reputation resplendent and renowned, and one's riches as high as Mount Meru; yet if one's mind be not centered upon the lotus feet of the guru, what then? What then? What then? What then?"

Glossary

amma: Malayalam word for 'mother.'

Amritapuri: the international headquarters of Mata Amritanandamayi Math, located at Amma's birthplace in Kerala, India.

AmritaSREE: Amrita Self-Reliance, Employment & Empowerment, a network of self-help groups managed by the Mata Amritanandamayi Math and aimed at empowering unemployed and economically vulnerable women by providing them with skill and vocational training and by encouraging those who are interested to become entrepreneurs.

ārati: a traditional ritual involving the waving of a lighted lamp to the Guru or deity usually done towards the end of *pūjā* or worship. At some of Amma's programs, multiple devotees take turns waving the lighted lamp to Amma as she showers them with flower petals and the *ārati* song is sung.

archana: chanting of the 108 or 1,000 names of a particular deity (e.g. '*Lalitā Sahasranāma*').

Arjuna: great archer and one of the heroes of the *Mahābhārata*. It is Arjuna whom Kṛiṣhṇa addresses in the *Bhagavad Gītā*.

āśhram (ashram): 'place for striving.' A place where spiritual seekers and aspirants live or visit, in order to lead a spiritual life. It is usually the home of a spiritual master, saint or ascetic, who guides the aspirants.

ātmā (ātman): the true self. The essential nature of our real existence. One of the fundamental tenets of *Sanātana Dharma* is that we are not the physical body, feelings, mind, intellect, or personality. We are the eternal, pure, unblemished self.

AYUDH: 'Amrita Yuva Dharmadhara' or 'Amma's Youth for Unity, Diversity, and Humanity' — the youth wing of the Mata Amritanandamayi Math.

Āyurvēda (Ayurveda): the 'science of life.' Ancient Indian, holistic health and medical system. Ayurvedic medicines are usually prepared from medicinal herbs and plants.

Bhagavad Gītā: 'Song of the Lord,' it consists of 18 chapters of verses in which Lord Kṛiṣhṇa advises Arjuna. The advice is given on the battlefield of Kurukṣhētra, just before the righteous Pāṇḍavas fight the unrighteous Kauravas. It is a practical guide to overcoming crises in one's personal or social life and is the essence of Vedic wisdom.

bhajan: devotional song or hymn in praise of God.

bhakti: devotion for God.

brahmachārī (brahmachari): celibate male disciple who practices spiritual disciplines under a guru's guidance.

brahmachāriṇī (brahmacharini): the female equivalent of *brahmachārī*.

brahman: the absolute reality, supreme being; the whole; that which encompasses and pervades everything, and is one and indivisible.

Brahmasthānam: 'the abode of *brahman*.' Born out of Amma's divine intuition, these unique temples are the first to show multiple deities on a single stone. The stone is four-sided displaying Gaṇēśha, Śhiva, Dēvī, and Rāhu emphasizing the inherent unity underlying the manifold aspects of the divine. There are twenty-one such temples throughout India and one in Mauritius.

darśhan: audience with a holy person or a vision of the divine. Amma's signature *darśhan* is a hug.

Dēvī: goddess; the Divine Mother.

Dēvī Bhāva: 'the divine mood of Dēvī;' the state in which Amma reveals her oneness and identity with the Divine Mother; a special all-night program where Amma gives darśhan wearing a colorful sari and crown.

dharma: 'that which upholds the universe.' From the root 'dhri' = to support, uphold, hold onto. Often translated simply as 'righteousness.' Dharma has many meanings, including the divine law, the law of existence, in accordance with divine harmony, righteousness, religion, duty, responsibility, right conduct, justice, goodness and truth. Dharma signifies the inner principles of religion. It signifies the true nature, proper functions, and actions of a being or object. It is, for example, the dharma of fire to burn. The dharma of a human being is to live in harmony with the universal spiritual principles and to cultivate a higher consciousness.

Duryōdhana: eldest son of King Dhṛitarāṣhṭra; rival of the Pāṇḍavas and chief antagonist in the *Mahabhārata* epic, often cited as an example of the harmful effects of unrestrained ambition, jealousy, and pride.

Gaṇēśha: deity with an elephant head and human body, son of Lord Śhiva and Goddess Pārvatī, widely worshipped as the remover of obstacles and the lord of beginnings.

gōpī: milkmaid from Vṛindāvan. The *gōpīs* were known for their ardent devotion to Lord Kṛiṣhṇa. Their devotion exemplifies the most intense love for God.

guru: 'one who removes the darkness of ignorance.' Spiritual master/guide.

Guru Pūrṇimā: the full moon ('*pūrṇimā*') day in the Hindu month of *Āṣhāḍha* (June – July) in which disciples honor the guru; also, the birthday of Sage Vyāsa, compiler of the *Vēdas*, and author of the *Purāṇas, Brahma Sūtras, Mahābhārata* and the *Śhrīmad Bhāgavatam.*

haṭha yōga: a system of physical and mental exercises, developed in ancient times, with the purpose of turning the body and its vital functions into perfect instruments, in order to help one attain self-realization.

hōma: ancient Vedic fire ritual in which oblations are offered to the gods by offering ghee and other sacred items into a consecrated fire.

japa: repeated chanting of a *mantra.*

Kaḷari: formerly a cowshed belonging to Amma's birth house, it became a small temple where Amma started giving *bhāva darśhan*, embracing her devotees while revealing her oneness with Kṛiṣhṇa and Dēvī. It is also the place in the Amritapuri *āśhram* where fire rituals are conducted on a daily basis.

Kālī: goddess of fearsome aspect; depicted as dark, wearing a garland of skulls, and a girdle of human arms; feminine of *kāla* (time).

Kālī Bhāva: divine mood of Kālī.

Kālī Temple: main temple in Amritapuri dedicated to goddess Kālī.

karma yōga: union through action.' The spiritual path of detached, selfless service and of dedicating the fruit of all one's actions to God.

Kauravas: the one hundred children of King Dhṛitarāṣhṭra and Queen Gāndhārī, of whom the unrighteous Duryōdhana was the eldest. The Kauravas were the enemies of their cousins, the virtuous Pāṇḍavas, whom they fought against in the *Mahābhārata* war.

Kṛiṣhṇa: from '*kṛiṣh*,' meaning 'to draw to oneself' or 'to remove sin;' principal incarnation of Lord Viṣhṇu. He was born into a royal family but raised by foster parents, and lived as a cowherd boy in Vṛindāvan, where he was loved and worshiped by his devoted companions, the *gōpīs* (milkmaids) and *gōpas* (cowherd boys). Kṛiṣhṇa later established the city of Dvārakā. He was a friend and advisor to his cousins, the Pāṇḍavas, especially Arjuna, whom he served as charioteer during the *Mahābhārata* war, and to whom he revealed his teachings as the *Bhagavad Gītā*.

Kurukṣhētra: battlefield where the war between the Pāṇḍavas and Kauravas was fought; also, a metaphor for the conflict between good and evil.

Lalitā Sahasranāma: thousand names of *Śhrī* Lalitā Dēvī, a form of the Goddess.

Mahābhārata: ancient Indian epic that Sage Vyāsa composed, depicting the war between the righteous Pāṇḍavas and the unrighteous Kauravas.

mahātmā: 'great soul;' term used to describe one who has attained spiritual realization.

Mahiṣhāsura Mardini Stōtram: hymn in praise of the Divine Mother who slayed the buffalo demon Mahiṣhāsura.

mantra: a sound, syllable, word or words of spiritual content and power. According to Vedic commentators, *mantras* are revelations of *ṛiṣhis*, arising from deep contemplation.

māyā: cosmic delusion, personified as a temptress; illusion; appearance, as contrasted with reality; the creative power of the Lord.

mōkṣha: spiritual liberation, i.e. release from the cycle of births and deaths.

Nārada: wandering sage ever engaged in singing the praises of Viṣhṇu. He composed the *Nārada Bhakti Sūtras*, aphorisms on devotion.

Ōm: primordial sound of the universe; the seed of creation. The cosmic sound, which can be heard in deep meditation; the Holy Word, taught in the *Upanişhads*, which signifies *brahman*, the divine ground of existence.

pāda pūjā: ceremonial washing of the feet of a deity, guru, or saint as a form of worship.

panchakarma: set of five traditional *Āyurvēdic* therapies for detoxification and rejuvenation aiming to cleanse the body and restore balance.

Pāṇḍavas: the five sons of King Pāṇḍu, and cousins of Kṛiṣhṇa, who are the main protagonists in the great *Mahābhārata* epic.

pīṭham: a small platform; seat for the Guru; also: a center of learning and power.

prasād: blessed offering or gift from a holy person or temple, often in the form of food.

pūjā: ritualistic or ceremonial worship.

ṛiṣhi: seer to whom mantras are revealed in deep meditation. Also the authors of many scriptural texts.

sādhanā: regimen of disciplined and dedicated spiritual practice that leads to the supreme goal of self-realization.

saṁsāra: the cycle of birth and death; the world of plurality.

saṁskāra: imprints or impressions left on the mind as a result of past experiences, actions, and thoughts (in this birth as well as in prior births). These imprints shape an individual's character, tendencies, and reactions in future situations. *Saṁskāra* can also refer to the prevailing culture, or a particular deep-seated conditioning that shapes individuals, families, and society. The ritualistic ceremonies performed at significant stages of life, such as birth, marriage, and death, are also called *saṁskāras*.

Sanātana Dharma: 'Eternal Way of Life,' the original and traditional name of Hinduism.

saṅkalpa: divine resolve, usually used in association with *mahātmās.*

sannyāsī: a person who has renounced the material world, including family, career, and other attachments, to pursue a life devoted to spiritual practice and the pursuit of enlightenment or liberation (*mōkṣha).*

satguru: 'true master.' All *satgurus* are *mahātmās*, but not all *mahātmās* are *satgurus*. The *satguru* is one who, while still experiencing the bliss of the self, chooses to come down to the level of ordinary people in order to help them grow spiritually.

satsang: 'communion with the supreme truth.' Also, being in the company of *mahātmās*, studying the scriptures, and listening to the enlightening talks of a mahātmā; a gathering of people to listen to and/or discuss spiritual matters; a spiritual discourse.

sēvā: selfless service, the results of which are dedicated to God.

sevite: person who performs *sēvā* (plural: *sevites*).

śhabad: in Sikhism 'divine word' or 'sacred hymn,' regarded as the *guru* itself.

Shivaji (Śhivājī): Shivaji Shahaji Bhonsale, 1630 – 1680, King of the Marāṭha Empire. Also known as Chhatrapati Shivaji and for being the disciple of Samarth Ramdas.

śhraddhā: in Sanskrit, *śhraddhā* means faith rooted in wisdom and experience, whereas the same term in Malayalam means dedication to one's work and attentive awareness in every action. Amma often uses the term in the latter sense.

śhrī (sri): a title of respect originally meaning 'divine,' 'holy,' or 'auspicious.'

swāmī (swami): title of one who has taken the vow of *sannyāsa* (see *sannyāsin*); *swāminī* is the female equivalent.

Upaniṣhad: portions of the *Vēdas* dealing with self-knowledge.

Vaikuṇṭha: the divine abode of Lord Viṣhṇu, often described as a realm beyond birth and death, full of bliss and free from suffering.

vairāgya: dispassion.

vāsanā: latent tendency or subtle desire that manifests as thought, motive and action; subconscious impression gained from experience.

Vēdānta: 'end (portion) of *Vēda*.' The philosophy of the *Upaniṣhads*, the concluding part of the *Vēdas*, which holds the ultimate truth to be "one without a second." A *Vēdāntin* is a follower or practitioner of *Vēdānta*.

Vēdas: the most ancient of all scriptures. Originating from God, the *Vēdas* were not composed by any human author but were 'revealed' in deep meditation to the ancient seers. These revelations came to be known as the *Vēdas*, of which there are four: *Ṛig*, *Yajur*, *Sāma*, and *Atharva*.

Vedic: pertaining to the *Vēdas*.

Viṣhṇu: 'all-pervader,' Lord of Sustenance in the trinity of Brahmā (Lord of Creation), Viṣhṇu, and Śhiva (Lord of Destruction).

viśhvāsa: faith.

Vṛindāvan: sacred site in Mathura district in Uttar Pradesh, celebrated as the place where Kṛiṣhṇa passed his early days as a cowherd.

yōga: 'to unite.' Union with the supreme being. A broad term, it also refers to the various methods of practices through which one can attain oneness with the divine. A path that leads to self-realization.

yoga: practice of yoga postures. (See *haṭha yōga*).

yōgī: a practitioner or an adept of *yōga*; *yoginī* is the female equivalent.

yuga: according to the Hindu worldview, the universe (from origin to dissolution) passes through a cycle made up of four *yugas* or ages. The first is *Kṛita* or *Satya Yuga*, during which *dharma* reigns in society. Each succeeding age sees the progressive decline of *dharma*. The second age is known as *Trēta Yuga*, the third is *Dvāpara Yuga*, and the fourth and present epoch is known as *Kali Yuga*.

Pronunciation Guide

Vowels can be short or long:

a – as 'u' in 'but' **ā** – as 'a' in 'far'

e – as 'a' in 'may' **ē** – as 'a' in 'name'

i – as 'i' in 'pin' **ī** – as 'ee' in 'meet'

o – as in 'oh' **ō** – as 'o' in 'mole'

u – as 'u' in 'push' **ū** – as 'oo' in 'hoot'

ṛi – as 'ri' in 'rim' **ṛu** – as 'ru' in Spanish 'Peru'

ḥ – pronounce: **aḥ** like 'aha,' **iḥ** like 'ihi,' **uḥ** like 'uhu,' **ēḥ** like 'ēhē,' and **ōḥ** like 'ōhō.'

Some consonants are aspirated (e.g. kh); others are not (e.g. k):

k – as 'k' in 'kite' **kh** – as 'ckh' in 'Eckhart'

g – as 'g' in 'give' **gh** – as 'g-h' in 'dig-hard'

ch – as 'ch' in 'chat' **chh** – as 'ch-h' in 'staunch-heart'

j – as 'j' in 'joy' **jh** – as 'dgeh' in 'hedgehog'

p – as 'p' in 'pine' **ph** – as 'ph' in 'up-hill'

b – as 'b' in 'bird' **bh** – as 'bh' in 'rub-hard'

Pronounced with the tip of the tongue against the teeth:

t – as 't' in 'teach' **th** – as 'th' in 'anthill'

d – as 'd' in 'door' **dh** – as 'dh' in 'madhouse'

n – as 'n' in 'night'

Retroflex sounds are produced by rolling the tongue back with the tip touching the roof of the mouth. The following examples can be used for practice:

ṭ – as 't' in 'tub'

ṭh – as 'th' in 'lighthouse'

ḍ – as 'd' in 'dove'

ḍh – as 'dh' in 'red-hot'

ṇ – as 'n' in 'naught'

ḷ – as 'l' in 'revelry'

ṣh – as 'sh' in 'shine'

zh – 'rr' in 'hurray' *(in Malayalam and Tamil)*

Other consonants:

y – as 'y' in 'yes'

r – as 'R' in Italian 'Roma'

l – as 'l' in 'like'

v – as 'v' in 'void'

śh – as 'sh' in 'shepherd'

s – as 's' in 'sun'

m – as 'm' in 'mother'

h – as 'h' in 'hot'

ṅ – as 'ng' in 'sing'

ñ – as 'ny' in 'canyon'

Double consonants:

chch – as 'tc' in 'hot chip'

jj – as 'dj' in 'red jet'

Acknowledgements

This book is the fruit of the wholehearted dedication of many individuals. I wish to especially express my gratitude to Ramana Erickson, Veena Erickson, Rajani Menon, and James Conquest for their invaluable editorial support. My thanks also go to Jagannath Maas for diligently preparing the layout, and to Arun Raj of the Amrita Office of Communications (AOC) for yet another captivating cover design. I am grateful to Swami Vidyamritananda Puri for his instrumental role in developing the glossary. I would also like to acknowledge Swami Jnanamritananda Puri, whose steady encouragement and unwavering support have been our backbone. This work has been made possible only through Amma's unconditional love and boundless grace that ties us all together.

Julius Heyne

www.ingramcontent.com/pod-product-compliance
Lightning Source LLC
Chambersburg PA
CBHW051414090426
42737CB00014B/2663
9781680379396